RESHAPING THE HOLY

Reshaping the Holy

DEMOCRACY, DEVELOPMENT,

AND MUSLIM WOMEN IN BANGLADESH

Elora Shehabuddin

Columbia University Press　New York

Columbia University Press
Publishers Since 1893
New York   Chichester, West Sussex
Copyright © 2008 Columbia University Press
All rights reserved

Library of Congress Cataloging-in-Publication Data
Shehabuddin, Elora.
Reshaping the holy : democracy, development,
and Muslim women in Bangladesh / Elora Shehabuddin.
p. cm.
Includes bibliographical references and index.
ISBN 978-0-231-14156-7 (alk. paper) —
ISBN 978-0-231-14157-4 (pbk. : alk. paper) —
ISBN 978-0-231-51255-8 (e-book)
1. Muslim women—Bangladesh—Social conditions.
2. Muslim women—Bangladesh—Social life and customs.
3. Women in Islam—Bangladesh. I. Title.

HQ1170.S464   2008
305.48'697095492—dc 22   2008007059

Columbia University Press books are printed
on permanent and durable acid-free paper.

Printed in the United States of America
Designed by Audrey Smith

c 10 9 8 7 6 5 4 3 2 1

p 10 9 8 7 6 5 4 3 2 1

To my parents

CONTENTS

ILLUSTRATIONS

ACKNOWLEDGMENTS

This book has taken longer to complete than I care to calculate, and I have incurred innumerable debts in the course of the years. The project grew out of my doctoral dissertation, which was itself inspired by earlier research I had done on the women members of the Grameen Bank. I remain grateful to the members of my dissertation committee—Amrita Basu, Atul Kohli, and Lynn White—for their advice and patience as my research interests took unexpected turns. Jim Boyce, Shelley Feldman, Paula Sanders, Dina Siddiqi, and Diane Singerman made valuable suggestions as I tried to make sense of my findings.

I could not have conducted research during my numerous trips to Bangladesh over the years without the generous hospitality of relatives in Dhaka and Chittagong: Abdur Rahim and Surma Chowdhury, Liaquat and Homaira Chowdhury, K. M. Fariduddin and Dil Afroze Farid, Mamun and Nasreen Khan, Nasrat Khan, Salim and Rehana Khan, Shafaat and Rehana Khan, Nurul and Naznin Mowla, Tanweer Nawaz, Tahera Salam, and M. A. M. and Parveen Ziauddin. I benefited enormously from discussions with Hasina Ahmed, Farida Akhter, S.M. Nurul Alam, Sonia Nishat Amin, Suraiya Begum, Anjan Ghosh, Meghna Guhathakurtha, Mirza Hassan, Manwar Hossain, Zakir Hossain, B. K. Jahangir, Rokeya Rahman Kabeer, Khushi Kabir, Lamia Karim, Kishwar Kamal Khan, Ainoon Naher, Tawfique Nawaz, James Novak, Hossain Zillur Rahman, Ataus Samad, Prashanta Tripura, and Muhammad Yunus. I am grateful to Hameeda Hossain, Sultana Kamal, the late Salma

Sobhan, and the staff at Ain o Salish Kendra (ASK), Dhaka, for allowing me to set up base at the ASK office. This study was greatly enriched by the research project I undertook at their request, and I thank them for the opportunity and our research assistants, who braved the monsoon rains to travel all over Bangladesh, for their hard work. Finally, I am grateful to the many women and men, in both rural and urban areas, who are not directly identified in the book and gave so generously of their valuable time to speak to my research assistants and me over the years.

This research was made possible by the generous support of the Department of Politics, the Council for Regional Studies, and the Center for International Studies/World Order Studies at Princeton University; the American Association of University Women; the Social Science Research Council (repeatedly!); the Andrew Mellon Foundation; the Woodrow Wilson Foundation; University of California, Irvine, Faculty Research Funds; and the Presidential Research Award at Rice University.

The book was written in various locations. I thank Judith Brown, then dean of humanities, for valuable office space at Rice University. I wish to thank my parents, Khwaja Muhammad and Khaleda Shehabuddin, in Paris, Bethesda, and Dhaka, and my in-laws, Samir and Jean Makdisi, in Beirut and Dhour Shweire, for providing ideal work environments. For the precious gifts of leave and teaching releases, I thank the Program in Women's Studies and the Department of Political Science at the University of California, Irvine, and Gary Wihl, the dean of humanities, and the Center for the Study of Women, Gender and Sexuality at Rice University. I was fortunate to be a research associate in the Women's Studies in Religion Program at the Harvard Divinity School in 2004–2005. Although it turned out to be a tough year, during which several of us faced personal difficulties, I benefited enormously from the close readings, insights, and support of my fellow associates Shawn Copeland, Nicola Denzey, Tonia Sharlach, and Susan Zaeske, as well as WSRP director Ann Braude and HDS colleagues Leila Ahmed and Karen King. Elora Halim Chowdhury, my fellow "Elora from Bangladesh" in women's studies in the U.S. academy, and Lynne Huffer read the entire manuscript carefully at short notice and made important suggestions, not all of which, I am sure, I have been able to incorporate to their satisfaction. Many thanks to Wendy Lochner at Columbia for her enthusiasm and infinite patience, to the anonymous readers for their thoughtful suggestions, and to Christine

Mortlock and the rest of the staff for their hard work. Special thanks to Sarah St. Onge for her meticulous editing.

My sisters Farhana and Sarah have been an unfailing source of support; their questions and comments have led me to think in novel ways about many of the issues surrounding Islam and gender that I explore in this book. My youngest sister, Sharmeen, was in elementary school when I started graduate school and is completing college as this book goes to press. I suspect she too cannot imagine life without this project and my preoccupation with it! My husband, Ussama Makdisi, has been involved with this project from the very start: he entered my life as I was studying for general exams and writing the very first draft of the dissertation proposal and has been a constant source of support in the years since. He has enriched this work in more ways than I can list here by reading and commenting on every line. I do not have the words to express my gratitude. The arrival of my *shonamonis*, Sinan and Nur, certainly delayed the completion of this book considerably, but I welcomed the enforced breaks from the manuscript. I dedicate this work to my parents, for all they have taught me over the years, for all they have encouraged me to explore and learn.

Earlier versions of parts of this book have appeared elsewhere: "'Development' Revisited: A Critical Analysis of the Status of Women in Bangladesh," *Journal of Bangladesh Studies* (December 2004); "Competing Discourses in Development and Modernity," in *Eye to Eye: Women Practicing Development Across Cultures*, ed. Susan Perry and Celeste Schenck (Zed, 2002); "Contesting the Illicit: The Politics of *Fatwas* in Bangladesh," *Signs: Journal of Women in Culture and Society* (Summer 1999); and "Beware the Bed of Fire: Gender, Democracy, and the Jama'at-i Islami in Bangladesh," *Journal of Women's History* (Winter 1999).

RESHAPING THE HOLY

1

GENDER, ISLAM, AND POLITICS

IN BANGLADESH

On January 10, 1993, in the eastern district of Sylhet in Bangladesh, a young woman called Nurjahan (literally, "light of the world") was dragged out of her home by her hair to be punished for adultery. Her life, even more than her tragic death, is representative of the lives of impoverished women in contemporary rural Bangladesh.[1] The seventh of nine children, Nurjahan was a young girl when her first marriage was arranged. After abusing her for several years, her husband suddenly divorced her and disappeared. Like millions of women throughout Bangladesh, Nurjahan joined a *mohila shomiti* (women's group) sponsored by a local nongovernmental organization (NGO). She also worked as a daily laborer for the Department of Forestry, collecting firewood in the hills to sell at the market. Some time after her divorce, the local imam, Maulana Mannan, and a number of elite men of the village approached her father with marriage proposals for Nurjahan;[2] he turned them down in favor of Mutalib, who was seeking a second wife to help his chronically ill first wife. Nurjahan did not wish to marry him, but her family prevailed. Her father obtained a divorce in writing from her first husband. Mannan confirmed the authenticity of the document for a fee of 200 takas and performed the marriage. Neither of the two marriages nor the divorce was formally registered with the state.

Before long, some people in the village began to protest that Nurjahan had not obtained a proper divorce from her first husband and therefore could not be married to Mutalib; they accused the couple of living in sin. A *shalish*, convened under the leadership of Mannan himself and composed of several members of the village elite, pronounced that Nurjahan's marriage to Mutalib was not in accordance with Islamic law and was hence invalid.[3] The shalish issued a fatwa that they should both be punished for engaging in unlawful sex. Thus, one winter morning in January 1993, Nurjahan and her husband were forced to stand in a waist-deep pit in the ground, and then each was pelted with 101 stones. Nurjahan's elderly parents were given fifty lashes each for their role in arranging their daughter's marriage to Mutalib. Some hours later, Nurjahan killed herself by drinking agricultural pesticide.

The story of Nurjahan highlights the dramatic intersection of gender, Islam, and politics in a contemporary Muslim state. Since independence in 1971, public political discourse in Bangladesh, by most accounts the fourth-largest Muslim country in the world,[4] has been characterized by acrimonious debates among politicians, development agencies, and urban elites over the appropriate public role of Islam. Poor women have long been at the heart of these disputes as the putative object of national and international concern, yet even in a polity in which since 1991 both the democratically elected prime minister and the leader of the opposition have been women, little attention has been paid to Bangladeshi women's own varied perspectives on the public role of Islam or indeed their own role in the recasting of what Dale Eickelman and James Piscatori (1996) call "Muslim politics." This book explores the profound implications of women's political and social mobilization for reshaping Islam. Specifically, it examines how Muslim women in Bangladesh, who have become increasingly visible, mobilized, and empowered by the activities of predominantly secular NGOs yet who desire not so much to unveil and abandon Islam as to retain, reclaim, and reshape it are fomenting change in an elite Islamist movement, namely, the Jamaat-i Islami (Society of Islam). In doing so, these women are actively refashioning the fundamental shape of the holy, creating a distinctly modern Muslim public arena in which women are both visible *and* pious.

The distressing story of Nurjahan vividly reflects many of the problems that plague rural society in Bangladesh and especially poor, illiterate women. Social norms that esteem marriage and motherhood as the primary callings in a woman's life prompted both of Nurjahan's marriages (see, for example, Kotalova 1996). Her first marriage occurred when she was still very young, and it is very likely that she had no say in the matter; as for the second marriage, even though she was not interested in remarrying, her parents thought it preferable that she join a household as a second wife rather than remain unmarried. In any case, gender discrimination and the limited opportunities for women in the formal economy meant that her meager wages ultimately left her financially dependent on a male wage earner, be it her father or a husband. Finally, the illiteracy and poverty of her family allowed elite men of the community to use the shalish to settle the score with both her father (for turning down their offers of marriage) and her new husband (over property disputes).

The story of Nurjahan brings to the fore two issues of significance to our understanding of gender, Islam, and politics. First, it provides a particularly vivid example of the consequences of a weak state. The state played no role in her marriages, divorce, trial for adultery, or death. Had her divorce and subsequent marriage been officially registered, she could have produced the relevant documents to quash all doubts regarding the validity of her second marriage. Remarkably, at no point did her family seek the assistance of the local police, who investigated the incident only after a journalist stumbled on the story of her suicide. At the same time, the shalish committee itself must have been fairly confident that the local police would not interfere in its activities. The national public furor that followed Nurjahan's death reflects the existence of distinct Islamist and secularist perspectives, each with its own analysis of the problems that afflict rural society and with different solutions to these problems. The limited reach of the state in Bangladesh has created a vacuum that has enabled secularist and Islamist forces, with financial support from international organizations, foreign governments, and Bangladeshi expatriate workers, to attempt to regulate society and poor women in accordance with their respective ideologies. Generally, for secularists, at the root of all problems lies the increasing Islamization of Bangladeshi state and society; according to Islamists, all problems stem from the absence of "true," formal Islamic institutions and government. The two groups, however, ultimately share a condescending assumption about the gullibility of the rural poor, especially women, and the overarching role of religion in their lives and decisions.

Second, the Nurjahan case prompts us to investigate, rather than assume, the precise role that religion plays in the efforts of traditionally underprivileged groups and individuals to improve their lives. While Nurjahan may have felt compelled to take her own life following the shalish, millions of rural women continue to struggle to survive under fairly dismal conditions. This struggle for survival has led many of them to overcome significant family and community censure in order to join an NGO. This book explores the manner in which rural women in Bangladesh negotiate between a customary and religion-based insistence on modesty, even seclusion, for all good Muslim women, on the one hand, and the need to work outside the home in order to keep themselves and their families alive, on the other. By most calculations, illiterate landless rural women in Bangladesh are situated at the bottom of all conceivable social, economic, and political hierarchies, and their material deprivation is reinforced by their subjection to strict cultural and legal codes of conduct. As this book shows, however, even they respond in unanticipated ways to rival attempts by the major political parties, NGOs, and members of the rural socioeconomic and religious elites to regulate their behavior.

The commonly assumed dichotomy between Islam, on the one hand, and modernity and secularism, on the other, holds little meaning for the vast majority of Bangladeshi Muslims who are poor and live in rural areas. In fact, impoverished rural women who have been targeted directly by international and indigenous NGOs, refuse to see their development as a choice between Islam and modernity. Even for those who claim to pray and fast regularly and consider themselves to be good Muslims, elite notions of religion and piety do not determine how they make decisions about such public matters as whether to join an NGO, which political party to support, and which laws to evade or follow.[5] Indeed, many impoverished women today adhere to neither the Islamist nor the secularist understanding of purdah. Rather than reject purdah outright, most women who join NGOs or take up factory work, often over the objections of relatives and neighbors, appear to be redefining the very meaning of purdah to bring it within their reach. Defining purdah as a state of mind, a purity of thought, something that they carry inside them rather than an expensive outer garment, permits these women to present and even see themselves as pious Muslims yet leaves them free to meet the basic needs of survival (see Siddiqi 1991 and Rozario 1998). Contrary both to the charges of Islamists and the wishful expectations of secularists, such women do not see themselves as either rejecting religion or embracing a secular modernity.

Although the beliefs and actions of poor women in rural Bangladesh often appear inconsistent and contradictory, they become comprehensible when one realizes that they are in fact motivated not by ignorance and gullibility, as secularist and Islamist elites alike claim, but by a knowledge, born of experience, of the limits of the *sarkar* (state or government) and of its inability to provide them with essential services such as education, legal protection, and health care.[6] While I do not wish to romanticize all poor rural women as shrewd survivors, it is nonetheless important to recognize the degree to which their public behavior reflects what could be termed a subaltern rationality. They make choices on the basis of both material and spiritual concerns, of how both to improve their lives in this world and to ensure a good *akhirat* (afterlife), in a manner that appears quite *irrational* in strictly secularist and Islamist understandings of self-interest and rationality. I contend, then, that while there do exist fundamental differences between the secularist and Islamist perspectives at the elite level, such contrasts become less clear when one descends to the realm of popular politics, among the poorer strata of society and among landless women in particular.

This book highlights the dynamic nature of the relationship among Islamists, secularists, and their common target, poor women in Bangladesh. Rather than assume these to be static categories, I examine not only how national Islamist and secular elites seek to effect change in the lives of poor women through NGOs and political parties and how women make sense of these overtures but also how the women themselves provoke changes in the different organizations targeting them, as well as how Islamists and secularists ultimately affect one another. The inordinate attention given to landless rural women in Bangladesh in recent decades, by international imperatives and local NGO initiatives, has created a large population of mobilized women in Bangladesh unparalleled elsewhere in the Muslim world. In the last few years alone, both secularist and Islamist elites have begun to undertake cautious modifications of their strategies, prompted by impoverished women's rejection of their traditional positions as well as by the wider democratic setting. The Jamaat-i Islami, for example, has been allowed and has chosen to operate as a political party in a democratic polity and is therefore now necessarily concerned with numbers; this has led it to make deliberate efforts in recent years to woo women voters by highlighting its (albeit qualified) support for women's education, employment outside the home, and participation in formal politics and by reaffirming its commitment to curbing violence against women. Secularist NGOs, for their part, increasingly recognize that their own relations with the poor will remain tenuous if they continue to disregard the latter's religious concerns. Many NGOs have recently found it useful to highlight Islamic sanction for girls' education and the use of contraception, for example.

At first glance, that mobilized women in a democratic context are forcing Islamist forces to moderate their ideology serves as a vindication of traditional modernization theory, of the assumptions that democratization, Westernization, and secularization go together and that these are indubitably positive developments. On closer inspection, however, we discover that both impoverished women and Islamists respond in ways unexpected in conventional narratives and, above all, in relation with one another as well as secularists. At its most ambitious, then, this book leads us to rethink our positions on one of the most contentious debates in the early years of the twenty-first century: can Islam be supportive of democratic rights generally and women's rights in particular? Fears about the incompatibility of Islam and genuine democracy have never been simply academic concerns but have always had very real and very grave policy implications. The focus in this book is not Islam as it is understood through canonical religious texts and legal manuals but as it is actually practiced by Muslims. This book also moves beyond the question of whether Islamists are willing to participate in democratic elections; after all, Islamists in Bangladesh, Egypt, Indonesia, Jordan, Lebanon, Turkey, and Yemen, for example, have certainly participated in elections, at the level of local politics and professional associations if not parliament. More productive ways of investigating the relationship between Islam and democracy include, first, examining an Islamist party's actual relationship to women, the poor, and non-Muslims and its pronouncements on their rights and, second, exploring how ordinary Muslim citizens themselves understand the role of Islam in their quest for a louder political voice and a better life.

WOMEN, POVERTY, AND ISLAM IN RURAL BANGLADESH

Approximately 76 percent of the population of Bangladesh lives in rural areas and almost 50 percent falls below the national poverty line (UNDP 2004). Poverty is disproportionately concentrated in rural areas, with 93

FIGURE 1.1 Paddy fields in rural Bangladesh.

percent of the very poor and 89 percent of the poor living in the country's villages (Oxford Policy Management 2004). In these predominantly
landless households, the adult men usually work in the fields or homes
of wealthier villagers for daily wages or come to a sharecropping arrangement with them. Sometimes the women also work for payment in cash,
though more often in kind; this is particularly true of female-headed
households, which are on the increase and disproportionately so among
the poorest in the country (Mannan 2000).[7] A small number of men
and women may leave the village in search of work elsewhere, but the
majority remain. Rising poverty and landlessness are fast transforming
traditional family networks: for example, where in the past a divorced,
abandoned, or widowed woman with children would have sought refuge
in her parents' or brothers' homes, today she is likely to be compelled to
fend for herself. It is these very men and women who remain in the villages but do not have access to an income from agriculture who are typically the targets of the various NGOs in the countryside. Because of their
sheer numbers, they are also of growing importance to political parties
during elections, representing in effect a reserve army of voters. Women
are of particular significance, not only because they are perceived as more
malleable by various organizations vying for their support but also because

they occupy an increasingly important and visible position in national politics, domestic policies, and international donor prescriptions.

Following the restoration of democracy in 1991 after fifteen years of military rule, Bangladesh has found itself in the remarkable position of having two Muslim women—Khaleda Zia of the Bangladesh Nationalist Party and Sheikh Hasina of the Awami (People's) League—alternate as prime minister in 1991, 1996, and 2001.[8] At the same time, NGOs and successive governments have turned their attention to ordinary rural women, channeling a variety of education, credit, and employment opportunities in their direction. They have exalted poor women for their ability to attract foreign aid, to contribute to the nation's GDP, to participate in international attempts to control the country's population, and to present positive images of Bangladesh on foreign television and at international meetings on women's rights and poverty alleviation.[9] The efforts of Bangladesh's Grameen Bank, or Rural Bank, which provides microcredit—small loans—to women who have no collateral, have attracted worldwide attention, and its methods have been replicated throughout Africa, Asia, and the Middle East, as well as in several American cities.[10] Other development organizations in Bangladesh have also gained prominence through their innovative strategies for imparting legal literacy, economic expertise, and organizational skills. Throughout the 1990s, the increasing social, political, and economic mobilization of rural women converged with growing Islamist participation in formal democratic politics as well as in heated discussions about the role of religion in the public sphere.

Thus, while it would be inaccurate to argue that rural women in Bangladesh have been ignored by academic scholarship as have many other underprivileged groups, it cannot be denied that they have been portrayed consistently as victims—of rape, warfare, natural disasters, corrupt and inefficient governments, culturally insensitive and infrastructure-centered donors and aid agencies, and local fundamentalists—or, on a more positive note, as the targets of new development schemes. And it was again as victims of local miscarriages of justice via extralegal fatwas and shalishes that poor women moved to center stage in the consciousness and public discourses of domestic urban elites and international human rights organizations in the early 1990s. For many local observers, these fatwa incidents reflected a backlash by the conservative elements in society against women's increased public visibility. The term "fatwa," which

FIGURE 1.2 Khulna-based NGO Rupantar performing *pot-gaan* (displaying elaborate painted images accompanied by spoken and sung narratives), which it uses to communicate to an overwhelmingly illiterate population about issues ranging from water resource management, arsenic contamination, the conservation of the Sundarbans, and the rights of the disabled to women's rights and relations between men and women.

in Islamic jurisprudence refers to a clarification of an ambiguous judicial point or an opinion by a jurist trained in Islamic law, had gained world-wide notoriety following the fatwa against the British writer Salman Rushdie in 1989 and some years later that against the Bangladeshi writer Taslima Nasrin.[11] Fatwas, however, have not been reserved solely for such high-profile figures. According to Ain o Salish Kendra (ASK), a law and mediation center in Dhaka, as many as two hundred women, mostly impoverished and rural, were subjected to fatwa-instigated violence in Bangladesh between 1993 and 2000; at least eighteen of them committed suicide. The Bangladesh Mohila Porishad (Women's Council) estimates that thirty-nine women were subject to fatwas as recently as 2002, in contravention of a 2001 high court ruling banning fatwas (Islam 2003). Members of the rural elite had charged the women with adultery and issued fatwas that they be whipped, stoned, or, in one instance, burned at the stake. In addition, following fatwas by several local and national religious leaders declaring that NGOs were converting girls and women to Christianity, villagers in various parts of the country set fire to NGO schools imparting basic literacy skills to women and chopped down mulberry trees planted by women with the assistance of NGOs. In certain districts, women were prevented from going to the polls in recent elections following fatwas that it was inappropriate for women to vote. These incidents have a number of factors in common: the targets were predominantly women from the poorest stratum of rural society; the fatwa givers were the elite men of their villages, such as landowners and religious leaders; and the state was slow to take action against the perpetrators and did so only following the intervention of women's and human rights groups (Shehabuddin 1999b).

The public outcry that followed the fatwa incidents, as manifested in articles and editorials in the printed media, reflected a polarization in the literate public between Islamist and secularist perspectives. The most vocal members of the secularist camp belong to the urban intelligentsia and professional class, many of whom are activists, in women's and feminist organizations, among others, and also employed by foreign-funded NGOs. As far as they are concerned, the fact that over 83 percent of the country's population is Muslim is of no political significance: in their view, Islam should have no role in the public sphere. They regard fundamentalism as perhaps the greatest obstacle to their vision of development and the spate of fatwas as a medieval, barbaric backlash against women and NGOs that was coordinated at the national level by the Jamaat-i Islami.

The Islamists, on the other hand, believe that in a Muslim-majority state it is only natural that Islam be recognized as an important determinant of both cultural identity and formal politics. The position is taken to its logical conclusion and most clearly articulated by the Jamaat, which calls for the establishment of an Islamic state. While it distanced itself from the outbreak of fatwa incidents in the 1990s as well as the more recent Taliban-style reign of terror in northern Bangladesh by an organization called Jagrata Muslim Janata (JMJ, or Vigilante Muslim Masses) (see Shehabuddin 1999a; Griswold 2005), the Jamaat has criticized NGOs for leading the rural poor away from the path of truth and righteousness with their international funds and talk of progress. As far as the Jamaat is concerned, the solution to the myriad problems facing Bangladesh lies in the establishment of a true Islamic state that would meet the basic needs of each citizen, educate the masses about its interpretation of the Quran, and do away with the need for foreign and so-called un-Islamic ideas and institutions.

This battle is not, of course, waged only in the pages of newspapers. Secularist and Islamist elites in Bangladesh have been locked in a struggle both over what women should and should not do and also over what meanings inhere in specific acts they undertake. This contest over meanings is perhaps most apparent in the issue of purdah.[12] For the secularist camp, purdah and by extension religion itself represent the primary obstacles to development and modernization. According to this view, the modern woman is one who has cast off that all too visible symbol of tradition, the veil, and a modern society is one in which Islam plays no role in the public domain. Against this model, there has emerged an Islamist vision of modernity. For example, according to the Jamaat, a modern Muslim woman is one who observes purdah as the party defines it, is aware of and enjoys all the rights granted in the Quran, and turns to activities outside the home only after she has fulfilled all her domestic obligations, the most important of these being the bearing of children and the transmission of Islamic values to them.[13] Both Islamists and secularists seem to agree, however, that the rural poor, especially illiterate women, naively believe anything that is said in the name of religion. Concerned that rural women may be misled by the other side, the two groups compete to direct the women's behavior. Secularists and Islamists in Bangladesh are divided

FIGURE 1.3 Banchte Shekha women's group meeting, Jessore.

in their visions not only of women but of the future of the Bangladeshi nation (Rashiduzzaman 1994); they both insist, however, on the incompatibility of Islam and a modernity that is understood as Westernization and secularization.[14]

As I show in the chapters that follow, major political parties, members of the rural socioeconomic and religious elites, and various NGOs are competing for the hearts, minds, and souls of poor rural women. At the same time, feminist and women's organizations are engaged in a range of activities revolving around women's rights and issues, such as violence against women, trafficking, legal aid, advocacy and reform, reproductive rights, and social and political empowerment. Many of these groups function as or work closely with development NGOs. To be clear, although almost all NGOs in Bangladesh today pay special attention to women's issues because most Western donors make funds available for women-related projects, not all NGOs can be described as dedicated to women's rights or feminist concerns. At the same time, almost all organizations in Bangladesh that are primarily concerned with such matters can be subsumed under the category NGO if we go by the local understandings of the term that I discuss in Chapter 4. The NGO traits in question pertain to agendas in keeping with universal conventions on human rights and access to external donor funding. While these women's rights NGOs are more interested in addressing women's rights than in winning women's support during bids for public office, their effectiveness over the years has depended a great deal on their ability to navigate among the interests and influence of Western donors, transnational feminist networks, the government, development NGOs, and the women they seek to help. As Santi Rozario points out, the women's movement in Bangladesh is far from united, and individuals and groups have come down on opposite sides on issues such as the Uniform Family Code (Rozario 2004: 7). Such disagreements notwithstanding, major women's and feminist groups and NGOs are far more likely to be prosecular than not. A coalition of women's groups, Oikyo Bodhyo Nari Shomaj (United Women's Forum), for example, was at the forefront of the opposition to the bill to declare Islam the state religion in 1988 (D. Choudhury 2000; Azim 2001; T. Murshid n.d.). Having just observed the impact on women of recent Islamization in Iran and Pakistan, activists in the women's movement in Bangladesh had grounds for concern and for their insistence on a secular stance (Mumtaz and Shaheed 1987; Hussain-Patel 2003; S. Khan 2004). Shelley Feldman and Farida Shaheed point out, however, that many women's groups' espousal of secularism and targeting of religion as a source of oppression in Bangladesh and Pakistan reflects the "exclusion of poor women as a voice among their membership" (Feldman 1998: 41; Shaheed 1998). In this book, I focus on how the women who are such important objects of attention for NGOs, political parties, and women's rights activists perceive, resist, and choose between competing secularist and Islamist attempts to mobilize their support. National and local elites have sought to direct rural women's activities in three interrelated arenas: they have tried to control women's social and sexual behavior by demanding reform in the nation's legal framework or even by taking the law into their own hands, women's economic behavior by regulating their involvement with NGOs, and women's formal political behavior by influencing their participation in local and national elections. They have succeeded to some extent in rural areas largely because the state has effectively been absent and unable to provide services such as health care, education, legal protection, and *unnoti* (improvement, development, a better life).

Today few would dispute that the Bangladeshi state has had a limited impact on the poorest of the country's citizens. Ambitious schemes have been proposed at the center; however, the state has consistently failed to attain the lofty goals outlined in the national constitution, such as the commitment to "emancipat[e] the toiling masses ... and backward sections of the people from all forms of exploitation" as well as to provide the "basic necessities of life, including food, clothing, shelter, education and medical care" (GoB 1994: articles 14, 15). Bangladesh's aid-dependent status has meant that successive governments have generally been more concerned about their accountability to international financial institutions and donors than to the local populace; the entrenchment of global neoliberal policies in the 1980s, which regarded the state as an obstacle to development, only served to weaken the Bangladeshi state even further. Today, the state institutions that most of the rural poor are likely to encounter, those at the local level, operate on the basis of bribes or, as many refer to it, "kichhu cha kabar taka" (a little money for tea).[15] Since impoverished rural women and men lack both money and influence, it is easy to understand why they generally do not seek out government assistance in times of trouble. The ineffectiveness of the state thus compels them to fend for themselves as best they can and has permitted certain members of the rural elite to commit and get away with their criminal excesses. While the poor may accept a local fatwa, however, they do not automatically support religion in the public sphere; similarly, when they join an NGO despite fatwas against it, this should not be interpreted as a rejection of Islam. They are simply choosing the course of action that they believe best serves their interests, given that God, NGOs, the local elite, and their neighbors are right there, while the state is far away. In the end, poor women in rural Bangladesh make choices with their own interests in mind, interests that often turn out to be very different from those of Western liberals and domestic elites, even those, secularist and Islamist alike, who claim to be concerned about the poor, the needy, and women. A woman in rural Bangladesh is likely to be anxious both about whether there will be enough food for her family the following day and whether she is conducting herself in such a manner that society and God will regard her as a good Muslim. What is interesting, ultimately, is how women weigh these often antagonistic claims and what factors influence their decisions and actions.

THE APPROACH OF THE STUDY

As an ethnographic study of Muslim women's activism in a non-Middle Eastern, formally democratic Muslim country, this book addresses topical discussions and important lacunae in the existing scholarship on politics, religion, and gender studies. Research in the field generally referred to as Islamic studies has long tended to privilege the study of texts rather than the lived experience of Muslims and to privilege the experience of Muslims in Arab countries, Iran, and Turkey over that of Muslims elsewhere. This is even true of the exciting new scholarship on Islamic activism and Muslim politics (see, e.g., Wiktorowicz 2004). Following in the footsteps of valuable recent books on Bangladesh (Riaz 2004), Indonesia (Bowen 1993; Hefner 2000), Malaysia (Peletz 1996 and 2002), and Pakistan (Nasr 1994, 1996), I redirect attention to South and Southeast Asia, home to the vast majority of Muslims in the world; however, in contrast to most of this earlier scholarship, women and gender as well as Bangladesh's formally democratic context are central to my inquiry and analysis. Closely contextualized attention to the relationship between Islam and politics accentuates not only the internal diversity of formal Islamist politics in different Muslim countries today but also, and of special significance to this study, highlights the multiple understandings of Islam among Muslim women and the consequences of these perceptions for women's decisions and activism. These issues converge in recent developments in Bangladeshi politics, especially in various attempts by secularist and Islamist elites to influence gender in society as well as national politics by respectively diminishing or enhancing the role of Islam in politics and society.

There has long been a propensity to presume and privilege the significance of Islam in the lives and decisions of Muslims rather than interrogate and rigorously investigate it (see Waines 1982; Lazreg 1990; Hale 1998; Minault 1999). Such assumptions about Islam continue not only to prompt academic generalizations about Islamic civilization as a monolithic entity but also to inform the views of elites, both secularist and Islamist, within Muslim societies. Assumptions regarding the centrality of Islam have led to characterizations of Islamic societies as unfit for democracy, development, human rights, and, above all, modernity, all of which, in contrast, are deemed to be the pillars of Western civilization (Lewis 1990; Huntington 1993a, 1993b, 1996; Lakoff 2004; cf. Hefner 2001; Stepan 2003; Stepan and Robertson 2004; Moghadam 2005; Voll 2005). Depictions of Muslim women as veiled, oppressed, and passive have fueled perceptions of Islam as oppressive, undemocratic, even misogynist and have contributed, as is now well known, to a very specific construction of Islamic civilization, such as the Huntingtonian variety (Huntington 1993a).

Very much at the heart of Samuel Huntington's fears regarding an imminent "clash of civilizations," for example, is the belief that the actions of a state in the international arena are determined by the religious identity of the citizens of that state. He claims that "in the modern world, religion is a central, perhaps the central, force that motivates and mobilizes people" (1993b). If we accept, as recent research compels us to do, that neither states nor societies are monolithic undifferentiated wholes, then how can we find credible the portrayal of states and societies as driven almost entirely by any one of the multiple civilizational affiliations of the groups and individuals who make up these complex states and societies (Migdal, Kohli, and Shue 1994)? Huntington himself concedes, for example, that Islamism and other fundamentalist ideologies are largely middle-class phenomena, yet he concludes that entire countries are experiencing a religious revival. One of the problems with his argument is that he does not disaggregate state or society sufficiently to realize that, in most of the poorer nations of the world, the middle class does not yet constitute a majority of the population, that its views are not representative of the whole, that the state may cater to certain groups but not others, and that therefore one may need to seek the catalysts of social change somewhere other than among the elites or the middle class. The recent conflicts between vehemently secularist political elites and democratically elected Islamist parties in Algeria and Turkey and the complicated negotiations between reformist and conservative Islamists in Iran point to the internal tension and lack of consensus over the role of Islam in public life even in predominantly Muslim countries. Given the numerous instances of conflict within what Huntington would identify as a single civilization and of cooperation between countries from different civilizations (Halliday 1997), it is more useful to focus on individual states rather than on entire civilizations. And furthermore it is as important to focus on societal actors as it is to focus on the state.

The state is an important actor in this study, though often more by virtue of its limitations and absence rather than as an overbearing presence. While I recognize that the state is not a "freestanding entity" (Mitchell 1991) and that the boundaries between state and society are blurred, difficult to delineate, and constantly shifting, I posit that the poor women in rural Bangladesh who are the subjects of this study demonstrate a clear sense of what the state is and what they can expect of it. Disaggregating both state and societal actors allows me to study the different implications of state policies for women and men at both the local and national levels and, at the same time, draw attention to different responses by the women themselves to the different levels of the state. An exclusive focus on the national level, for instance, would emphasize the achievements of prominent women's groups; it would obscure, however, less dramatic instances of activism and resistance undertaken by ordinary village women, individually or in small local groups, against local officials and branches of government in different arenas such as legislation, development, and formal politics. All three arenas are conceived and defined at the national and international levels through global agreements such as the Convention for the Elimination of Discrimination Against Women (CEDAW), the World Bank's decision to support microcredit for women, or the National Democratic Institute's declaration that Bangladesh's parliamentary elections were free and fair. Yet the final, practical implementation of these policies depends a great deal on the local police, NGO workers, party activists, and the populations they target: ordinary men and women (see John 1999). Thus I also pay attention to intermediate groups, such as political parties, development NGOs, and activist organizations, that inhabit the blurred margins between state and societal actors and that, in Bangladesh, can be classified as generally prosecular or pro-Islam.

Assumptions about women and gender have been central to relations between state and society and among different groups within the state and within society. Similarly, gender has played a pivotal role in the very creation of received notions of a dichotomy between Islam, on the one hand, and the West, modernity, democracy, and rights for women, on the other (L. Ahmed 1992; Kahf 1997); it can, however, also prove crucial to endeavors to reveal weaknesses in these same notions. In an effort to move beyond unproductive assumptions and generalizations about women, Muslim women, or Bangladeshi women, this book focuses on a very specific class of women within a specific political system: landless, rural women in Bangladesh, the majority of whom are Muslim. In addition, it also discusses women involved in what many would see as a clearly antifeminist cause, religious politics: namely, women in the Jamaat-i Islami (see Jeffery 1998: 223). In the process, I draw attention to differences among women of different classes, as well as differences among women within classes, differences prompted by their families' backgrounds and their differential access to education, employment, and NGOs. In addition, I emphasize these women's experience of and interaction with wider structures such as religion, state, and community rather than privilege the last's capacity to determine and dominate their actions. Thus the women are recognized as actors operating within multiple constraints rather than merely as objects of community codes of conduct and state-defined policies. To paraphrase Karl Marx and, more recently, Verta Taylor and Leila Rupp (1991), Muslim women make their own history, but not just as they please.

Today there is a growing body of literature that challenges traditional characterizations of the poor in general—and women in particular—as "unimportant, politically apathetic, or acquiescent" (Singerman 1995: 3).[16] In his highly influential study of Malaysian villagers, *Weapons of the Weak*, James C. Scott argues that even the most exploited groups rarely take up revolutionary activity when aware of their exploited status; rather, they engage in what he refers to as "everyday forms of resistance" or "off-stage" forms of struggle, such as "foot-dragging, dissimulation, desertion, false compliance, pilfering, ... sabotage and so on" (1985: xvi). Revolutions in the traditional sense are indeed rare, but rural society in Bangladesh today is undergoing profound changes catalyzed by the introduction of new ideas, technologies, and products. Some changes are reinforcing long-standing hierarchies and aggravating harmful practices,[17] but others are enabling some members of impoverished groups to challenge the status quo and move beyond hidden resistance in an effort to bring about significant change in their own lives and those of their families.[18]

I argue against scholarship that begins from assumptions that Muslim women are more oppressed than other women, that the source of their oppression is only and always Islam, and that poor and uneducated Muslim women are particularly vulnerable to the supposed dangers of tradition, religion, and superstition, politically apathetic, or resigned to their lots. They are, it would seem, most in need of "saving," from Muslim men and Islam generally (Spivak 1988; Hirschkind and Mahmood 2002; Abu-Lughod 2002; Balchin 2003). Supporters of modernization theory, for example, have argued that women's awareness of their oppression and movements to overcome these injustices are dependent on a certain stage of development, urbanization, and education (Basu 1995: 2).[19] While it is true that differences in demands and methods of mobilization exist among women of different classes within particular societies, there are no empirical grounds for assuming that all women in poorer societies are less capable of articulating an awareness of male-biased injustice simply because their countries are behind according to some linear model of development. Similarly, although it is true that upper- and middle-class women have greater access to education and can often afford to hire poorer women to take over household responsibilities, thus permitting them to devote more time to women's organizations, it does not follow that impoverished illiterate women have no understanding of gender inequality and have no means to combat it. As Sonia Alvarez (1992) has shown in her study of women's mobilization in Brazil, the concerns of poorer, less-educated women may be different from those of their wealthier, more educated sisters, as may be their means of demanding and effecting changes. In the context of Pakistan, Farida Shaheed (1998) has found that while urban, educated middle-class women regard religion as a grave threat and secularism as the solution, neither is perceived as such by most poor rural women.

Interestingly enough, while there has been a great deal of scholarship on underprivileged women in Bangladesh in recent decades, this work has examined them in the context of economic development, factory work, and public health initiatives, most of it applauding women for their potential to contribute to national progress, population control programs, and microcredit enterprises rather than recognizing them as social and collective actors in their own right and for their own interests. Like the inhabitants of poor Cairo neighborhoods that Diane Singerman has written about, ordinary women in Bangladesh have been studied as "objects of political rule rather than as the architects of political change and struggle" (Singerman 1995: 5).[20] Research on women and gender in Bangladesh is certainly undertaken at academic institutions and independent research organizations such as Women for Women, founded in 1973 (Roushan Jahan 1995: 95). A primary reason for the many gaps in knowledge on the subject is the unusually prominent role of donors and development NGOs, which regularly commission studies in order to learn more about the groups they target as well as to evaluate their ongoing projects. As Dina Siddiqi notes in her assessment of the field of women's studies in Bangladesh, women are now "hypervisible. . . . However, most research tends to be located within a narrow WID [Women in Development] framework, thereby reproducing a depoliticized and ahistorical understanding of women's lives." Much of the research undertaken is "donor driven contract research," which means that the research agenda is determined externally, with little attention to local priorities (Siddiqi

2003b: 14; see also Guhathakurta 1997).[21] Because these reports are generally produced for internal distribution only, outsiders have typically had limited access to them, though it should be noted that some organizations have started to take advantage of the Internet to make reports more widely available.

Because of the limited and specific nature of donor and NGO interest, religion and politics have been conspicuously neglected areas of study. This book seeks to help fill this gap by speaking directly to debates within women's studies in religion.[22] As is well known, there is a long history of suspicion between Islamists and secular feminists, Muslim and non-Muslim (e.g., Moghissi 2000; Winter 2001; Hilsdon and Rozario 2006). Feminist activism and scholarship have tended to dismiss all religion, but especially Islam, as inherently patriarchal, while on the Islamist side the obsession with the veil has led most Islamist ideologues and movements, in the nineteenth century and today, to ignore far more pressing needs facing Muslim women. After all, most Muslim women in the world are citizens of nondemocratic polities, live below the poverty line, struggle for daily survival, and are subject to discriminatory personal status laws. While the recent gender-sensitive readings of the Quran by scholars such as Barbara Stowasser, Amina Wadud, Azizah al-Hibri, Fatima Mernissi, and Asma Barlas have sparked talk of a Muslim reformation and indeed provided desperately needed alternatives to the dominant interpretations of the last millennium, it will be some time before these works receive the attention they merit from parties like the Jamaat or become available, accessible, and relevant to the vast majority of Muslim women. By directing attention to Muslim women's actual spiritual and material concerns, this book elaborates in an impoverished, rural South Asian context the insights of Jenny White's study of Islamist women in Istanbul (2002), Shahla Haeri's on elite professional women in Pakistan (2002), Saba Mahmood's on women in the piety movement in Cairo (2005), Lara Deeb's on Shia women in a Beirut suburb (2006), and Pieternella van Doorn-Harder's research on women religious leaders in Indonesia (2006). However, while most of the women in these studies are literate and, with the exception of Haeri's subjects, involved in movements that have led them to shed the traditional Islam of their parents and practice, a new, self-conscious, or, to use Deeb's term, "authenticated" Islam, the women in this book have little to no formal education and negotiate direct overtures by both secularist and Islamist groups.

Poor women in rural Bangladesh do not regard Islam to be the source of their problems but espouse their own understanding of Islam, one that is supportive of their struggles to improve their lives. Rather than rely exclusively on globalized Islamist or secularist explanations of their situations, they form their own analyses and devise their own strategies to improve their condition, many of which entail very public and very visible acts, such as joining NGOs and voting during elections, that fall outside the realm of hidden resistance. An investigation of the interests and concerns of those on the ground makes a valuable contribution to our understanding of political behavior by shedding light on aspects of women's behavior that tend to remain in the shadows in studies focusing on formal politics and national elites. In the process, it forces us to rethink generalizations about Islam and politics that are based on the assumptions that there is a single monolithic Islam and that most Muslims do not differentiate between public and private roles of religion.

SOURCES

I bring together recent work on gender, formal politics, religion, and development and my own primary research into Muslim women's lived experience of and interaction with wider structures of religion, state, and community in order to understand how nonelite, uneducated, impoverished Muslim women can be viable and important agents of change within Muslim societies. To be sure, the women who inhabit the villages of Bangladesh were never a mere distant object of study for me in the way that term is usually understood. Although a citizen of Bangladesh from the moment the state was born, I had in fact spent only four years in Bangladesh by the time I arrived in the United States to attend college. My father's profession required living overseas, and I had spent most of my childhood and teenage years in Europe, with brief stays in India and Lebanon. My sisters and I had, however, made regular visits home to Bangladesh and to our parents' *desher bari*, their ancestral village homes. In our father's village, our *dadu* (paternal grandmother) had been in charge of the family home and agricultural property since our grandfather passed away, before I was born, before even our parents' marriage. In our mother's village, it was her grandmother, our great-grandmother, also long widowed, who sat at the helm of a large extended family. Some years later, our *nanu* (maternal grandmother) retired to the village after a lifetime spent traveling around the country with first her father and then her husband. All three women commanded much respect in their communities by virtue of their age, wealth, the status of their deceased husbands, and, no doubt, the fact that they had all borne sons. Yet local women and men also valued them for their wisdom and knowledge, which went far beyond what they had gleaned from their limited formal education. Similarly, my own relatives regularly turned to village women for advice and help on all sorts of matters ranging from ailments to festivities to entertaining us children. "Backward" and "modern" were never terms used to distinguish "them" from "us"; rather, there was a clear recognition that, at least today, any difference was a matter of wealth and education. Over the years, I watched my great-grandmother and two grandmothers converse with countless poor village women who came to see them, sat on a low stool or squatted on the floor (depending on their age and status) in front of them (they were always seated on a chair or a bed), and discussed their joys and sorrows over *paan-shupari* (betel leaves and nuts). These visits would very often wind down with requests for financial assistance, for a good word with someone, or for *doa* (blessings) that all would turn out right but invariably ended with requests for one last *paan* for the walk home.

Academic interests in college in the United States led me to begin reading the scholarship on village women in Bangladesh, a body of work that grew exponentially in the 1980s and 1990s, with increasing focus on health- and reproduction-related issues (the Matlab studies, for instance) and the impact of pioneering development organizations like Grameen Bank and BRAC. I found the women in these accounts both familiar and unfamiliar. I could easily visualize the settings described— the homes, the paths, the fields, the ponds—but remained unsatisfied by the women who populated these locales in the scholarship, including in my own early work on Grameen Bank borrowers (Shehabuddin 1992). A convergence of personal experiences and national and international developments led me to become interested in questions of faith, religious practice, and the regulation of morality. What exactly did Islam, laws, and local customs mean to the village women I'd gotten to know over the years, who tried to be the best Muslims they could and also delighted in performing at weddings what urban relatives considered risqué songs and dances? How had their ideas and attitudes changed over time? And why?

I was taught to read the Quran and say my daily prayers at an early age and was regularly reminded of the importance of these activities. I still remember a dire warning from my *hujur* (as we called the teacher hired to teach us how to read the Quran) in Dhaka when I was around ten that women who did not cover their hair would pay a heavy price on Judgment Day. I spent several sleepless nights wondering what this meant for the women of my mother's generation who prayed and fasted but did not cover their hair. It was not until my own visits back to Bangladesh from England and Poland during my teenage years that some relatives started to tell me that I should dress more appropriately. They never invoked Islam. Rather, they phrased these rebukes in terms of "we don't dress that way here" or, for that matter, walk or talk or behave "that way," either. It was simply understood that young girls of my family's religious, class, and educational background behaved in certain ways and not others. Such rules also led many relatives and family friends to object to my parents' sending me to college in the United States, to a coeducational institution in a country I had never even visited before. Interestingly, those who supported my parents quickly responded by invoking the Quranic verses encouraging the pursuit of knowledge!

The (im)modesty of my clothing would emerge again as a topic of discussion during fieldwork. Whenever in Bangladesh, I allowed Dhaka- and Chittagong-based female cousins to take me to their favorite shops and tailors and help me put together a small collection of *shalwar-kameez* (coordinated three-piece suits comprising a long shirt, loose pants, and an *orna*, or long scarf) to update my expatriate wardrobe (invariably a few years behind the latest local fashions). In my own way, I tried to resist the pressures of class and fashion trends by wearing simple inexpensive cotton saris whenever possible but this symbol of Bengali nationalism in its mainstream configuration—with a short-sleeved blouse and a bared midriff—was not appropriate for all occasions. Concerned about being properly dressed when interacting with Islamist activists, I was careful to wear only long-sleeved *shalwar-kameez* to those meetings. Loose clothing thus covered everything except my head and hair. I considered covering my hair also on those occasions but decided it would be hypocritical since ordinarily I did not cover my hair.

As it turned out, this outfit did not pose any problems for the Jamaat men I met. Suitably accompanied by a younger male cousin on my very first visit to a Jamaat office in Chittagong, I had a long and productive conversation with three high-ranking men; they sat on one side of a long table and my cousin and I on another. In the course of our conversation, they gave me the name of a woman who was actively involved with the Jamaat, and I paid her a visit a few days later, this time without my cousin. Although she did not comment on my dress for much of the afternoon, she became visibly uncomfortable when I made a move to go into the next room to speak to her husband, also a Jamaat member, while dressed "like that." She had herself suggested that I speak to him directly to learn more about the Jamaat's position on contraception, but she insisted that I conduct this conversation by speaking to him loudly while we sat several yards apart, separated by a curtained doorway (Shehabuddin 1999a: 170). Some months later, during Ramadan, another Jamaat woman chided me for not covering my hair, pointing out that my obligatory fast would not count because I was not also observing purdah: "Are you fasting? Do you pray? Don't you think that it would be a shame if your difficult fast were rendered invalid because you don't observe purdah? I see you as a daughter, and I make this request of you: observe purdah. You said that you had met Mrs. M— in Chittagong. Do you know that she grew up in London, completed secondary school there, and used to wear dresses this short? [She pointed to her upper thigh.] Now look at what [her husband] has made of her with God's blessings." Indeed, this Mrs. M— was none other than the woman who had forced me to speak to her husband through a curtain.

While elite Islamist women expressed disapproval of my uncovered hair and many non-Islamist urban friends and relatives grumbled about the outmoded length of my hemlines, the rural women with whom I spent most of my time were far more concerned about whether I was married, whether my husband was good to me, why I did not have a nose stud, and why I did not have children yet. In the villages in Chittagong, they laughed kindly at my initially pathetic attempts to speak my parents' native Chittagong dialect and took it upon themselves to teach it to me. In our distant homes away from home, our parents had taught my sisters and me to speak only *shuddho bangla*, or standard Bengali, instead of their own dialect. In northern Bangladesh, the local women delighted in my relatively simple, unbookish Bengali. Although I had learned to read and write Bengali quite early, because I grew up overseas and often with few other Bengalis around, my spoken Bengali never developed beyond a certain level of complication and eloquence. This ended up serving me extremely well in the villages of Bangladesh, though not in academic seminars in Dhaka.

This book is based on a combination of ethnographic research, open-ended interviews, survey questionnaires, and close textual analysis undertaken on numerous prolonged visits to Bangladesh between 1990 and 2003. Over this period, I had the opportunity to interact in informal as well more formal interview settings with large numbers of impoverished rural women and men, members of different political parties, NGO workers, and government officials. I also collected and analyzed newspaper articles, government documents, political party and NGO literature, and recordings of Islamist lectures and relevant television programs. In addition to my own fieldwork and primary research, I also draw on the results of a large research project I supervised (in 1996)[23] and two others I co-organized (in 1996 and 2001).[24] In all three cases, I worked with several research assistants, and as a team we were able to cover much greater ground than I could have alone. We all kept journals during the period of research, and these have been an invaluable source of insights and observations that do not come through in interviews and surveys. The names of all respondents have been changed, of course, in order to preserve their anonymity.

Not surprisingly, we encountered a variety of problems in the course of our work. There were a number of occasions when the husband or father of the woman being interviewed expressed grave objections to her spending so much time talking to the researcher instead of putting the rice on the stove or taking care of the children. Local elected officials in some areas suspected that we were working for a rival political party and were therefore reluctant to grant interviews, while the impoverished rural women and men expressed hope that these conversations would somehow help improve their lives. The Islamist elites I interviewed were concerned about how I would portray Islam to my Western readers; this became particularly urgent after 9/11. The secularist elites, while accustomed to the constant flow of researchers from overseas, were suspicious of my interest in religion, both in their own (private) lives and in my willingness to listen to what Islamist men and women had to say. They felt strongly that the latter were all *razakars* (those who collaborated with the West Pakistanis in 1971) and should not be granted a forum. In the end, by employing a variety of research methods, by taking seriously social actors (Islamists and impoverished women) and issues (religion) that have tended to be neglected for reasons informed by politics, elitism, and nationalism, I believe I have been able to capture a clearer picture of the lives of women in Bangladesh, the factors that constrain or enable their behavior and actions, the issues that matter to them, and the actual role of Islam in their lives.

STRUCTURE

Chapter 2 traces the historical antecedents to current debates about gender, religion, and politics within South Asia generally and within Bangladesh specifically. As in other parts of the Muslim world, international and indigenous elite discourses in South Asia since the colonial era have stressed the role of Islam as a determinant in the lives of Muslims. Thus prescriptions for reform and progress have tended to center almost exclusively on the need either to privilege or to abolish completely religious considerations, principally in the matter of women's rights and gender roles in society. These opposing viewpoints have influenced the policies of the state over the years, culminating in present-day Bangladesh in Islamist and secularist perspectives. In this chapter, I examine the conflicting societal pressures on, first, the British colonial state (in the nineteenth and early twentieth centuries), second, the Pakistani state (1947–1971), and, third, the Bangladeshi state (since 1971) and the implications of the state's decisions for the lives of women, rich and poor, during these different periods. The preoccupation with religion has blinded successive governments as well as national elites to the real needs and concerns of poor women and men in rural Bangladesh. This historical overview reveals a remarkable shift over time in the agents of change. While in the nineteenth century the most vocal proponents for reform in the lives of Muslim women were elite men like Syed Ahmed Khan in India and Qassim Amin in Egypt, in the early twenty-first century, we find that not only educated urban women but also uneducated, impoverished rural women are poised to be a viable force for change within Muslim societies.

Chapter 3 examines the nature of poor women's encounters with the state in rural Bangladesh today. Since laws are among the most direct means by which the modern state can intrude in the most private aspects of its citizens' lives, I focus on the legal arena in this chapter. I investigate the extent to which the Bangladeshi state reaches the rural poor and the implications of its limits for poor women's perceptions of the state. I find that in the absence of a strong state, multiple legal codes govern the lives of poor rural women, and they in turn do not automatically turn to the state's legal system in times of trouble but seek out different forums for dispute resolution. As the case of Nurjahan clearly demonstrates, the judicial system of formal courtroom and judge in rural Bangladesh competes with and indeed is often superseded by shalishes. Competing notions of legality regarding marriage and divorce are central to the Nurjahan incident and others like it. Different groups within both poor and elite circles have different ways of ascertaining whether a couple is cohabiting legally and different perspectives on a community's right to take action against what it considers to be illicit or immoral activity. What is of interest is how rural men and women select between these different codes, at times even choosing to disregard them all. In Bangladesh, as in other Muslim countries, both secularists and Islamists consider legal reform an important means of promoting women's interests. However, for legal reform, whether undertaken by secularists or Islamists, to trickle down to the masses and into families, it is necessary that the law be known, followed, and implemented at the grassroots level. The question then is: to what extent does state law actually influence gender roles within society?

Contrary to secularist and Islamist elite claims that the rural poor go along with fatwa decisions such as that against Nurjahan because they are ignorant or easily swayed by religion-based claims, I argue that the poor do not always submit to fatwas (understood here to mean shalish decisions) and that, when they do, it is not necessarily because they believe they are following the word of God; rather, however religious they may be, they are concerned that if they disobey, in the context of a weak state, they risk incurring the wrath of the local elite with little likelihood of state protection. Thus it is not merely ignorance of the laws but also the knowledge that the state lacks the will and ability to enforce them and protect its most vulnerable citizens that influences the decision making of the rural poor. In the end, it is often more important for the ordinary villager to maintain good relations with the local elite than to follow the rules of a state that neither enforces its laws nor is likely to defend the individual against wealthier and more powerful neighbors.

The failure of the state to provide for the vast majority of its citizens is particularly damning in the postcolonial context. In Bangladesh, as in other developing societies, it was decided after independence that the state would be the primary actor in the new nation's struggle to modernize and catch up with the industrialized world rapidly, as well as to improve the situation of the lower strata of the population; in other words, it would bear primary responsibility for the twin objectives of economic development and redistributive reforms. Over thirty years after independence, it is clear that the state has failed to reach the vast majority of the population. As I show in chapters 4 and 5, the rapidly growing presence of NGOs and the recent restoration of democracy offer poor women in rural Bangladesh some hope of change.

In chapter 4, I examine government and NGO attempts to foster development in rural Bangladesh and ameliorate the lives of poor rural women and the nature and extent of support for such initiatives among Islamist and secularist elites as well as the women who are the intended beneficiaries of these various projects. While educated, urban-based critics of NGOs routinely criticize the state for not doing enough, they also often charge the NGO community that seeks to fill the gaps with attempting to function as a parallel government. Left-wing and nationalist groups argue that NGO activity simply hastens the destruction of class solidarity among the rural poor, for example, by pitting individual microentrepreneurs in competition with one another. Islamist organizations, for their part, articulate concern about the spread of un-Islamic values that accompanies the microloans and educational curricula of the Western-funded NGOs. While there is some validity to all these claims, it is also true that NGOs do present impoverished women in rural Bangladesh with new opportunities not simply to earn some money but also to interact with other village women, to think about the issues that impinge on their lives in new ways, and, in effect, to dream about the possibility of a different life. Many defenders of NGOs contend that Islam is the primary obstacle to NGO attempts to reach out to poor women and to women's ability to benefit from involvement with NGOs; in their view, then, Islam serves as a major impediment to attempts to modernize the nation. I find, however, that rural women perceive religion to be less momentous an obstacle to their involvement with NGOs than is their fear of indebtedness to NGO microcredit providers. As it turns out, millions of rural women throughout the country are taking advantage of NGO programs providing microcredit and legal aid as well as attending NGO classes on topics ranging from cow fattening, nutrition, and hygiene to basic literacy and voter education; the problem is that NGO programs have not always reached the poorest of the poor.

With the restoration of democracy in Bangladesh in 1991, NGOs and political parties of all persuasions launched programs to encourage rural women to vote. Of course, NGOs themselves have much at stake in who exactly comes to power at the national level; the government, after all, is responsible for and, more important, has a mandate for defining the development agenda for its five-year term, with clear implications for the very survival of NGOs. While most NGOs have been nonpartisan in their voter education programs, focusing on the act of voting itself rather than whom citizens vote for, others have openly opposed the Jamaat-i Islami on the grounds that if it came to power it would hinder women's attempts to improve their lives through NGO activities. The Jamaat, for its part, has insisted that a vote in its favor would constitute a vote for Islam and therefore a vote for God. These competing claims for women's votes led me to explore, in the last chapters of the book, the possibilities for change afforded by the formal electoral channel.

In chapter 5, I discuss the extent and nature of women's participation in formal politics, including the factors that influence, first, their decision to vote or not to vote and, second, their choice of party or candidate. On examining the role of Islam in these decisions, I find that it is significant to the extent that the women voters interviewed felt that pious men and women made the best leaders; however, their notions of what connotes Islamic or religious leadership differed significantly from those of both secularists and Islamists. Again, of greater significance to their decisions were their perceptions of the state. Many women who voiced little faith in the state saw elections as an opportunity to receive presents such as saris or cash from the different political parties vying for their votes: since their vote was worth little to them, they saw no harm in casting it in favor of the most generous party. On the other hand, voting constituted a deeply meaningful activity for women who believed that the state actually could effect change in their lives. Following recent elections, secularists have been jubilant that the votes of rural women mobilized and conscientized by NGOs defeated the "backward" and "medieval" forces of Islam, that is, the Jamaat-i Islami. My research shows that large numbers of women who considered themselves very good, observant Muslims indeed did oppose the Islamist party, but, in doing so, they did not see themselves as voting against Islam but simply against a political party that they perceived as being opposed to their interests.

In chapter 6, I examine how the unforeseen responses of impoverished rural women have compelled the elites to proceed, albeit cautiously, with their own accommodations and responses to current social and political exigencies. Thus the Jamaat-i Islami now finds itself attempting to shape an alternative modernity without sacrificing its Islamic credentials just as secularists struggle to accommodate mobilized women's piety within their own views of nation and society, to take seriously their religious concerns rather than expect them to disappear. In this chapter, I focus on some specific ways in which the Jamaat has been trying in recent years to reach out to and win the support of poor, illiterate women. Long enfranchised but only recently mobilized by democratic politics and the activities of secularist NGOs, impoverished women themselves are fomenting change in Islamist politics and rhetoric.

In essentializing Islam and positing an opposition between Islam and democracy and modernity, as do Samuel Huntington, Bernard Lewis, and other like-minded scholars, Bangladesh's secularist and Islamist elites seem to share much common ground. They also both assume that the rural poor, especially women, constitute a singular unproblematic category, that they are easily attracted by religious symbols, and that they want a more Islamic polity. Working from these assumptions, both groups propose solutions that invariably center on women. But because both take for granted a singular doctrinal version of Islam rather than varied local understandings and lived experiences, the solutions they propose appear to have little significance for most poor rural women.

In the end, greater attention to women's actual interests and needs as they themselves articulate them—rather than elite perceptions of their interests—can only enhance the effectiveness of projects designed to help them. The failure of urban-based elites, backed by foreign donors and global networks, to incorporate the real-life concerns and experiences of the rural poor into their elaborate blueprints for the future ultimately belies their claims of representing the nation. The various feminist organizations and NGOs that work to promote women's rights are less removed from the realities of impoverished women's lives, yet their suspicion of religion, piety, and religious authorities prevents them from fully understanding the worldview of many of the women they seek to help. While secularist and Islamist elites are engaged in a zero-sum game, impoverished rural women fuse Islam and modernity. And, in doing so, they bring about further democratization of social, economic, and cultural power. My research thus challenges the proposed incompatibility between Islam and modernity. I find that both the Jamaat and unlettered, impoverished rural women are adapting to existing conditions and shaping their own modernities without sacrificing their Muslim-ness. A recognition of the diversity of perspectives within Muslim populations and the mutability of Islamist politics, a recognition, in other words, that there is no single, unchanging Islam, can better inform policies of Western states vis-à-vis Islamist parties and development projects targeting the impoverished and "oppressed" women of the third world.

This empirical study of the lives, struggles, and reflections of landless women in Bangladesh and their interaction with wider structures of society in the arenas of law, development, and formal politics shows that Islam is understood very differently and employed to different ends by different groups within the same society. More important, this book shows how ordinary, unlettered, landless Muslim women can use their particular understanding of their religion to carve out a space for themselves in a traditionally male public sphere and, largely by virtue of their sheer numbers, alter it dramatically and perhaps irrevocably. Before I discuss these more recent changes, however, it is necessary to turn back to the nineteenth century, when many of these debates about women's rights and visibility first occurred. A recollection of the long history of elite (male, then female) intervention in the lives of poor women in South Asia allows us to appreciate the revolutionary potential of the present moment, when Muslim women, despite a high incidence of both illiteracy and poverty in rural Bangladesh, are actively trying to represent themselves rather than allow themselves to be represented by elite men and women.

hope that they themselves can then question unlawful shalish verdicts, and provided assistance with litigation when a case had to be taken to a formal court. An overwhelming majority of the people interviewed (88 percent of the women and 90 percent of the men) were in favor of shalishes that included NGO workers; they explained that such shalishes tended to be more impartial, whether between rich and poor or men and women, than the traditional shalishes run entirely by the local elites, such as the one that condemned Nurjahan and her husband to public stoning.

Most disputes in rural Bangladesh arise over property and marital matters (Siddiqi 2003a: 9). Villagers listed the following among reasons for convening a shalish: to determine if a divorce is valid or how much mohrana and maintenance an ex-husband should pay following a divorce and for how long; to settle complaints of violence perpetrated against a woman by her husband and/or in-laws; to settle disputes between husband and wife over dowry; to resolve disputes over property; and to deal with cases of polygamy, premarital pregnancy ("a major problem these days with young girls increasingly frequenting hotels in the nearby town"), extramarital relationships ("on the rise particularly among women whose husbands are abroad"), and cases such as "a wife killing her husband so that she can run off with another man."[13]

Given their informal nature, traditional shalish committees have not operated in a uniform manner; instead, each committee draws on its own understandings of state law, religious law, village customary law, or a combination thereof, to resolve the matters before it. Many NGO programs targeting shalishes were developed precisely to ensure that shalishes worked in accordance with state law. They did this by providing legal aid training to shalish committee members. Nagorik Uddyog thus described its own goals: "Legal aid training provides a comprehensive understanding of existing state laws, so that members will be able to identify violations of laws as well as decisions that are insensitive to gender and class interests. The objective is to ensure that *shalish* rulings are consistent with the framework of state laws. Sessions cover the legal rights of citizens, women's rights and personal laws (custody, marriage, divorce, maintenance and inheritance laws)" (Siddiqi 2003a: 13). Such endeavors have permitted increasing numbers of poor women and men to present their perspectives and get fair hearings. The problem, however, is not simply that the rural poor and elite shalishdars do not know state laws; as Sultana Kamal reminds us, "even the fullest application or implementation

FIGURE 3.1 A shalish hearing organized by Nagorik Uddyog. (Courtesy of Nagorik Uddyog.)

of [existing] laws will not deliver the desired justice to women" (1995b: 79). Many state laws, after all, are discriminatory toward women. A more important problem is that the laws, as they are phrased, do not always reflect the concerns and realities of the lives of poor women and men; furthermore, they are not enforced consistently enough to be relied on to address injustices or even to serve as a deterrent. Thus, even when they know the law, rural men and women often violate it if they consider it to be contrary to their interest; this is particularly true in the areas of marriage and sexual relations. Rural men and women also violate the law by seeking the assistance of a shalish rather than the local police in criminal matters such as domestic violence and rape, over which shalishes have no legal authority, and extramarital relationships, which the law does not recognize as a crime.

Marriage Registration

In rural Bangladesh today, most marriages are solemnized simply with a maulana reciting the Surah Fatihah, the opening chapter of the Quran, followed with a feast hosted by the bride's family. Under the Muslim

Marriages and Divorces (Registration) Act of 1974, however, all marriages must be registered with the local *qazi* (marriage registrar). The *kabin-nama* (marriage registration form) is important because, at least in theory, it stipulates in writing the amount of the dower, serves as a means of checking the ages of the couple getting married, allows the husband to grant his wife the right to divorce him for any reason they specify on the form, and furnishes documented proof of marriage that can be used by either party to seek legal redress in the event of marital breakdown. A marriage is not legally invalid if not registered, and although the parties involved may face imprisonment or a fine of up to five hundred takas, this is rarely enforced (Selimuddin 1996). Given the state's tepid enforcement of this law and the shortage of qazis to serve the entire population, it is not surprising that relatively few marriages are actually registered (*Daily Star*, February 27, 1998).[14]

About 72 percent of the men and women we interviewed claimed that their marriages were indeed registered and that there had been a kabin. An overwhelming majority recognized the advantages of registering one's marriage: the kabin serves as documented proof of marriage, thus a man is less likely to divorce, drive out, or abandon his wife if their marriage is registered, whereas, without a kabin, he can do so at any time because he has nothing to fear. With a kabin, it is possible to seek legal recourse in the event of problems such as a second marriage, divorce, or desertion; it guarantees a wife's rights and makes the marriage solid.

Minimum Age at Marriage

Under the Child Marriage Restraint Act of 1929 (amended 1984), the minimum legal age at marriage is eighteen for women and twenty-one for men. Relatives, parents, and even the officiating qazi may face legal charges for allowing an underage marriage to take place. Approximately 60 percent of the men and women interviewed were aware of the precise minimum legal age for marriage for women, while responses to questions about the minimum age at marriage for men ranged from twenty to thirty years, with the largest number of responses (37 percent) clustered at twenty-two years. Although some respondents identified benefits to a woman's early marriage—namely, her character would remain pure, intact, and chaste, and she would cease to be a financial burden on her family at an early age—the majority were very conscious of the dangers that early marriage posed to a woman. They pointed out, for instance, that her health would suffer from early and frequent pregnancies in an immature body and that an early start to childbearing would lead to her having too many children and, most likely, weak, underweight children and increase her likelihood of dying at childbirth. They also expressed concern that such a young girl would not understand how to run her husband's household or even how to serve him and that she would be unable to work properly because of her various psychological and physical problems.

Such compelling reasons for later marriage and the law notwithstanding, all the interviewees conceded that underage marriages were very much the norm in their communities. Among the reasons they offered to explain this were ignorance or lack of education on the part of the parents of the bride and groom, a family's dire financial need, and the desire to avoid having villagers start to talk and focus unfavorable attention on a home as a daughter grows up. Many alluded to the dangers of having an unmarried grown-up daughter at home: once she becomes *shiana* (mature), she risks getting involved in an illicit relationship, losing her chastity, and tarnishing her own character and hence her parents' reputation and *ijjot* (honor); if a suitable groom is found, he should not be allowed to get away, especially if he does not demand a dowry.[15] Many respondents explained that a girl who is "fair-complexioned"—almost always a synonym for beautiful—is all the more likely to marry early because prospective grooms are less likely to demand a hefty dowry, while she herself is seen as being in greater danger of becoming involved in an extramarital relationship. On the other hand, a "dark-complexioned" (read "unattractive") girl may need to compensate for her looks with some education and a dowry; this may mean a later marriage since, if her parents are poor, they have to wait until they have saved enough to cover all the wedding-related expenses.

One might expect that the very need to record one's age on a *kabin* would hinder underage couples from marrying; however, first, registration is not as widespread as it ought to be, and, second, the absence of official birth records makes it nearly impossible to verify any information that is provided on the form. As one qazi said, "We know that underage marriages are against the law and we know what the minimum ages are. But how can we know what a woman's age is? I can roughly guess the age of a man, but that's impossible to do with a woman." Another qazi asked,

"If her guardian tells me that she is 20, how can I insist otherwise?"[16] The local union parishad chairman is supposed to maintain a record of all births, deaths, marriages, and divorces in his area, but few people take the trouble to inform him.

Dower

The mohrana (dower) is one of the conditions of Islamic marriage and constitutes a payment by a husband to his wife. It can come in the form of money, jewelry, or other assets; it may be paid in full at the time of marriage or partly then and partly on demand at a later date. Some regard it as an insurance policy for women in the event that they find themselves without male support. This money is for her personal use, to do with as she wishes, with no expectation that she should use it to contribute to household expenses. Islamists are quick to point to this as an example of Islam's special provisions in favor of women. According to Jamaat orator and former member of parliament Delawar Hossain Saidi, "Even if his wife becomes a millionaire by wisely investing the mohrana money, a man is still fully responsible for her food, clothing, health care, and happiness."[17] Others, however, regard the dower as a payment to the bride for the right to sexual access and for the use of her womb to produce future members of the husband's lineage; thus even though the mohrana may provide women with some financial assets, it comes at the cost of affirming her role as wife and mother.[18] This is reflected in shalish decisions: a man is under no obligation to pay his wife mohrana if he divorces her before their marriage is consummated. Similarly, it is fairly common for women, of different classes and educational backgrounds, to absolve their husbands of this commitment on their wedding night, that is, before the marriage is typically consummated.[19]

Villagers of diverse educational and economic backgrounds referred to the dower as khotipuron that a man must pay only if he initiates divorce. At an ASK-sponsored gathering of union parishad members and community leaders in July 1996 in Sitakundo, some men demanded to know why the husband should have to pay mohrana or khotipuron in situations when the wife initiates the divorce. When a lawyer present explained that, under the law, the den-mohr is one of the requisites of marriage and has nothing to do with divorce (except, of course, that divorce is not relevant unless all conditions for the marriage have been met in the first place), a local journalist retorted, "So then, a woman could basically make a business out of this—getting married, getting mohrana, getting divorced, getting married again, forever?"[20] The parallels between this hypothetical scenario and the numerous reported instances of a man who takes on multiple wives, contemporaneously or serially, in order to get more and more dowry, is very striking. The difference is that a woman is permitted to have only one husband at a time, so it would be a very drawn-out process; moreover, a man who has been married several times remains far more marriageable than his female counterpart.

In practice, most women—and this is true across classes—do not know the actual amount of the den-mohr set at the time of their own marriage and, if they do, are wary of demanding that it be paid for fear that this would antagonize their husband. Local officials concede that, in any case, it is very difficult to claim mohrana from the ex-husband after a divorce. Very often, the man simply does not have the money. In that event, the shalish committee has no option but to excuse him from paying part or all of the mohrana.[21] In some cases, a woman's family agrees to forgo the mohrana in exchange for the groom's granting her a divorce. As the following account of a dispute in the western district of Rajshahi shows, the dower is often set at the same amount as the dowry, so that in the event of a divorce, it simply becomes a matter of the groom having to return what he received as dowry. If the marriage has not been consummated, however, the groom can argue that there is no need to pay a dower, and he keeps the dowry.

When Shirifa Begum was about seven or eight years old, she was given in marriage to Najmun Huda, then twenty-five, on the understanding that she would remain with her parents until she attained puberty. Her father paid ten thousand takas in dowry at the time of the wedding and den-mohr was set at the same amount. Soon afterward, the groom's family began to insist that Shirifa come live with them, but the young girl refused—she was terrified of her husband—and her parents did not force her. Two years later, Najmun Huda remarried secretly, and Shirifa's parents found out just as they were finally preparing to send her to live with her in-laws. Shirifa's father, Selim Miah, persuaded the village elders to call a shalish. The committee decided that Najmun Huda should return the money he had received as dowry at the time of the marriage. He asked for two months in which to return the money. At the time of the interview, it had already been several months since the shalish, but Shirifa's family had not yet received all the money. Shirifa was then fifteen years old, and her parents had begun receiving marriage proposals on her behalf. Before discussions with prospective grooms could proceed too far, however, Najmun would begin to spread all sorts of lies about Shirifa and her family, and the proposals would invariably be withdrawn. Najmun claimed, for example, that he had had children with Shirifa when in fact they had not even consummated the marriage. Shirifa's parents were devastated. Selim Miah lamented, "They didn't take my daughter into their home. They didn't return the dowry money. Now they're out to make sure she can't get married into a good family." He had approached many *matbors* (local community leaders) with his problem, but to no avail. "Am I not to get any justice in the matter?" he asked.

Divorce

There was widespread agreement among rural men and women that the high incidence of divorce was driven by greed, ignorance, and high unemployment. These factors were also seen as having contributed to oppression and violence, increased prostitution, illicit love affairs, and excessive dowry demands. Villagers described a very common scenario: a man gets married with the understanding that his in-laws will give him a generous dowry. He receives part of it at the time of the wedding and expects the rest to follow shortly. When it does not—usually because it was set at an amount beyond the means of most people—he sends his wife back to her parents to fetch money, "sometimes, even before the wedding *mehendi* [henna] on her hands has dried." He beats her and abuses her in between demands for more and more money. Finally, he divorces her and sends her home for good, so that he can marry someone else and get more dowry.

Although the MFLO declared invalid the verbally pronounced divorce (whereby a man simply need utter "talaq" or "I divorce you" three times), men retain a unilateral right to divorce their wives without having to show due cause. The law requires that the man inform the local government official, usually the chairman of the village union or municipality, of his decision in writing; the latter then sends a copy of this notice to the often-unsuspecting wife. Within thirty days of receiving this notice, the chairman has to convene a shalish committee that includes representatives of both husband and wife. The primary objective of this committee is to attempt reconciliation. If reconciliation is not possible, then the divorce is effective ninety days after the wife is first notified of her husband's intent. The *iddah*, or three-month waiting period, allows all concerned to ascertain whether the woman is pregnant and provides a final opportunity for reconciliation. The law requires that all divorces be registered at the Marriage Registration Office. If the man does not follow this procedure, he may face a jail sentence of up to a year, a fine of ten thousand takas, or both.

A woman does not have an automatic right to initiate divorce; however, by responding "yes" to question 18 of the marriage registration form, a man can grant his wife the right to initiate divorce (*talaq-i-taw-fiz*). This means that she would not have to go to court for a divorce but could instead inform the chairman of the local council of her decision and generally proceed as above. Some officials openly admitted, however, that they do not bother to ask if the man wishes to grant his wife the talaq-i-tawfiz and simply mark it "no." One qazi thus rationalized this practice: "Parents are desperate to get their daughters married. They are even paying dowry to the groom's family so that they will take their daughter off their hands. They are not going to insist on her right to initiate divorce since that might jeopardize all chances of marriage!"[22] Under the Muslim Marriages Dissolution Act of 1939, a woman can go to the Muslim family law court and file a case if her situation meets one or more of nine conditions: for example, if her husband has been missing for more than four years; if he has not supported her for more than two years; if he has taken another wife without following the legal procedure for doing so; if he is impotent; or if he has been sent to prison for more than seven years. A woman can also get a divorce in exchange for relinquishing her claim to den-mohr or something else (*khula*) or in the event of mutual consent. Taslima of Madaripur, for example, married her husband without the involvement and approval of his family. Her family gave him four thousand takas cash, a bicycle, and a ring. She had been to her husband's home only twice over the course of a year before he started demanding ten thousand takas more in dowry. He beat her up, left her at her parents' home, and refused to pay her any maintenance. Her family sought the help of the Madaripur Legal Aid Association. They called a shalish and got a *khula* divorce in exchange for a payment of five thousand takas.

The majority of the men and women we spoke with seemed far better informed on the procedures involved when a man seeks a divorce than when a woman does. They were aware that a man simply needed to notify the union parishad chairman of his intention to divorce his wife and pay her all he owes her, specifically, her den-mohr or, some said, her den-mohr plus maintenance for herself and any children. A few interviewees believed that the man had to go to court in order to get a divorce. Most respondents did not know that a woman seeking divorce must go through formal legal channels like the court or qazi in order to initiate the divorce and to ensure that she receives whatever money she is owed. There were also important misconceptions pertaining to divorce initiated by the wife: that she must return all the man's money to him and that she automatically loses all rights to the den-mohr.

If the marriage is not registered, then no proof exists, and the situation is very different. Indeed, it is nearly impossible for a woman to initiate divorce under those circumstances: obviously, she does not have a written right to initiate divorce since that can be granted only during registration, and neither can she demand a divorce in the event of desertion, nonmaintenance, and so on, since she cannot prove that she was married in the first place. Although all divorces too must be registered with the local qazi, this is seldom done in rural areas, with the exception, according to one chairman, of government employees. Because their spouses are entitled to benefits such as pension payments, these men are interested in ensuring that a former spouse does not receive these benefits.

Tied to divorce is the matter of the custody and guardianship of any children involved. Under the law, boys can stay with their mother until age seven and girls until puberty; the father, however, remains the guardian throughout and is responsible for all expenses. The operating assumptions here, of course, are that children belong to their father's lineage and that the father is responsible for their maintenance; that the mother may remarry and therefore become part of a different lineage; and that, in any case, women are dependent beings themselves and thus cannot bear full responsibility for the children (Kamal 1995a: 41–42). Usually, the father gladly leaves young children with their mother. As soon as sons are old enough to work and earn money, he takes them away, but he leaves daughters with the mother, who then has to bear the costs and responsibility of getting them married.[23]

Polygamy

Under the MFLO, a Muslim man in Bangladesh is allowed up to four wives at the same time; however, he must make a formal application to the local Union Arbitration Council for permission each time he wishes to remarry, and his application must show that he has obtained the permission of his current wife or wives. The union parishad chairman then convenes a shalish committee that includes individuals representing the man as well as his present wife or wives. This committee discusses the need for this additional marriage to take place. If the present wife/wives are dissatisfied with the committee's decision, she/they can petition that the case be heard in a family law court. If the man remarries without the permission of the shalish committee, he is required immediately to pay his present wife/wives their den-mohr, or his assets can be seized; if the prior wives file a complaint in court, he may be jailed for up to a year, fined ten thousand takas, or both. Finally, marriage without approval from the shalish committee is sufficient grounds for the wife to seek divorce.

In practice, an important reason that the rules regarding polygamy are almost impossible to enforce is that, as I mentioned earlier, few marriages are actually registered, making it extremely difficult to keep track of an individual's marriages, particularly if they are contracted in different villages. Polygamy, in the sense of a man openly living with more than one wife, is rare in Bangladesh. The Quranic stipulation that multiple wives must be treated equally—financially, emotionally, and physically— undoubtedly serves as a deterrent to having cowives live together. More commonly, when a man wishes to take a second wife, he simply goes ahead and marries her and usually does so without informing his first wife, in contravention of state law. In some cases, the man may desert his first wife or throw her out of the home; in such a case, she is still married, hence unable to remarry herself but without any form of financial support. The legal sanction of polygamy for men means that, in practice, an illiterate rural woman lives in great uncertainty since, ignorant though a man might be about all other aspects of the law, he knows very well that he can have up to four wives at any given time, and he makes sure that his wife is aware of that. Sadly, the mere threat of divorce, desertion, or a cowife ensures compliance in many rural women.

A woman whose husband has taken a second wife without first obtaining permission from her and the local arbitration council has certain options. Under state law, she can press charges against him, and, given recent widespread campaigns against polygamy on TV and radio, most women are aware of the conditions under which multiple marriages are legally valid. In reality, however, displeased though they may be and even if they are aware of their legal rights, women often quietly accept the second wife. There are a number of reasons why they do so. Very often, they simply cannot spare the time, money, and hassle involved in filing formal charges in court; in addition they don't want to be deprived of what security they are afforded by having a husband. A woman may prefer to put up with an abusive husband or a cowife than risk the financial, social, and sexual vulnerability to which his absence would subject her. With her husband in jail, a woman's financial situation is likely to deteriorate further, and, living alone, she is also likely to be harassed by male relatives and neighbors. Cognizant of the realities of poor rural women's lives and the limited options available to them, some NGOs often encourage women to accept a cowife.[24]

Among the hundreds of people we interviewed, not a single person, male or female, of any socioeconomic class identified any advantage in polygamy. Of course, it is possible that, following media campaigns, even men who supported the practice were wary of expressing their true opinions. Almost all the respondents, however, cited a number of disadvantages to a household with multiple wives. Among them were: it would be harder to make ends meet because of greater expenses; more wives would generally mean more children and so more mouths to feed; there would be no peace in the home; there would be constant quarreling between cowives and disputes over finances. In fact, one man admitted, "After a while, even the husband realizes that it is a bad idea to have more than one wife at a time!"

Proposals for Reform of Polygamy Laws. Secularists and Islamists have adopted extreme positions on the issue of polygamy: the former wish to outlaw it completely under a secular code, while the latter resist any regulation of the practice on the grounds that the Quranic verses on the subject already have restrictions built into them. And there is, of course, a range of positions between the two extremes. When BNP member of parliament Farida Rahman presented a bill in parliament in 1993 to reform certain aspects of the MFLO, she was greeted with little enthusiasm and criticized for not having discussed the matter with women's groups. The bill, which sought to amend article 6 of the 1961 MFLO, proposed that a man wishing to take additional wives seek the permission of an assistant judge court rather than the local arbitration council. In an editorial in the *Daily Star*, Hameeda Hossain, a prominent Dhaka-based activist for human and women's rights and cofounder of ASK, dismissed the proposal as "more crumbs for women" on the grounds that it did nothing to challenge man's right to polygamy, an instance of gender inequality that violates article 28 (1) of the constitution: "As long as a man's superior rights in marriage and divorce are not challenged, women will remain vulnerable to oppression and violence.... If such laws are meant to be a deterrent, how effectively can women use the court system, given their social and economic dependency? And is the woman expected to abdicate her marital decisions to the court?" (1994). At a discussion organized by the magazine *Ananya* in Dhaka, the late Nileema Ibrahim, another renowned bulwark of the women's movement in Bangladesh, stated, "One man, one woman—it is on this basis that relations between men and women in society should be organized. There is no difference between having or not having the first wife's permission. A man should simply not be permitted to take on a second wife." Columnist Syed Muhammad Saadullah pointed out that it was necessary and possible to reform Islamic law to keep up with the times: "In today's world, there is no justification for maintaining the right given to men by Islam at the time of the Battle of Uhud of marrying up to four women. Islam is a modern religion. It is possible in Islam to keep up with the times." Advocate Sigma Huda listed some of the problems inherent in men's right to polygamy: "Because the majority of the country's population is poor, there is no regular registration of marriages. There is a large floating population. If a woman seeks legal recourse to protect her rights, she has difficulty producing the necessary documents. Moreover, the punishment for polygamy is not sufficiently severe—given all this, there is no alternative but to pass a law outlawing polygamy completely" (*Bhorer Kagoj*, January 22, 1994). In its publications, ASK questions the fairness of some of the conditions under which, according to the 1961 MFLO, an arbitration council can give a man permission to take an additional wife. For instance, a special issue of the ASK magazine *Sanglap* titled "Polygamy and the Law" states that one justification is that the first wife is childless; ASK points out that this assumes that the woman alone is responsible for the couple's inability to have children. Second, a man can remarry if his first wife is an invalid or handicapped; ASK asks, "What should a wife do if her husband is an invalid or handicapped[?] Can she not go to a doctor or hospital?" Third, a man can remarry if his first wife refuses to lead a proper conjugal life with him; ASK's response is, "Should a human being be forced to do something against his/her will? Would this not be a violation of their human rights?" (ASK 1994b: 6).

Just as there are vocal individuals and groups who wish to curb male license to marry at will, there are those, such as members of the Jamaat, who believe that polygamy "is sanctioned by Islam and hence . . . should not be banned. [It] should not be encouraged, but banning this practice would create more problems than one can solve" (Women for Women 1995: 32). During a Bangladesh Television program just before the 1996 elections, three veteran journalists questioned Jamaat leaders about their positions on various issues. Matiur Rahman, editor of *Bhorer Kagoj*, asked the Jamaat's secretary-general, Matiur Rahman Nizami, about the party's position on polygamy. Nizami began by identifying differences between the MFLO and Islamic law: "There was a great deal of opposition to this law during Ayub Khan's rule. Islam permits multiple marriages, but there are also certain restrictions. To completely prohibit it is wrong. What is important is to ensure that it is not misused. What the ordinance does is add to and take away from a God-given rule." When asked specifically about the MFLO requirement that a man wishing to take a second wife obtain the permission of his first wife, Nizami responded: "Look, this matter is tied up with conjugal life. There should be some degree of understanding between the two people. However, if one person experiences a practical need and the other person does not recognize that need and it is not dealt with, if a person feels a need and it is suppressed, then he may drift in the direction of antisocial behavior and indiscipline. There is seen to be no problem if a man has illicit relations with innumerable women; however, objections arise when he wishes to marry a second woman legally. God has given this law with the entire society's well-being in mind and in order to minimize social disorder."[25]

Rahman pressed Nizami, "Do only men feel this need? Do women not experience any such needs? What would your rules be on that matter?" Nizami conceded that women too could have such needs, but he dismissed the notion that a woman might be permitted to have multiple husbands:"Women can certainly experience such needs. . . . As one of our female writers [Taslima Nasrin] has demanded to know, if men can have multiple spouses, why can't women? We do not believe that that is practicable. And no woman would really think it appropriate either." Maulana Abdus Sobhan, a member of the Jamaat's Central Working Committee (Karmo Parishad) added, "Society needs to be enlightened. According to the shariah, if a man takes two wives, then he is expected to treat them both equally. It is a problem now because we don't have an enlightened society, because we don't have Islamic rule. What Ayub Khan's law has done is make it even more difficult."[26] During an interview with me, a senior Jamaat leader explained that it was only out of ignorance that the right to polygamy was routinely abused: "The Quran does not *call* for polygamy. It simply specifies the circumstances under which it is permissible. Unlike other religions, it at least deals with the issue! . . . Those who don't know what the Holy Quran says about it assume that it simply provides a license for polygamy. . . . Polygamy is like medicine. It is not meant for everyone—only for those who need it. In the West, you have extramarital affairs. In Islam, this situation is averted by the institution of polygamy. So you have a legally and socially recognized and maintained wife as opposed to a 'girlfriend.'"[27]

In rural Bangladesh, Quranic stipulations and the state's attempts to regulate the practice have combined to prevent the situation from getting out of hand somewhat, but by no means can they be deemed to have been effective in protecting women's rights.

Dowry

An integral feature of marriages in Bangladesh today is dowry, a payment from the bride's family to the groom's, that is, a transfer of wealth in the opposite direction from the den-mohr. An increasingly important factor behind domestic abuse, it is called *joutuk* or *dabi* in local parlance, the latter a literal translation of "demand" (R. Ahmed 1987; R. Ahmed and Naher 1987; Rozario 1998; Oldenburg 2002; Bates et al. 2004; Suran et al. 2004). Islamists and secularists both condemn the practice, but their explanations for its growing prevalence and their proposed solutions differ considerably. The main laws governing dowry are the Dowry Prohibition Ordinance 1980 and Dowry Prohibition (Amendment) Ordinance 1982 and 1986, under which anyone who gives or takes dowry may be sen-

tenced to one to five years' imprisonment, a fine, or both; t
be reported within a year of its being committed. Even
there are a number of problems with the manner in wh:
phrased. First, a bride's family is unlikely to press charges
giver and the taker can be held liable. Second, given a social
marriage remains the ideal for all women, parents are unlik
prospective grooms by refusing to pay dowry, let alone by reporting them
to the authorities.

The rural respondents in the ASK study concurred that dowry was
a fairly recent phenomenon in Muslim households in Bangladesh, having become prevalent only in the last fifteen to twenty years.[28] Of those
who admitted that dowry was given at their marriages, most had married within the last twenty years. In contrast, older women recalled how,
at the time of their marriages, it was the grooms' families that had provided gifts such as saris and jewelry. When asked if, today, the den-mohr
from the groom's compensated for the dowry a woman's family has to pay,
respondents laughed at the improbability of that ever happening: after
all, the overriding concern of the parents of a grown daughter is to get her
married; if they have to pay a dowry and even forgo the appropriate den-
mohr in order to accomplish their goal, they are prepared to do so.

Asked to speculate on the factors driving the increasing prevalence of
dowry, respondents pointed to male unemployment, greed, new social
norms (one family imitated another until everyone was doing it), an
increase in the number of women in the population, and the scarcity
of suitable grooms. Whatever the reasons for it, almost all respondents
agreed that it was practically impossible to get one's daughter married
today without a dowry. Indeed, dowry has become so commonplace in
rural Bangladesh that if a man does not ask for dowry, the bride's family
may suspect that that he is willing to waive it because there is something
wrong with him. At the same time, a family may pay dowry but then
choose not to discuss it in public, preferring to let their neighbors think
they did not have to pay any. The opposite, however, has also happened:
dowry has become a status symbol, with neighbors anxiously comparing
the dowries they have paid at their daughters' weddings. When asked to
suggest solutions to what was often referred to as the "curse of dowry,"
many respondents evinced great faith in the legal system and the government: 68 percent of respondents thought that the government, national
or local, could put an end to dowry. Other possible solutions included

more jobs for men, more education generally, and a social movement and collective protest.

Women's rights groups condemn dowry for the misery it inflicts on young girls and their families. The practice reflects the devaluation of women: grooms' families are in effect demanding that brides' worth be supplemented with consumer durables like watches, bicycles, and cassette players. Jamaat members also denounce dowry, attacking the practice as un-Islamic and a reversal of what is stipulated in Islam: that a dower be given by a man to a woman at the time of marriage, for her to use in any way she wishes. In his waaz mahfils, Saidi laments the deviation from Islam's imperative: "The Quran has made the mohrana compulsory, but today, who is receiving the mohrana?—Men! The situation has been reversed!" In contrast to women's groups, Saidi holds women directly responsible for this reversal. He contends that women's "worth" has indeed fallen, primarily as a result of their increasing "immodesty": "the *attraction* that is supposed to exist toward women has been transformed into *repulsion*. That which is available easily, cheaply, has no value. . . . If you wear a burka, male strangers cannot see you, therefore they will develop attraction towards you. Your value will rise. Your status will increase. And your chastity and your body will be protected." The present lack of modesty, he argues, has led to the need for compensation in the form of a hefty dowry.[29]

EXTRAMARITAL RELATIONSHIPS

By extramarital relationships, I refer to intimate relations between a man and woman who are not married to one another. When one or both are married to other individuals, the affair is commonly referred to as *bhyabi-char* (adultery). This is distinct from *prem* (love), which, in rural parlance, is more often used to refer to relations between an unmarried man and an unmarried woman. While physical punishment for adultery is specified in the Quran, adultery is not a criminal offense under Bangladesh's penal code; the only law on the books regarding extramarital relations dates back to British rule and allows a husband to bring charges against the man who is having an affair with his wife (Penal Code, 1860, sections 497–498).[30] As the late Salma Sobhan, a prominent lawyer, human rights activist, and cofounder of ASK, pointed out, adultery is seen very much as a legal matter between two men, with no real role for the woman herself: "Adultery, if it is an offence, is surely between the man and woman who are married where one or the other has been unfaithful, and not an offence against the man whose wife has been seduced unless the wife is regarded as a piece of property. There is an unmistakable hint of indignation at the violation of property rights rather than for the breach of any code of morals or honour—'You have used my car without my permission'" (1978: 14).

According to article 35 of the constitution, there is no law outside the nation's law and no punishment outside what is specified by law; yet, in rural Bangladesh, shalishes have awarded a variety of punishments to women deemed guilty of adultery: Nurjahan was stoned 101 times; a few months later, a second Nurjahan was tied to a stake, doused with kerosene, and burned to death; later that year, Firoza was given 101 lashes for her involvement with a Hindu man and then committed suicide; in June 1994 a fatwa was issued in a Rajshahi village to expel a young Hindu woman, Anjali Karmakar, from the community for engaging in the "immoral" activity of talking to a Muslim man (ASK 1996; see also Lucas and Kapoor 1996). Yet another particularly shocking incident is the 1994 shalish case of Rokeya in the southeastern district of Feni. After her husband's death, she moved back into her parents' home with her two young children. With assurances of marriage, her neighbor, Dulal, initiated sexual relations with her, and she became pregnant. When he refused to marry her, she filed a case against him but then dropped the charges under pressure from him and more powerful villagers. Shortly thereafter, Dulal came into her house and raped her. The following day, he dragged her out of the house naked and beat her up in public; he then took her back inside and kept her locked up for several days. Following a fatwa from a local shalish that had found her guilty of zina—she was, after all, a pregnant widow—she was dragged, half-naked, to an open field near the village school and tied to a large tree.[31] In front of a few hundred people, her hair was cut short and her face and breasts were smeared with soot.[32] At that point, local elected officials arrived at the scene, untied her, and proposed what they considered to be a more humane punishment: she was made to wear a garland of shoes and parade herself, in her half-naked state, around the village (M. R. Khan 1996: 28).

Scholars, novelists, and ordinary villagers bear ample witness to the time-honored use of the institution of the village council in South Asia to regulate the conduct of villagers, especially women, Hindu and

Muslim alike (e.g., Kaiser 1993; S. Begum 1994; Moore 1998; P. Singh 1996; Shehabuddin 1999b). The novelty of incidents of shalish-related violence in rural Bangladesh in the mid-1990s lay in the use of the term "fatwa" and the invocation of a pure form of Islam to settle village problems. Historically, prominent religious leaders in South Asia had issued fatwas to justify different positions vis-à-vis British colonial authority, Western education, or "modernity." In contrast, these more recent fatwas were used to evoke Islamic law and the authority to regulate the social, economic, and political behavior of poor village women specifically; moreover, they were issued by men who, by the standards of Islamic jurisprudence, were not qualified to do so and who, as far as the state was concerned, lacked the authority to mete out such judgments and sentences. In any case, in many of the incidents reported in the press, the problem was not even one of adultery as it is normally understood, that is, as a sexual relationship between a married person and someone other than his or her legal spouse. In the case of Nurjahan, for example, she was charged with living in sin with a man whom she, her parents, and her "husband" believed to be her lawful spouse. Neither shalishes nor local elites had any legal authority to sentence and punish, but it was not until January 1, 2001, that the High Court Division of the Supreme Court of Bangladesh announced a landmark ruling declaring all fatwas "unauthorized and illegal" and a "punishable offence" under section 508 of the Bangladesh Penal Code (*Daily Star*, January 7, 2001; Pereira 2002a).[33]

Local perceptions and shalish treatments differ across three distinct kinds of illicit relationships: those in which neither the man nor the woman is married, those involving a married man, and those involving a married woman. (If both the man and woman involved are married to other individuals, the case is treated as a mixture of the latter two, though the burden of blame tends to fall disproportionately on the woman.) *Prem*, relationships (not sexual activity) between unmarried young people appear to be increasingly acceptable in rural society, unless the man and woman are of different socioeconomic backgrounds. Usually, the first time a premarital affair is brought to the attention of a shalish, the committee simply issues a stern warning to the couple to desist from their "unlawful" activity and get married. If they do not, the next step is a fine. When asked if they were aware of any legal prescriptions on the matter, many of our respondents reiterated that both the man and the woman must consent to the marriage. Other respondents did not think there was anything at all in the law on the subject.

Villagers strongly disapproved of a married man being involved with another woman, and shalishes were often summoned about this. Generally, if the man could get his first wife's permission, he was expected to marry his mistress and take her as his second wife. Alternatively, he could divorce his first wife and then marry the other woman. In practice, as discussed above, most men remarried and divorced without bothering with the legal procedures. If the man did not marry the other woman, the shalish committee required that he pay a fine and/or that they both be punished publicly, perhaps caned. A few respondents claimed that the man was sent to prison, but this was unlikely since shalishes do not have the power to do that; it is possible, however, that in certain situations, if it turned out to be something other than a simple affair—rape, for instance—the committee decided to refer the matter to the police. When asked what the law might have to say on the subject, a large proportion of our respondents cited the much-publicized legal requirement that the husband needed permission from the first wife and, in the event of divorce, must pay maintenance for the wife and children.

The most brutal condemnation and the most abusive language were reserved for married women engaged in extramarital relationships. From the responses received regarding the usual shalish resolution of such affairs, it appears that physical punishment is meted out to the married woman and her lover far more often than to an adulterous husband and his lover. The punishment might include one or more of the following, most of which entail some form of public humiliation: the pair might be let off with just a fine and warning; they might be beaten, flogged, or caned; they might be half-buried in the ground and have dogs let loose on them; in certain cases, they might even be expelled from the village. Although I use the pronoun "they," very often the woman receives a more severe punishment than her lover does—even in instances where the lover himself is married. Many respondents pointed out that the more drastic of these punishments were used only if the woman paid no heed to an initial warning; usually, serious efforts would also be made to reconcile the woman with her husband. If the husband was willing to give her a divorce, then she received a lighter punishment and married her lover after the divorce became effective. When asked if they knew what the law had to say on this matter, some respondents mentioned a fine and imprisonment, but most said that they were not aware of any legal provisions regarding such incidents.

The gender bias in these traditions is patent. While a married man who is discovered having an affair can simply take his mistress as a second wife, matters are considerably more complicated in the case of a married woman having an affair: it is far more difficult for her to obtain a divorce, and she is not permitted to take on a second husband. Ideally, her husband grants her a divorce, and she marries the other man. As one woman, Akhlima Khatun, of the southwestern district of Jessore, put it, "If the woman no longer wants to eat her husband's rice and if the other man's family consents, then they get married. Usually, however, they don't. Instead, they are flogged and fined." Abdul Aziz of Dinajpur conceded that punishment varied with gender and class: "An adulterous couple is usually beaten with shoes. But, sometimes, when the man is well-off but the woman isn't, only the woman gets punished." According to Samiyara, a landless woman in Rajshahi, common punishments for zina in her community are public flogging and being paraded around the village wearing a garland of shoes.

VIOLENCE AGAINST WOMEN

Since the 1980s, there has been an alarming increase in incidents of violence—rapes, acid attacks, murders—against women of all classes (and no doubt also an increase in the reporting of such incidents). In response to prolonged activism and campaigning by women's groups, the government passed the Violence Against Women (Deterrent Punishment) Ordinances in 1983 and 1988 and Repression Against Women and Children's Acts in 1995 and 2000 (Anwary 2003; F. Khan 2005). Under these laws, the infliction of physical injury, rape (with the exception of marital rape), provoking suicide, trafficking in women, kidnapping of women, and murder are all recognized as crimes and deemed punishable by law. What these laws do not cover is the mental and physical abuse to which countless women are subjected within their own homes, which often even leads to their deaths; these cases are filed away as suicides or accidents. These laws also exclude deaths resulting directly from illegal fatwas. An additional problem is that only the police can file a case under this law; this means that, more often than not, perpetrators of violence against women go free because the police have not investigated the cases (Kamal 1995a: 30).

Domestic Violence

Under the 1939 Dissolution of Muslim Marriage Act, cru~~~
nine grounds under which a Muslim woman can seek divo~
court. Nevertheless, in rural areas, ~~battered women hesitate~~
~~recourse through the police because of corruption in the po~~____ _____ ____
~~the complexity and expense of court cases.~~ Even though such matters
fall outside the jurisdiction of shalish committees, villagers very often
opt for some sort of resolution through a shalish. As mentioned earlier,
a financially dependent woman may prefer to have her abusive husband
around rather than in jail. Thus, even if she decides to discuss her abuse
in public, she is likely to prefer a resolution through a shalish precisely
because a formal hearing may lead to a jail sentence. Following a shalish,
an abusive husband is often excused after a public beating and humiliation. More often, however, as the following quotations suggest, it is not
obvious to the community or even to a battered wife that an abusive husband deserves censure, even punishment. During a group discussion at
a gender issues workshop organized by the NGO Banchte Shekha, one
middle-aged woman described what happens when a wife charges a husband with domestic violence at a shalish.

> The matbor asks the wife what happened.
> "He beats me," she responds. "Just like that."
> "Why would he beat you just like that?" comes the immediate
> retort. "You must have done something wrong."
> "Why is there a shalish about this?" demands another member
> of the committee.
> The shalish is then dismissed without further ado.[34]

The following quotations from the 1996 ASK survey illustrate the
manner in which many women understand their husbands' authority and
rights over them: "My husband clothes me and feeds me. So, of course he
has the right to hit me if I do something wrong." "My parents handed me
over to my husband when I got married. It is up to him now to discipline
me if I do something wrong." "A man does have the right to hit his wife. . . .
I know this from what I've seen around me growing up." "*Murobbis* [the
elders] say that women make mistakes all the time; that's why their husbands can discipline them." When we asked rural men and women why

so many men believed they were within their rights in hitting their wives, a common response was, "Well, their rationale is, 'I feed her, clothe her, take care of her . . . and she disobeys me!!!' And they use the slightest instance of 'disobedience' to beat up their wives." The argument that a man has the right to hit his wife if she does something wrong was stated repeatedly by both men and women throughout the country. According to Ahmed Ali, a day laborer in Rajshahi, "I know from our elders that if your wife does something wrong, if she goes down the wrong path, then she can be beaten and disciplined. However, you cannot hit her if she hasn't done anything wrong. I know this from a waaz."[35]

When asked where they learned about men's right to discipline their wives, most respondents cited their own experience or that of their parents, relatives, or neighbors, as well as sources such as village elders and the hadith. According to others, "Wife beating has become an addiction. A man will say that he is 'disciplining' her, that she has become unruly and disobedient." Some men pointed out that violence should be avoided. For instance, Aziz Miah, a farmer in Rajshahi, explained, "It is said in the hadith that our Prophet never raised a hand against his wives; therefore, no, I do not believe that I have a right to hit my wife." Amirul Islam, a union parishad member from Jessore, clarified, "A man can 'control' or 'discipline' his wife but not hit her." Several women also insisted that domestic violence had no religious sanction. Majida Begum of Madaripur pointed out, "According to the hadith, men are not allowed to hit their wives—but they do it anyway." Similarly, Omisa, a day laborer in Dinajpur, said she knew from her murobbis that "a man cannot hit his wife."[36]

There is a close link between demands for dowry and violence against women within the home. In the words of a Banchte Shekha member at the workshop I mentioned earlier, "Very often, under pressure from her husband, a woman goes back to her father to ask for more dowry. Her father shrugs helplessly, 'Where shall I get this money?' The woman returns to her husband empty-handed and gets beaten up. In this way, a woman is often driven to suicide, killed, or kicked out of the home by her husband and in-laws, just so that her husband can remarry and get more dowry from another family. If the woman's parents can take her in when she's kicked out, that's good; otherwise she's homeless." According to another Banchte Shekha member, "If a woman dies (i.e., murder or suicide), the police may actually show up, but if they receive a bribe, they'll turn around and walk away." Another woman added, "If the matter is taken to a shalish, the matbor usually dismisses the case by saying 'Allah has taken back what belongs to Allah.'" Very often, the woman's family may choose not to have an autopsy because "it won't bring their daughter back." In the end, then, "the family of the husband goes untried. They get away with what they've done."[37]

Rape

As elsewhere in the world, incidents of rape are notoriously underreported in rural Bangladesh, primarily in order to avoid the stigma that would be attached to the woman. A second reason is the expected response of the authorities to the incident and the woman. Under the Repression Against Women and Children's Act, 2000, rape is a criminal offense, punishable by death or life imprisonment. While essentially identical to its predecessor act of 1995, the 2000 act expands the definition of rape in significant ways, although it does not include marital rape unless the bride is under thirteen years of age (Pereira 2002b: 194–195; Monsoor 1999: 332).[38] For a conviction to be obtained in a court of law, the victim must provide medical proof that she was indeed raped. This proof can be provided only by a medical examination conducted within six hours of the crime and by a doctor who has a rape kit on hand. In addition, the burden is on the woman to prove that any evidence of penetration is from the rape rather than prior sexual activity.

Even for the women and their families who are willing to reveal that a rape has taken place, the formal law and order system are not the natural place to seek justice. Some villagers hesitated to take a rape case to court because they had heard that the rapists would be killed (that is, given the death penalty) if found guilty; that struck them as incommensurate punishment. Moreover, a court case entails expenses beyond the means of much of the rural poor. Many therefore seek redress through the village shalish. Just over a third of the respondents in the ASK study admitted that they had heard of rape having been committed in their village; only half of this group said that a shalish was actually summoned following the incident. A shalish may not have been held for a number of reasons: the rapist could not be found; he was a powerful member of the village and no one dared speak out against him; he refused to come to the shalish.

When a shalish is held following a rape incident, the committee may use a variety of means to establish guilt and arrive at a suitable resolution.

It may insist on medical proof in accordance with state law, or it might insist on following Islamic law, which requires that four honest Muslim men must have witnessed the actual act of penetration for a crime to be established. It may also listen to testimonies from both sides and attempt to come to some sort of compromise. Should the committee decide that no crime was committed—because, for example, the woman actually consented to the activity, or she is considered to have deserved what happened because of her past flirtatious or immodest behavior or dress, or four honest Muslim men did not witness the incident—the case against the defendant is dismissed. The woman herself is then rebuked for her provocative behavior and indeed may be charged with illicit sex and punished for it; in any case, her reputation is permanently tarnished for having had sex, or claiming to have had sex, with a man other than her husband.[39]

Should the committee members decide that a crime was indeed committed, they are very likely to recommend that the rapist marry the woman. Their rationale for this is fairly straightforward: the committee is aware that an unmarried woman who has publicly admitted to having been raped will have a very difficult time finding a husband, and since marriage is considered incumbent upon all men and women, they believe that they are in fact assisting her. Many respondents mentioned that committees require that both the man and woman consent to the marriage for it actually to take place. Another common outcome is that a marriage is arranged for the woman, and the rapist has to pay all the attendant expenses, such as the near-obligatory dowry and the costs of the wedding feast. In an alternative shalish resolution, the rapist must give the woman a sum of money and plot of land. If the woman is able to maintain control over these, she is guaranteed an independent source of income. Money and land, however small its value, ensure that she is not left utterly destitute. Since it is inevitable that, if she is unmarried, she will have trouble finding a husband and that, if she is already married, her husband may seek a divorce because she has been touched by another man, this money and land can be crucial to her survival. Respondents also reported shalish sentences that the man be publicly beaten or caned for his crime, in addition to having to pay compensation to the woman. Sometimes, especially in the event of the woman's death, the man is handed over to the police, despite valid concerns about corruption and fears that a wealthy rapist might bribe his way out of retribution.

While secular, feminist legal activists like Faustina Pereira applaud the government's willingness to pass stricter laws against violence against women, they recognize that such laws are of little use without better implementation. They call for the recognition of domestic violence and nonconsensual sex within marriage as crimes and for improved evidentiary procedures relating to rape (Pereira 2002b: 195–196). The assumption by courts that the past sexual history of rape victims, but not of the perpetrators, has relevance to their understanding of an incident ties quite neatly with Islamist explanations for the rising violence against women.

Regarding violence against women—notably rape, acid attacks, and murder—the position of the Jamaat leadership is quite clear: it is the prevalence of sexual messages in the media combined with women not observing purdah that has led to the increase in assaults on women and to a general increase in promiscuity in society.

> You live in America. You've seen what goes on there. Coeducation is very bad. Free mixing of the sexes leads to illegitimate children— children with no clear paternity. Animals are identified by their mother, but not humans.
>
> And where women don't observe purdah, you have the problem of rape. You must admit that the first step in a rape is sight. The eyes are all important. It is only when a man can see a woman that he will be attracted to her. This would not happen if she were properly covered.[40]

Begum Rokeya Ansar, a prominent member of the Jamaat, echoes this sentiment in her writing, arguing, in effect, that men are under constant visual assault from immodestly clad women. In a widely circulated pamphlet entitled *A Woman Worker's Responsibilities and Duties in the Islamic Movement*, she expresses outrage that, "given the manner in which women are walking about on the streets without purdah, any man who wishes to respect purdah has no choice but to avoid all markets and other public areas and confine himself to his house." As far as she is concerned, it is not just men but "shameless young women" who have brought women down from the positions of respect and honor they enjoyed in the past (1991: 10). One of the most shocking cases discussed in the national media in recent years was the gang rape and murder of fourteen-year-old Yasmeen in August 1995 by three policemen who offered her a ride home. Farida Akhter, a prominent women's rights activist in Dhaka, reports that at a meeting of women representatives from the main political parties and major NGOs, the Jamaat representatives practically held Yasmeen herself responsible for her rape and murder. They argued that had Yasmeen been observing purdah, she would still be alive today—with her chastity intact.[41]

CHOOSING AMONG GOD, LOCAL ELITES, AND THE STATE

In the media furor that followed Nurjahan's tragic death and numerous similar incidents in the 1990s, both secularist (including feminist) and Islamist elites argued that fatwas work as a weapon because the rural poor are gullible and believe anything that is said in the name of Islam. I contend, however, that the poor do not always submit to fatwas and that, when they do, it is not necessarily because they believe that they are following the word of God but because they would incur the wrath of the local elite if they disobeyed. Thus it is not merely ignorance of the laws but also knowledge that the state lacks the will and ability to enforce its laws and protect its citizens that influences the decision making of the rural poor. For the ordinary poor villager, it is often more important to maintain good relations with the local elite than to follow the rules of a state that neither enforces its own laws nor is likely to defend the villager against wealthier neighbors. To illustrate better how the poor do not always accept shalish decisions, I present a second example of a case of illicit sexual relations, one with less tragic consequences than that of Nurjahan and Mutalib but perhaps more representative of rural Bangladesh. By coincidence, this case also involves a young woman called Nurjahan.

This Nurjahan lives in Savar, not far from the capital city, Dhaka, and she too was accused of living in sin with a man she knew to be her husband.[42] The following is her husband's, Fazlu's, account of the incident that sparked the controversy: "I came home from the fields one afternoon. I asked Nurjahan to fetch the water for my bath. We started arguing over something. At some point she locked the door. I knocked for a little while. Because I couldn't hit her, I angrily said, 'I divorce you.' Then people rushed over and stopped the argument." Nurjahan claimed that she could not hear what he was saying from the other side of the door. After they stopped fighting, she came out, and life continued as usual— that is, until a few days later, when the local imam and some villagers issued a fatwa that they could no longer live together, that they should each be whipped or stoned 101 times in order to purify themselves, and that they should perform *hilla* if they wish to remarry.[43]

Fazlu explained to the imam that he had said "I divorce you" in a flash of anger and not really meant it. He had also already sought the advice of religious experts in Dhaka, who had informed him that, according to Islamic law, the man must say "I divorce you" three times over the course of three months, giving the matter much thought between each pronouncement, for the divorce to be final. Fazlu and Nurjahan had also found out that under the Family Laws Ordinance of 1961, they were not considered divorced and, in any case, divorced couples wishing to remarry were no longer required to perform hilla. Thus reassured, Fazlu and Nurjahan refused to go through hilla and resumed conjugal life. The elders and religious leaders of the village, however, declared these opinions from Dhaka completely invalid, arguing, "This was passed by the government. It has nothing to do with Islam because it was not passed by an Islamic government. Even if it means going against the government's law, we stand by our fatwa." They in turn sought a fatwa from another source in Dhaka, which confirmed that Fazlu had indeed divorced his wife and that the couple must indeed perform hilla if they wished to remarry. After local government officials were brought in, the imam lost his job, and Nurjahan and her husband now live together.

As this story so aptly demonstrates, a number of legal codes coexist, albeit in great tension, in Bangladesh: the state's own reformed Muslim Family Code, which is derived from Islamic law; the state's secular criminal code; Islamic laws, which tend to be interpreted very differently by the urban-based Jamaat and rural religious leaders; and a more international human rights perspective that is espoused by numerous secularist development organizations. What is of interest is how rural men and women select from these different codes or even choose to disregard them all at times.[44] Central to both the Nurjahan-Mutalib and Nurjahan-Fazlu stories are assumptions about the legality of certain procedures for marriage and divorce. Various groups, within both the poor and the elite, have different ways of ascertaining whether a couple is cohabiting legally and have different perspectives on a community's right to take action against what it considers to be illicit or immoral activity. I argue that this legal pluralism exists precisely because the state has failed to enforce its own legal system as *the* law of the land.

Despite the growing prominence of rural women in recent years, the discussions regarding the problem of fatwas remain elitist, with both secularists and Islamists looking down on the rural poor as naive and ignorant. If only we had secular laws, argue the secularists, these mullahs could be locked up for good. Or, if only we had true Islamic rule, argues the Jamaat, only properly trained religious leaders would be permitted to issue fatwas, and there would be no abuse of religion. The main problem, however, is not ignorance of the law but cynicism, on the part of both the rural poor and the rural elite. Even those who do know the law often choose to ignore or break it, for a number of reasons. First, they may simply believe that they can get away with it. Time and again, interviewees expressed little faith in the ability of the state to protect the weak and vulnerable or to punish wrongdoers, because they felt the state to be weak, corrupt, and inefficient. Second, they found that existing laws did not suit their social and economic concerns, for example, in the matters of child marriage or dowry. The ordinary villager may often be unaware of the differences between the laws of the land and what the local elite claim is true Islamic law, but she chooses to follow the latter because, from her perspective, she has to answer to God and to the local elite for her actions, while she may go through life without ever directly encountering any branch of the state. In the case of the first Nurjahan, her father himself later admitted that, as the elite men of the shalish were demanding that his daughter step into the pit, he urged her forward, telling her, "Daughter, do as they tell you." In contrast, Nurjahan and Fazlu tried to bypass the local elite by obtaining a written fatwa from a religious center in Dhaka, yet they too did not seek the assistance of the local police. An unscrupulous elite has no interest in undertaking the reform of a corrupt law-and-order system; as the first Nurjahan protested the fatwa against her, even as she was being dragged into the pit, the shalish committee kept repeating, "The law is in our hands" (ASK 1994a).

Secularists express concern that the rural poor, through their support of religion, may well destroy the secularist foundations of the country. Many poor rural women who described themselves as pious Muslims have been known, however, to resist local religious decrees when they seem contrary to their own interests, to what they perceive to be the true spirit of Islam, or to the law of the land. This is not to say that the rural poor are firmly planted in the secularist camp. The example of Nurjahan and Fazlu demonstrates that some may be willing to privilege the 1961 Muslim Family Code, which is basically reformed Islamic law, over traditional interpretations of Islamic law. The couple insisted that because Fazlu had said "I divorce you" in a fit of rage and because his declaration had not been registered with local officials, he had not actually divorced Nurjahan. But not all their fellow villagers agreed with this interpretation of the situation. Although Nurjahan and Fazlu ultimately resumed conjugal life, with state sanction, their fellow villagers were not sure how to react. Many still believed that they were divorced in the eyes of God and were therefore sinning by living as a married couple. The result was a social boycott of the couple and many of their relatives.

Rural men and women repeatedly complain that they do not believe that the state can protect them and that therefore state laws as distinct from God's laws (as interpreted by members of the rural elite) may not be worth following. Consequently, a marriage that is not formally registered with the state may still be socially acceptable, or, as in the case of Nurjahan and Fazlu, a divorce that is not recognized by the state may seem perfectly valid to the local community. Recall that a man and woman are usually considered married if an imam has said the necessary prayers and declared them married, although according to state law all marriages must be registered with the local qazi. Another area of gross disparity between law and practice is that of underage marriage. Most people interviewed considered it the solemn, God-given duty of parents to arrange the marriage of their children at as early an age as possible, though they conceded there were known disadvantages to a girl's being married too young. Similarly, the giving and taking of dowry is a perfect instance of a practice that violates both Islamic and state law but persists throughout the country because of myriad sociocultural as well as economic reasons. When asked if she was afraid of getting into trouble with the law for demanding and taking dowry at her son's wedding, a woman in Tangail retorted, "If someone from the *sarkar* comes and charges me with it, I'll simply turn around and say, 'Why do *you* take bribes?' We're both just trying to supplement our incomes."[45] At the same time, poor parents being forced to give dowry at their daughters' weddings are unlikely to seek legal help from the state, not only because the law as it exists calls for the punishment of both the givers and takers of dowry but also because they know that while wealthier guilty parties can bribe their way of out any legal difficulties, the local legal bureaucracy may well choose to show its efficacy by prosecuting them. The poor are left to face the wrath of the law.

In the end, poor rural men and women's minimal interaction with, even avoidance of, the state's formal legal structures is not an outcome of *gramyo* (rural) ignorance, as urban elites often assume. Rather, it is a result of their lack of faith in the state's ability to protect them in their time of need and their sense that the laws as currently formulated do not reflect their needs and priorities. When Ashrafullah stood by as his daughter was being stoned, it was not because he was ignorant or persuaded that the shalish committee was carrying out the word of God or state law. Rather, he knew that the state's local agents, specifically the police in this case, would be ineffectual, while he would still have to face the powerful shalishdars every day. Perhaps because they lived closer to the capital city, Fazlu and Nurjahan had the courage and means to seek out a fatwa to challenge the one issued in their village. The rural poor, then, make the choices they do in light of their knowledge and experience of the state's ability—or more often inability—to help them during crises; they have little incentive to learn the details of laws that are seldom enforced or enforced only at the discretion of corrupt local police. This attitude toward the state's legal machinery directly influences both the villagers' faith in the state in general and in its ability to improve their lives with the rhetoric of *unnoti* (development) and *gonotantro* (democracy).

4

CONTESTING DEVELOPMENT

Between Islamist and Secularist Perspectives

In the spring of 1995, shortly before a scheduled trip by then–First Lady Hillary Clinton to visit some of Bangladesh's renowned indigenous NGOs, the enmity between groups for and against NGOs spilled out onto Manik Miah Avenue in Dhaka. This grand avenue runs in front of the national parliament complex, a starkly modern set of buildings designed by American architect Louis I. Kahn in 1962 and constructed of marble and concrete to be the "Second Capital" of united Pakistan. Members of the NGO community had applied to the government for permission to hold on Manik Miah Avenue on March 31, 1995, a "national conference . . . of those village poor who are trying to stand on their own feet" with NGO assistance (Samad 1995). The government denied the application. According to Maulana Mufti Fazlul Huq Amini, secretary of the Shommilito Shangram Parishad (United Action Council, or UAC), a coalition of various Islamist organizations that had come together with the stated goal of having all NGOs shut down (Rashiduzzaman 1994: 983), NGOs wanted to use the rally to demonstrate their own power: "That rally would have been a direct challenge to Bangladesh and Islam. However, as a result of objections from vigilant members of the public, that rally was forced to be postponed. . . . The NGOs should know that at no point in any of the twelve months will they be allowed to hold such a meeting. They will be hindered by all means" (*Inqilab* 1995a). He called on all concerned citizens to attend instead the anti-NGO rally scheduled for the same day and at the same venue originally chosen by the NGOs. The government denied permission for this rally too; however, by the afternoon of March 31, hundreds of UAC activists had broken through the police cordon and assembled on Manik Miah Avenue. Not surprisingly, NGOs and intellectuals immediately charged the government with a double standard and with at least tacitly supporting the anti-NGO rally (*Daily Star*, April 2, 1995). Over several hours that afternoon, various speakers proceeded to attack NGOs, the government, and the women involved in NGOs. From their speeches, it was clear they believed that NGOs posed a threat to what they saw as the Islam-based culture of Bangladesh and that the NGOs' point of entry into this culture was through women. In other words, women represented the chink in the nation's cultural and religious armor. A national convention of the poor was finally held on Manik Miah Avenue some months later, on January 1, 1996. Over a hundred thousand poor men and women from all parts of the country converged on the avenue in front of parliament. This gathering adopted a declaration calling for greater attention by the government to poverty alleviation, the environment, and gender issues (*Daily Star*, January 2, 1996).

In recent years, in Bangladesh as elsewhere, NGOs have been celebrated for their innovative strategies to reach the poor and vulnerable and have been rewarded with generous funds from Western governments and donor agencies. While all political elites within the country publicly admit the need for change and the need to help the most underprivileged members of Bangladeshi society, opinions differ, however, on the role of the state versus that of NGOs in meeting these needs and in the content and substance of the measures used to bring about the desired changes. Islamists are critical, for example, of the content of textbooks used in NGO schools, the high interest charged by microcredit lenders, and the near-exclusive focus on women. Secularist critics, for their part, focus their attention on the relative strength of NGOs vis-à-vis the state, the efficacy of their strategies, and the growing involvement of NGOs in business ventures. Both groups express concern about NGO accountability. These national debates have had repercussions for the lives of ordinary rural women and their ability to join NGOs in their areas. For example, in some parts of the country, local religious leaders have condemned women's involvement with NGOs, calling it un-Islamic and the women, by extension, bad Muslims; there have also been physically violent attacks on NGOs and NGO women.

While such attacks have certainly prevented some women from joining NGOs, millions of others throughout the country have become and remain NGO members. The near-absence of reliable state-sponsored services compels women to turn to NGOs, often at the risk of alienating members of their families and communities. They do not see themselves as rejecting religion, contrary to some secularist claims, or becoming bad Muslims or even apostates by joining NGOs, contrary to some Islamist claims. Much as both Islamist and secularist elites insist that Islam is irreconcilable with what each side understands to be modern or Western, this is not a distinction that is relevant to rural women trying to decide whether they should become involved with an NGO. As the targets of anti-NGO discourses and, to use NGO language, the "intended beneficiaries" of NGO measures, impoverished rural women have their own understandings of both the processes and the desired outcomes of externally defined development and modernization.

DEVELOPING THE WOMEN OF BANGLADESH

Gender inequalities in Bangladesh have generally been tackled within a framework of development defined by NGOs, the state, and their donors. Rather than characterizing conflicts between Islamist groups and NGOs as a clash between the forces of tradition and development, however, it may be more useful to recognize that there are, to borrow Judith Nagata's term, "contested models of development" (1994), as presented by Western-oriented NGOs, Islam-oriented organizations, the state, and, finally, those generally targeted by most development policies, the rural poor. At the national and international levels, it is possible to discern two competing models of development and modernity that vary primarily on the issues surrounding the role of religion and women in society. The secularist approach is espoused and imposed by most Western international donors and aid agencies and, consequently, by those who depend on them for their funding, that is, several of the development NGOs now operating in Bangladesh as well as feminist and women's rights groups. While I am not suggesting that these organizations adopt a secularist position only because their donors impose it—after all, compliance with universal agreements such as CEDAW presupposes a diminished public role for religion—it is nonetheless true that donor priorities do affect the agendas of local organizations (see, e.g., Karim 2004; E. Chowdhury 2005; Mahmood 2006). The second approach, the Islamic model, also receives support from international donors, though a different set, of course. The term "Islamic NGO" can be taken to refer to "organisations which, while carrying out developmental work, have Islam as their uniting ideological conviction and run programmes which include an element of Islamic preaching, whether evangelical or non-evangelical" (Kalimullah and Fraser 1990: 73). A small number of NGOs and Islamist political parties such as the Jamaat use money from certain Muslim countries to promote a polity, a society, and gender relations governed by Islamic rules as they understand them. Unwilling to alienate either set of donors, the Bangladeshi state finds itself caught between these competing ideologies. All the parties that have attained national office have ratified international conventions, such as CEDAW; at the same time, while none of them has called for an Islamic state, each has made concessions to Islamist forces in its policy making, particularly in matters pertaining to women, as is evident from the persistence of reservations to CEDAW (*Daily Star*, March 8, 1998; Salma Khan 2001).

In her foreword to Bangladesh's national report to the 1995 Beijing Conference on Women, Sarwari Rahman, then minister of state for women and children's affairs, announced: "We are part of the worldwide movement for the emancipation of women and their full participation in policy and decision-making at all levels" (GoB 1995b: 1). In the report itself, the government asserted: "Bangladesh considers the issue of Women in Development . . . one of the top priorities on account of its own need to transform its potentially rich human resources into enduring assets. In the economic sphere the government is making all out efforts to integrate women in the development process and to create opportunities for employment and income generation of women. . . . The government is also seriously keen to increase the female literacy rate to enable women to participate in various socio-economic activities" (4). In the conclusion to this report, the government identified as its "most remarkable achievement" during and after the UN Decade of Women "[the] focusing and highlighting [of] the indispensable role of women in national development. . . . The most spectacular achievement of the International Decade in Bangladesh is its influence on the government to formulate plans, programmes and policies for improving the socio-economic condition of women" (40). The report ended, "Bangladesh is committed to the upliftment of women's status backed by adequate allocation of resources to implement policy decisions and an integrated and holistic multisectoral approach to women's development where they can play a central role as agents of change in their own right as well as beneficiaries of economic growth and social and political development. The vision of Bangladesh is of an ideal society where men and women are equal as human beings and are entitled to equal access to opportunities for the realization of the goals of Equality, Development and Peace" (41).

It is true that the Bangladeshi state has paid attention to women's issues from the very beginning, but its efforts have been less than adequate, at times even misplaced. As noted in chapter 2, one of its first tasks was to "rehabilitate" the thousands of women who had been raped by the Pakistani army and its collaborators during the 1971 war of independence or whose husbands had been killed or crippled during the war. With the onset of the UN Decade for Women and similar measures in other countries, the military government of Ziaur Rahman established a women's affairs division in the president's secretariat in 1976. According to Rounaq Jahan, a veteran of the women's movement in Bangladesh, this top-down move came as a surprise to women's organizations, which had not asked for it. She believes that the military government in power at the time was attempting "to project a modernist, development-oriented image and found WID [Women in Development] to be a good vehicle for that purpose. The regime also wanted to increase the volume of donor assistance, and therefore picked up on some of the donors' favourite themes: population and women. An additional incentive was the recruitment of political support among new groups, and women were identified as a potentially large constituency" (1995: 42).

In 1978 the Ministry of Women's Affairs was created; this was redefined later as the Ministry of Women's and Children's Affairs.[1] Under the Ershad military government in the 1980s, the ministry was downgraded to a department under the social affairs ministry; the democratically elected government of the early 1990s restored its ministry status. According to Anne Marie Goetz, the changes that came and went with each new government "owe less to any significant variation in the official commitment to the WID/GAD agenda than to its utility at various times in generating international political capital in demonstrating a progressive national position. What has remained constant . . . has been an unclear mandate, and deficiencies in staff, financial resources, and administrative privileges." She points to the ministry's inability even to follow through on its mandate—which includes the authority to oversee programs for women proposed by other ministries—because of limited staff and little time. Similarly, poor resources restrict its ability to implement projects (1998: 59–60).

On March 8, 1997, International Women's Day, Prime Minister Sheikh Hasina announced the adoption of the National Policy for the Advancement of Women (Najma Chowdhury 2001: 221). This policy spelled out the government's "commitment and policies for women on Human Rights, Education and Training, Health and Nutrition, Political Empowerment, Administrative Reform, Violence and the Oppression of Women" (CEDAW 2003: 8). In 1998, in keeping with the requirements of the Beijing Platform for Action, the Bangladesh government approved the National Action Plan. Drafted by the Ministry of Women and Children's Affairs, NGOs, the NGO preparatory committee for the NGO Forum for Women, the planning commission, and thirteen ministries, it promised greater coordination among the different ministries and organizations.[2] Six years later, however, in 2004, important changes were made to the document, and they were made very quietly, without any announcements (Tahmina 2005, cited in Siddiqi 2006b). For example, the revised document emphasizes constitutional rights, unlike the original version, which had been explicit about equality in inheritance, assets, and ownership of land. The new document supports women's employment in "appropriate" professions and no longer stipulates that more women should be appointed to the cabinet and to "the highest positions in the judiciary, diplomatic corps and key administrative bodies." Curiously enough, the government has not implemented any aspect of the new document, and indeed the country's official Poverty Reduction Strategy Paper, finalized in late 2005, "retains the spirit of the 1997 policy" (Siddiqi 2006b). For instance, in this document, prepared by the government in broad consultation with its development partners, including the World Bank and the IMF, equal inheritance rights for men and women remain a stated objective (IMF 2005: 337). Once again, then, the Bangladeshi government seems to be caught between two competing visions of gender roles in society, this time between Western donors and the Beijing platform and its Jamaat allies in the cabinet and parliament.

Since the early 1980s, NGOs have emerged as increasingly important actors in international development; some would say they even compete with states to lead the development process. According to the United Nations' 2002 human development report, there were thirty-seven thousand registered international NGOs in the world in 2000, 20 percent more than just ten years earlier (UNDP 2002). This has coincided with a loss of faith on the part of international agencies in the ability of states to deliver the goods of development, though, of course, one must keep in mind that it is precisely structural adjustment programs imposed on third world governments by these same international bodies that directly targeted social services and reduced these states' abilities to help the poorest of their populations (see, e.g., Bergeron 2004). Many tasks that in the past had been the responsibility of the state were privatized, that is, turned over to NGOs. Because NGOs are generally more in contact with the target populations than are government bureaucracies, many assumed that not only would NGOs spend more of the money on providing services to the poor than would government officials, that is, be more efficacious, but also that NGOs would be more aware of the concerns and needs of those at the grass roots (Pearson and Jackson 1998: 4).

Despite the recent proliferation of NGOs throughout the world and, subsequently, of scholarly literature on NGOs, a clear definition of the term "NGO" is yet to emerge. Strictly speaking, an NGO, as the term suggests, refers to any nongovernmental organization and in theory could encompass everything from neighborhood soccer clubs— Robert Putnam's civic associations (1993)—to BRAC, the largest NGO in Bangladesh and perhaps the world. Richard Holloway, for instance, specifies that NGOs are neither government nor for profit. He posits that "in common parlance in Bangladesh, [NGOs] refer to organizations started in Bangladesh, or brought in from overseas that claim to do development work, and usually do this with foreign money." NGOs' main tasks are to "help the government" and to "do things the government cannot do or does not do well" (1998: 19–20). Others believe that development NGOs "mobilize the poor through education and conscientization to develop their own organization, and create demand for their social rights and distributive justice, and provide various support services to help them achieve a sustainable, people-centered development" (cited in Westergaard 1996: 28). While Bangladesh certainly has its share of NGOs that focus on areas that are not strictly related to development—for example, human rights work or academic research—as noted earlier, the poverty of the population and the nature of donor involvement mean that most issues are connected to creating a better life for the country's inhabitants, and so almost all such organizations are versions of development NGOs.

According to a recent calculation, there are 7,643 NGOs in Bangladesh, including all NGOs registered with the NGO Affairs Bureau as well as the registered field offices of Grameen Bank, BRAC, ASA, Proshika, and Caritas (Fruttero and Gauri 2005: 785 n.7). It is estimated that NGOs have received about $300 million a year in foreign funding in recent years (Stiles 2002a: 34). By the end of 2003, the Grameen Bank alone had 3.1 million members in 43,681 villages, while BRAC had over 4 million members in over 65,000 villages and an estimated coverage of 78 million people in Bangladesh (Grameen Bank 2004; BRAC 2004: 6).[3] In recent years, NGOs in Bangladesh have focused primarily on the following goals: the establishment of effective democratic processes at the grass roots, poverty alleviation, women's rights, education, health and family planning, and the environment (Rahman and Mustafa 1995). Scholars and media alike recognize that Bangladesh is unusual in terms of the high concentration of NGOs within the country and the level of influence they exert in not simply the development arena but also the legal and political arenas (Fruttero and Gauri 2005; M. Ahmad 2001; *Economist* 2003).

A category of NGOs in Bangladesh that has long been neglected is that of the religious organizations, often referred to in the international arena as RINGOs or RNGOs (*Economist* 2000; Berger 2003; Hours 1993; M. Ahmad n.d.). The openly Christian organizations have featured prominently in Islamist criticism of the NGO community, often being seen, incorrectly, as representative of all NGOs in the country. This stems largely from a general acceptance of a dichotomy between Islam and development and of a neat congruence between development and Western Christianity, which today is seen as quite secular. As Jo Rowlands observes, "A particular view of 'development-as-Westernisation' has come to dominate to such a degree that it has become virtually impossible for any different possibility even to be imagined" (1998: 12).

But there are, of course, also Islamic and Islamist NGOs and social service providers, even though "general discussions of NGOs in Bangladesh (within the discourse of development) implicitly tend to exclude

'Islamic NGOs'" (Naher 1996: 35). The Islamic NGOs in Bangladesh focus on charity, disaster relief, and rehabilitation. Muslim Aid, for example, has provided humanitarian assistance not only in Bangladesh following numerous devastating floods and cyclones but also in war-torn regions of the world such as Rwanda, Bosnia, and Afghanistan. Others, like the Islami Samaj Kalyan Samity (Islamic Social Welfare Association) in Dhaka, run orphanages, adult literacy classes, and medical clinics. While these organizations clearly provide invaluable services, they do not purport to encourage their beneficiaries to question the status quo or transform society. In contrast, organizations such as the Bangladesh Masjid Samaj (Society of Mosques), Bangladesh Masjid Mission (Mosque Mission), and the state-run Islamic Foundation have grander objectives and claim to propound an alternative vision of development, one that they see as being in line with Islamic principles. Even if recognized for doing good work, they are distinguished from traditional NGOs in both their orientation and activities. The Islamic prohibition on interest keeps these organizations off the microcredit bandwagon, and their views about gender in society also dictate their programming. According to Bernard Hours, these organizations seek to enhance "the social and religious role of mosques" by training imams to participate in the task of economic and social development within an Islamic framework. Members of these organizations believe that the moral reform and development of individuals must precede any societal development and that social justice will follow only after virtue and peace have been established in society. They understand "welfare" not as "material prosperity and well-being" but as "an intimate harmony between individuals and nature, a gift from God" that in turn generates a respect for the teachings of Islam (1993: 72–78).

As Mokbul Morshed Ahmad points out, all religious NGOs in Bangladesh face some common problems precisely because of their religious orientation, in particular, suspicion about their motives. RNGOs in Bangladesh have been found as guilty of corruption as more secular organizations, and they have been charged with directing their efforts to coreligionists only. And while Christian NGOs are suspected and often charged with proselytizing, Islamic NGOs are often seen as training camps for terrorists (M. Ahmad n.d.). The most lucid proponent of an Islamic development in Bangladesh is the Jamaat-i Islami, which, while officially a political party and not an NGO, sees its task as far greater than merely contesting elections and seeking state power. (I discuss the Jamaat's perspective on various aspects of development later in this chapter.)

The term "NGO" has come to mean different things to different groups in Bangladeshi society and often something very different from the way NGO officials and other members of the development community understand the term. For young university graduates in Bangladesh, NGOs represent a "potential sector of employment" (Naher 1996: 34–35). Similarly, for many university professors, lucrative consultancies at NGOs have become an attractive source of supplementary income. Impoverished rural women we spoke with had other ideas about the main responsibilities of an NGO. These included giving loans; teaching poor men and women how to make marketable handicrafts; providing adult and health education; offering free legal services and arranging shalishes; providing training in fish, poultry, and cattle farming; eradicating poverty; helping the poor to improve their lives; "getting money for us from overseas"; and "making women independent." According to Hours, "for the Bangladeshis, the modern concept of NGO implies . . . above all a foreign—sometimes neocolonial—godsend, a supplier of funds, jobs, and material benefits of which one should take advantage. That is why the charitable dimension of aid is always perceived more rapidly than the more abstract notion of development, which makes no sense to the peasants" (1993: 71–72).

As I described at the beginning of the chapter, relations between NGOs and Islamists have not always been smooth, and when summoned to intervene the state has found itself in a difficult position. Confrontations, direct and indirect, have occurred over specific policy issues too, both between NGOs and Islamists and between NGOs and non-Islamist individuals and groups. It is to these instances and arenas of conflict among the differing elite worldviews that I now turn.

ALTERNATIVE MODELS OF DEVELOPMENT

According to the *Country Paper—Bangladesh* written for the World Summit for Social Development in Copenhagen in March 1995, "A generation ago, it would be difficult to find a woman in a college or a university without a *Borqa*. Now not only in the universities and colleges, but the streets of Dhaka and even in *mofussil* towns [smaller district towns] women are not only found without *Borqa* and dressed in traditional sarees but also one finds scores of women in [the] latest fashionable modern dress in the educational institutions, offices and work places. This is a change which was unthinkable for the previous generation. . . . Women are developing fast and are increasingly participating in every walk of life" (GoB 1995a: 18). Similarly, the explicitly feminist NGO Saptagram Nari Swanirvar Parishad (Seven Villages Women's Self-Reliance Movement) devotes a chapter in its Bengali textbook *A Guide to Enhanced Awareness: Adult Education Lessons Part 1* to the subject of purdah, discussing it in the following terms: "Because of purdah, we are unable to work outside [the home]. That is why we are unable to earn money. That is why we cannot improve our situation" (Afroze n.d.a.: 8). The teachers' guide, available both in Bangla and in English translation, advises instructors to tell the story of a woman who was kept in the strictest of purdah and then died in childbirth because her father refused to summon a doctor to see her. It continues, "The purdah is an obstacle in the path of women's freedom and development. We are suppressed through being kept locked away behind purdah in the name of religion and unless we break free from such superstitions, we shall never be able to obtain our rights" (Afroze n.d.b: 25–27).

These quotations illustrate well a preoccupation in the nation's development discourse with developing women and with linking development to women's dress, in particular their shedding of the burka. This attitude, of course, clearly echoes the colonial position on the veil.[4] While the state, in this instance, and many NGOs see this change in dress as a positive development, for Islamists, this transformation poses a threat to their idea of indigenous culture. As in the nineteenth century under colonial rule, women and the clothes they wear serve as positive markers of tradition for some, negative markers of backwardness for others. For some—namely, the development establishment based in the global north and those who work for them—poor women represent the very cause of backwardness in societies such as Bangladesh; they are seen as retarding development with their dismal illiteracy and ignorance (the two are often read as synonymous), unfettered fertility, and blind adherence to old traditions. At the same time, on a positive note, these same women represent a point of entry for outside influences, for what development planners regard as more progressive views on such matters as gender relations, family planning, and legal awareness. For Islamists, women serve a valuable role in society as repositories and transmitters of venerable old traditions; it is their responsibility to inculcate the next generation with the appropriate customs, mores, and manners. At the same time, on a negative note, Islamists consider these same women to be the most vulnerable to undesirable, un-Islamic, alien ideas and practices.

While acknowledging the contribution of NGOs to the nation's development, Allama Mufti Ahmed Shafi, who presided over the 1995 rally discussed earlier, called on God-fearing Muslims to develop alternative development-oriented institutions, so that "the poor would no longer have to run after NGOs." To that end, he urged the imams of the 250,000 mosques in Bangladesh to set up relief funds in order to collect money. It was not enough simply to give long speeches against NGOs, he pointed out; rather, it was necessary to inform the public about the NGOs' inappropriate activities and build up public opinion against them. The East India Company, he reminded his listeners, entered this region on the pretext of engaging in trade but then went on to take over the entire country; it was the ulama, he argued, who finally kicked out the British and brought about independence. Today, these enemies had put on new saris and returned in the guise of NGOs to transform the local people into their servants yet again. Once again, it was up to the ulama to play a part in rescuing the country from their clutches. He noted that in Chittagong illiterate destitute village women were being given loans only after they had secretly converted to Christianity. He cited incidents in which women had been given a proper Muslim burial, only to be exhumed shortly thereafter by NGO workers who insisted they were actually Christians and then reinterred them with Christian services. Amini, secretary of the Islamist coalition that sponsored the rally, stressed that the rally was being held for Islam, for an Islamic state in Bangladesh, and for the destruction of NGO strongholds in Bangladesh. Those who wished to transform the country into a Christian state, he continued, were the very same people who had tried to prevent them from holding the rally. He warned that God would not support for much longer a government that wished to root out Islam and put NGOs in power. He reminded the listeners that the NGOs had wanted to convene a meeting in order to destroy Islam, the Quran, and the traditional family structure, but God did not allow that meeting to be held. Addressing himself to Hillary Clinton,

due to arrive two days later, he entreated, "Please do not come. Your
NGOs are working against the Quran and against Islam in this country. . . . God is the greatest power. God destroyed Russia. Can God not
destroy America?" For Amini, Hillary Clinton represented the United
States, which he associated closely with the NGOs operating in Bangladesh. Another speaker, Lt. Col. (Rtd.) Khandaker Abdur Rashid,[5]
exhorted nationwide resistance to NGO schemes that targeted women
in order "to destroy our social system . . . and to create Taslima Nasrins
and Farida Rahmans.[6] The primary targets of NGOs are our mothers
and sisters. It is to ruin them socially that NGOs are enticing them out
of their homes with money and inciting them against their husbands"
(*Inqilab* 1995b).

Also in March, a "powerful Bangladeshi politician" told *Newsweek*,
"These NGOs have challenged the most basic traditions of Islam. They
have challenged the authority of the husband" (Klein 1995). In an article
in the *Dainik Shangram* a few months later, Muhammad Abdus Salim

FIGURE 4.1 "After you sweep the house, heat up the food, and wash my sari and
petticoat and put them out in the sun to dry. Don't get out of line. . . . If you do, I'll
tell the NGO Sir!" (*Daily Inqilab*, June 14, 1995). (Courtesy of *Daily Inqilab*.)

decried women's involvement in NGOs, arguing that it was ruining the "traditional" family structure and values of the country:

> [NGOs] cannot tolerate Bangladesh's traditional marriage system. With the goal of establishing a society without marriage and responsibilities, they are bringing in the Western world. Even though there are 20 million educated unemployed young men in the country today, NGOs are giving 90 percent of their jobs to beautiful young women. Then the[se women] . . . are sent off to places where they have no relatives, only unmarried young men for company. Men and women sleep in the same room. Illicit mixing of the sexes is just one aspect of the training courses for the job. By pitting these wanton women against unemployed men, having them "work" at all hours of the night, the NGOs are shredding families, especially in the villages, into little pieces. . . . Even though some of the male workers may lose their jobs from time to time, the "smart women" never do.
>
> (*Salim 1995*)

According to Abdur Rahman Siddiqi, national development and social care are not the true objectives of these NGOs; rather, he argues, NGOs are no more than Trojan horses left inside the country by Western imperialists to attack "our education, culture, religion in the homes of the weakest members of our society" (*Inqilab*, August 9, 1995).

Village elites we interviewed charged NGOs with violating local norms and attacking Islam, for instance, by encouraging women to work outside the home, by enrolling pregnant women in prenatal programs, by vaccinating infants, by providing un-Islamic education (in terms of curricular content) in an un-Islamic setting (coeducational), and by disrupting divinely ordained "harmonious" conjugal relations between husband and wife within the home. In a study undertaken by S. M. Nurul Alam following attacks on NGOs in 1995, rural religious leaders gave the following reasons for their hostility to NGOs: women's involvement in activities "outside the home boundary"; training sessions for women in distant places; overreliance on foreign money, especially funds seen to be coming from Christian or Jewish sources;[7] limited involvement of men; no provision for Islamic education; concerns about conversion from Islam to Christianity; high interest rates charged by the providers of microcredit. They had a clear sense of what they believed counted as "acceptable" development: it should reflect Islamic values and be in accordance with shariah; the country should draw on its own resources rather than be dependent on foreign aid; money should be raised domestically by coordinating the collection and distribution of *zakat* (obligatory tax on Muslims, to be used for charity); special attention should be given to tackling illiteracy and unemployment; there should be increased support of madrasas and Quranic teaching; the banking system and loans should be interest-free; men should play the primary role in development activities (S. M. N. Alam 1996: 19, 15).

To ameliorate the plight of the poorer strata of society, the Jamaat proposes a number of measures. According to a senior Jamaat politician: "The problem with the other parties is that they claim to work for the good of the country, but they end up working for the rich and powerful—and against the poor. Elimination of poverty is one of our primary objectives and our means to that is through an Islamic state. While Communist parties want to strip the wealthy—the capitalist class—of all their wealth, we do not want to do quite that. We just want to get rid of poverty." The Jamaat posits that the poor have a moral claim on their wealthier relatives, therefore there should some redistribution of wealth within extended families from the latter to the former. In interviews with me, male and female Jamaat members stressed the potential of the *bait al-maal*, a pool of funds to which everyone would contribute and from which anyone who needed money could draw what he or she needed. Jamaat women often cover a daughter's educational or marriage expenses by drawing on this fund.[8] They proposed that the government set up a zakat fund to coordinate the collection and distribution of the zakat; one Jamaat leader explained, "If we could raise our own money, as we could through zakat, we no longer would need foreign aid."[9] The notion of a *bait al-maal* featured prominently in Jamaat founder Maududi's own thoughts and writings, which remain central to Jamaat ideology to this day:

> Hoarding of wealth beyond one's needs is prohibited in Islam. Islam expects believers to consume what they have, or to share their surplus with the have-nots. The wealth must remain in circulation. . . . The Islamic way of Zakat administration is the collection in a pool for the common weal. . . . The pool is the deterrent of all evils which

a society is infested with in the absence of such an arrangement for the support of the less fortunate.

The pool called the Bait al-Maal is there like the "lender of the last resort." . . . If you die your children who are young shall not go a-begging. The pool should provide for them, and for you to face the hazards of old-age, sickness, catastrophe, invalidity . . . and all. The capitalist cannot capitalise on your need and offer you sub-standard wages. You shall never starve. You shall never be without clothes, without shelter, when the Bait al-Maal is there.

(Gilani 1978: 321)

To address women's specific financial needs, Jamaat workers pointed to the need to enforce the Islamic requirement for mohrana; if they received their mohrana, divorced women would not fall into such dire financial straits.[10] As a solution to the health care crisis in Bangladesh, Jamaat leaders proposed setting up an army of paramedics along the lines of Chairman Mao's "barefoot doctors."[11] High medical bills combined with substandard health care thanks to poorly regulated private and government doctors, both diminish the productivity of much of the population and contribute to the slide into poverty of marginal households (Hulme 2004).

Not all criticism of NGOs originates at the Islamist end of the spectrum. A variety of groups and individuals, who may or may not fully support what I call the hegemonic view of development espoused by the main NGOs, have expressed reservations about certain aspects of NGO activities. These criticisms come from the Left, from secular nationalists, and from feminists (often but not always overlapping identities). One of the most commonly aired grievances—and on this many Islamists would agree without hesitation—is the lack of financial accountability and transparency of NGOs to anyone other than their foreign donors (Hashemi 1996; Townsend and Townsend 2004; Bebbington et al. 2007); this is not a problem in Bangladesh alone of course.

Related to this is the lack of internal democracy or participatory decision making, or "'downward' accountability to members and beneficiaries" (Edwards and Hulme 1996: 6; see also Kilby 2006). Who gets to set the agenda and decide what programs should be undertaken: the donors, the NGO directors, or the NGO members? Syed Hashemi laments the top-down nature of decision-making in many of the larger NGOs:

Although government-NGO conflict in Bangladesh arose from the government's determination to enforce greater upward accountability from NGOs, NGOs have never developed a countervailing system of downward accountability to the poor. It is interesting to note that although terms such as "grassroots" and "participation" permeate NGO rhetoric, the consciousness-raising approach is reminiscent of the vanguard party of the Old Left. The underlying assumption is that declassed, urban-educated, middle-class NGO workers from the outside must go to the villages to raise the consciousness of the poor so that they will organize to form their own class. This approach denies poor people the capacity to organize and struggle for themselves. . . . In NGO strategies, there has never been a sustained faith in the ability of poor people to bring about their own transformations. It is this perspective that has disallowed any real participation of the poor in NGO activities or the development of systems of accountability to them. . . . A truly participatory development paradigm that integrates poor people effectively into the decision-making process remains largely unexplored in Bangladesh.

(*Hashemi 1996: 127–128*)

Secularist and Islamist groups alike have raised pertinent questions about the motives underlying NGOs' policy choices, accusing them of basing their decisions on the wishes of foreign donors rather than local needs and interests. To use Hashemi's language, "donor dependent" NGOs work on "donor-driven agendas for development rather than indigenous priorities" (1996: 129). Critics charge that as a result many NGOs have no deep attachment to the issues on which they work; rather, they switch focus in accordance with donor interests and priorities. One writer refers to this practice as:

the "flavour of the month" approach to development. What it basically means is that whichever buzzword or term is in common use to reflect the priorities being assigned by the funding agencies is then blindly recited by all the fund-hungry NGOs in the hope of obtaining more foreign funding. . . .

Over the last ten years, it has covered a variety of subjects. These have included women's rights (a longtime favourite, this one—a tired and overused term to describe just about any programme

which can in any way be linked to women as beneficiaries, no matter how tenuous the link) and family planning (another old favourite reflecting the western obsession with how to keep the third
world population—also known as "them"—in check) as well as
more recent innovations, such as the flood action plan (FAP), the
environment and children's rights.

(Nina Chowdhury 1995; see also White 1992: 15–21, 1999)

For instance, almost all NGOs in Bangladesh provide microcredit
because that is what has interested donors in recent years.[12] "Civil society
empowerment" has also been an important—and problematic—NGO
issue in recent years (Stiles 2002b). While one must not deny that many
effective programs have been undertaken through donor initiative and
support, such as nonformal education, immunization, and control of
diarrheal disease, the problem remains that as soon as important donors
lose interest in an issue, the program grinds to a halt; such was the fate
of adult literacy programs. As for the target group itself, at no point in
the decision-making process are its members consulted. Their assistance
is only sought at the implementation stage: their participation "is at the
level of deciding whether to get involved" (Hashemi 1991: 161; see also S.
Rahman 2006).

Like the Islamists cited earlier, some secular nationalists also see
NGOs as merely tools of Western imperialism. But while the former are
concerned that Western interests pose a threat to Bangladesh's Islam-
based culture, at stake for secular nationalists is the ancient Bengali
culture of the region. According to the late Dhaka University professor
Ahmed Sharif, the government had "leased the country to NGOs" that
represented the interests not of Bangladesh but of the foreign powers
who funded them (Bhorer Kagoj, July 23, 1995), while historian and political commentator Badruddin Umar attacked NGOs as instruments of
imperialist powers and goals (Umar 1996). Several observers were particularly critical of the oversight role adopted by NGOs during the 1996
parliamentary elections, pointing out that the country already had an
election commission and did not need outsiders' affirmation of its elections (Bhorer Kagoj, July 23, 1995).

Finally, recent critical evaluations of NGOs have questioned their very
effectiveness and the extent to which they have succeeded in making the
rural poor independent or challenging the rural power structure. Kirsten

Westergaard, for example, finds that impoverished villagers are simply transferring their dependency on the wealthier villagers to NGOs—for money and mediation in disputes, for instance. There are, of course, exceptions; a few NGOs, such as RDRS (Rangpur Dinajpur Rural Service), are "withdrawing direct supervision and support with the objective of creating self-reliant organizations," though it is still too early to assess the long-term sustainability of these efforts (Westergaard 1996: 53; 2000). Development NGOs, as the local representatives, so to speak, of a global development industry, have also been charged with institutionalizing a neoliberal agenda and with enacting "a shift in discourse from social welfare and redistribution to individualism, entrepreneurship, self-reliance and empowerment" (Feldman 2003: 5; see also Ferguson 1994).[13]

Syed Hashemi and Sidney Schuler (1992) contest claims that NGOs necessarily make better use of resources at their disposal. They point out that there is no empirical evidence that NGO provision of social services is cheaper than public provision; moreover, the fragmented nature of NGO provision means that not all areas of the country are equally covered. In short, it may be inappropriate to think of the NGO community as a substitute for the government. Nevertheless, this has not averted occasional hostility from various levels of government. Some bureaucrats, for example, perceive a threat from NGOs, concerned "that voluntary organizations are stripping away their conventional realm of power" (Rashiduzzaman 1997: 240). The government was particularly displeased that the first visit by a U.S. First Lady to Bangladesh was motivated by an interest in successful NGOs like Grameen Bank and BRAC rather than rather than by some more official purpose.[14] According to M. Saifur Rahman, the BNP finance minister at the time (and again in 2001–2006), "Providing Tk. 2,000 or 3,000 to a poor fellow or planting some saplings here and there without even ensuring who will look after them will not durably remove poverty" (Daily Star, March 20, 1995). Ambivalence regarding NGO accountability crosses party lines. In July 2000 the finance minister of the AL government then in power, the late Shah A. M. S. Kibria, expressed concern about the high interest rates charged by NGOs to their already impoverished clientele. He cautioned against the danger of their turning into "rent-seeking institutions" and called for "discipline in their financial matters" (Islam 2000b).

Despite reservations, many defend NGOs as the best available option and cite the indigenous ones as a source of national pride. Even Hashemi

FIGURE 4.2 New Grameen Bank borrowers in front of their temporary meeting-house, Chittagong.

maintains that NGOs are probably still more effective than government workers simply because they are more accessible to ordinary people in the sense that they maintain a presence at the village level and their doors are usually open to villagers. He also notes that the Bangladeshi government itself "also attempts to legitimize itself through donor support," quickly publicizing any signs of approval from foreign agencies and aid consortia (Hashemi 1996: 128–129). In the end, however, even though both NGOs and the state are dependent on foreign donor support, a democratic government, at least in theory, is ultimately accountable to the people while NGOs face no such constraints.

TARGETING RURAL WOMEN

In its report entitled *Women's Empowerment: Measuring the Global Gender Gap*, released in May 2005, the Switzerland-based World Economic Forum measured the size and nature of the gender gap in fifty-eight countries and ranked "countries according to the level of advancement of their female population" (Zahidi and Lopez-Claros 2005). The study focused on five areas deemed to be of "critical importance for development" in order to identify each country's "strengths and weaknesses":

FIGURE 4.3 Young girl minding her mother's shop, which was financed by a Grameen loan, Feni.

economic participation, economic opportunity, political empowerment,
educational attainment, and health and well-being (World Economic
Forum 2005). Bangladesh came out thirty-ninth, "much ahead of South
Asian countries like India (53) and Pakistan (56), and tops the list of
Muslim countries, surpassing Malaysia at 40," a Bangladesh news service wire story published in the *Daily Star* triumphantly declared (May
19, 2005; Zahidi and Lopez-Claros 2005: 8). The study ranked Bangladesh eighteenth in economic participation with remuneration, thirty-
seventh in both educational attainment and health, fifty-third in economic opportunity, and forty-second in political empowerment (*Daily
Star*, May 19, 2005).[15]

In Bangladesh, as in other impoverished nations, educational achievement, economic participation, and political empowerment have certainly
attained the status of shibboleths in recent years, lauded as the most
important tools to achieve women's empowerment. It is essential, however, that we delve deeper into each of these areas to problematize the
manner in which they have been conventionally understood. Not only
do the much-publicized success stories of high rates of loan repayment,

school enrollment, and voter turnout distract us from many problems associated with these very areas of development, but they also forge a sense of complacency—"We've already made enormous strides," "We're doing everything possible"—and obscure the relevance of alternative ways of measuring progress or positive change that merit immediate attention in order to help millions of disprivileged women of Bangladesh lead truly decent, dignified, and meaningful lives.[16] By focusing here on the specific arenas of education and employment (and links between them within Bangladesh and in the wider international context), I show that there is no hegemonic position in either area, permitting multiple perspectives to coexist.[17] In chapter 5, I take up the subject of women's political empowerment by looking at NGO voter education and mobilization programs for women and women's participation in recent elections.

Education

Since the nineteenth century, the education of girls and women has remained high on the agenda of reformers concerned with Muslim women's rights. Today, throughout the poorer countries of the world, the education of young girls has come to be viewed as a "silver bullet" policy instrument, largely thanks to studies that suggest a link between improvements in women's education and their status and in turn between their status and lower fertility and better health (Cochrane 1979; Mason 1985; Mayuzumi 2004). In the early 1990s, Lawrence Summers, then vice-president for development economics and chief economist at the World Bank, expressed his faith in women's education as the solution to the problems of poor women in poor countries: "An educated mother faces a higher opportunity cost of time spent caring for the children. She has greater value outside the home and thus has an entirely different set of choices than she would have without education. She is married at a later age and is better able to influence family decisions. She has fewer, healthier children and can insist on the development of all of them, ensuring that her daughters are given a fair chance. And the education of her daughters makes it much more likely that the next generation of girls, as well as boys, will be educated and healthy as well. The vicious cycle is thus transformed into a virtuous circle" (1993: vii).

Betsy Hartmann explains that education is a popular means of empowering women globally, not only because it is "a laudable goal in and of itself" but because "it is also politically safer than advocating other forms of empowerment, such as letting women organise independent trade unions in free trade zones or on plantations" (1995: 134). According to Patricia and Roger Jeffery, "Girls' schooling is often regarded as a basic requirement for other 'empowerment' policies to succeed or, at the very least, as a significant contributor to them. Advocating girls' schooling is also usually non-controversial, since it is hard for any group in most societies to argue against most schooling, particularly if the state (or the religious leadership) remains in control of the curriculum. Female education has indeed become a rallying cry for international agencies, most notably the World Bank" (Jeffery and Jeffery 1998: 244–245).

The Bangladesh government made one of its earliest policy statements on girls' education in its 1973 *First Five-Year Plan*, where it argued that "the level of schooling of women determines the efficiency of household management. Educated mothers pay greater attention to nutrition, health, and childcare than the uneducated one [*sic*]" (GoB 1973: 479). Thirty years later, on the occasion of the release in Dhaka of UNICEF's report *The State of the World's Children 2004*, Women's and Children's Affairs Minister Begum Khurshid Jahan Haque urged the education of girls, arguing that this would ensure the education and better health of the entire family, bring an end to social ills like early marriage and polygamy, and make women financially solvent (United News of Bangladesh, December 11, 2003). Recent governments in Bangladesh have paid increasing attention to the education of girls and have implemented a variety of strategies to further it, including a food-for-education program, scholarships for female pupils, free secondary education in rural areas, and a separate school for girls in each *upazila* (subdistrict). In these and other efforts to expand access to education, the state has been surprisingly successful. To quote a 1999 World Bank report: "Across Bangladesh a revolution is taking place in the schools. A peek into any secondary school classroom in rural Bangladesh is all it takes to see that enrollment trends are changing fast. It is becoming commonplace to see more girls there than boys." One World Bank–supported program provides stipends to girls in grades 6–10. "The stipends cover full tuition, examination costs, and an increasing proportion of school fees, textbooks, school supplies, uniforms, shoes, transport and kerosene (for lamps), reflecting families' rising educational costs and the need for an extra incentive in upper grades to reduce high dropout rates" (World Bank 1999). The success of the first years of the

World Bank–funded Female Secondary School Assistance Project led to its renewal through the end of 2006. The hope is that this scheme of stipends for female pupils will provide a "financial incentive for families to send girls to secondary school rather than arranging teenage marriages for them." World Bank task leader Ana Maria Jera thus expressed her satisfaction with the project: "It has been incredible. One of the risks was a conservative or religious backlash in communities, but none materialized. It has been a revolution. . . . There has been social acceptance, and there's no going back" (Nuthall 2002).

At the primary level, the ratio of girls to boys increased from 0.81 in 1990–1991 to 0.96 in 2000–2001. Thanks to numerous initiatives to boost female enrollment at the secondary level, the ratio of girls to boys stood at an impressive 0.99 in 2000–2001 (UNDP 2003: 204). Overall, the national literacy rate for girls and women five years and older rose fewer than ten points in a twenty-year period, from 14.8 percent in 1974 to 24 percent in 1994.[18] In 2001 the female adult literacy rate (age fifteen and above) was 30.8 percent, and the male equivalent was 49.9 (UNDP 2003). Thus there are indications that that the gender gap is closing, though not quickly enough (Chowdhury, Nath, and Choudhury 2002). Part of the delay can be attributed to the corruption that, according to newspaper reports, plagues the distribution of stipends to deserving students as well as the hiring of teachers at many schools (*Independent*, June 26, 2003; *Daily Star*, May 19, 2005). That aside, much progress has been made in promoting girls' education in Bangladesh, thanks primarily to a successful partnership between state and society whereby, generally speaking, the state, NGOs, and civil society have recognized each other's potential contribution and worked together toward their goals (Mia 2005).

While figures such as those presented above are useful, we should also be concerned about the quality and content of the education and the opportunity costs of focusing exclusively on schooling. Today, as Patricia and Roger Jeffery point out, it is hard to find any group anywhere openly arguing against girls' schooling. The debates focus instead on what and how children, especially female pupils, are being taught. In Bangladesh, as elsewhere, the educational system is seen as responsible for molding the citizens of tomorrow, and disagreements abound over whether students should be trained to be good Muslims, Bengalis, Bangladeshis, or all of the above, reflecting in turn contested visions regarding the future of the national community (see Hossain, Subrahmanian, and Kabeer 2002). Thus groups like the Jamaat have expressed opposition not to the idea of female education but to the content of curricula and to coeducation generally. Shortly before the 1996 elections, the party's secretary general, Matiur Rahman Nizami, outlined the party's plans for mass education and for girls' education specifically in an appearance on Bangladesh Television:

> We have an economical plan to increase access to education by using already extant institutions. In every village is a mosque. It is a wonderful social institution. With a little government assistance—none of the imams is uneducated—the mosques can be used as centers for the education of adults, children, and farmers. This can be done easily if a small salary can be arranged for the imam. Soon everyone will have access to education. . . .
>
> In keeping with the cultural and historical tradition of this country, women will be in separate institutions. . . . It is because we wish to increase women's education that we wish to establish separate institutions for women.

Maulana Abdus Sobhan, a member of the Jamaat's central working committee, added, "Girls' schools and colleges already exist. We simply wish to increase the number."[19] This point was also made by the Jamaat's women representatives at a meeting organized by the Dhaka-based research group Women for Women: "Women should have equal rights [to] men to educational and health facilities. But . . . separate arrangements should be made for the education of girls from primary to university level. . . . Girls should develop their talent and personality in a separate environment away from boys" (Women for Women 1995: 30).

The mid-1990s were marked by numerous instances of violent opposition to NGO-run schools. In many parts of the country, mullahs issued fatwas that such schools were inculcating rural Muslim children with Christian values and ideas. They expressed particular objections to the education girls received at such schools: they claimed that girls became shameless, too knowledgeable about their own bodies and "un-Islamic" legal rights, and irreverent toward religious authority.[20] About twenty-five BRAC schools were set on fire. Many parents withdrew their children, especially their daughters, from these schools (S. Begum 1994). Similarly, in Patiya in the southeastern district of Chittagong, BRAC was unable to open eighty new schools because of fierce opposition from local mullahs. [21]

In interviews S. M. Nurul Alam conducted shortly after a series of attacks on NGOs in 1995, he and his team found that among the points of conflict between local Islamists and NGOs are perceptions that NGO schools pose an alternative to Islamic schools and that they do not provide religious instruction (1995, 1996). Interestingly, writing as early as 1858, in the aftermath of what the British have referred to as the Sepoy Mutiny, the Indian Muslim leader and educationist Syed Ahmed Khan listed among the causes of the "Indian revolt" the British government's "interference . . . with the religious customs of the Indians," the emphasis on Urdu and English at the expense of Arabic, Sanskrit, and Persian, and the introduction of female education: "Man believed it to be the wish of Government, that girls should attend, and be taught at these schools, and leave off the habit of sitting veiled. Anything more obnoxious than this to the feelings of the Hindustanees cannot be conceived. In some districts the practice was actually introduced" (2000: 16–17, 19–21).

Today, the rivalry between NGO schools and Islamic schools is no doubt fueled in large part by the disparity in available funding (Shehabuddin 1999b). Local Islamists have also voiced concern about the content of the texts being used at many NGO schools and, in some cases, the coeducational classes. The NGO Saptagram was a frequent target of such attacks.[22] In its schools, it sought to provide an alternative education to its female members, to teach them to view the world differently. In the words of one of the top officers of Saptagram, "By 'education,' we do not mean simply literacy, but education for empowerment. That is, the kind of education that can enable women to target the causes of their oppression and socioeconomic misery—to see the 'bigger picture' and their own situation within that context—and can also provide them with the means to change their own lives" (Ghuznavi 1995). Saptagram's elementary reading books for girls and adult women alike include lessons that emphasize the need to register marriages; warn against child or early marriages, dowry, purdah, and exploitation; and list the grounds on which women can initiate divorce. The late Rokeya Rahman Kabeer, founder of Saptagram, explained in a preface why the organization had been compelled to develop its own textbooks: "Before taking the initiative to write [this book], we carried out a far-ranging research to find out whether any government or non-government organisation had issued

any 'gender-oriented' publications. We could find none. And that, inevi-
tably, made us deeply aware that although we were on the threshold of
the 21st century, there was still no true acknowledgement of women's role.
Instead, books were written about 'cowboys' portraying them to be such
good people and of course doing all the work. Or there would be Jack and
Jill with Jill, as always, meekly following Jack" (n.d.: 3).

Through its gender-sensitive educational programs, Saptagram sought
to bypass many of the pitfalls of schooling of concern to scholars like
Patricia and Roger Jeffery, who make a crucial distinction between education and schooling. They argue that "calling schooling 'education' bathes
the whole topic in a warm positive glow, and draws attention away from
the circumstances in which children are actually socialised and learn
about the world around them. Since schooling is usually only a small
part of this learning process, talking casually about differences between
educated and uneducated women ignores the ways in which unschooled
women are nonetheless highly educated in the specifics of their social
worlds." They point out that "in the demographic literature (and in much
of the policy debate) education is, in practice, usually measured simply
by years of schooling, rather than by taking cognisance of the quality and
content of schooling, or considering adult and non-formal education." It
is necessary, they argue, to examine the content of what they learn and
the conditions in which they learn: "Schooling is . . . usually regarded
unequivocally as a 'good thing', but feminists must surely ask whether
and how gendered school curricula critique gender inequalities. Indeed,
schooling often endorses images of the good wife and mother (as well as
class and other inequalities), and may provide an education for consent
rather than for independent thinking" (Jeffery and Jeffery 1998: 248).

The actual concerns and objectives of policy makers and parents can,
of course, turn out to be quite different. While policy makers clearly
assume that education prompts a young village girl to gain a higher sense
of status in her community and autonomy within her household, parents throughout South Asia are often willing to send their daughter to
school for a few years with very different goals in mind. For instance,
many parents worry that they will be unable to attract a suitable groom
if their daughter has no education at all (Mukhopadhyay and Seymour
1994). Their primary concern, then, is that she master basic reading and
writing, just enough to manage her household when she gets married,
as many put it (see Vlassoff 1996; Jeffery and Jeffery 1998). While in the

past this led many parents to withdraw their daughters from school after they completed elementary school, not only because they believed they had learned enough to equip them for married life but also because the secondary school was often a great distance away, stipends to encourage secondary school enrollment for girls plus enhanced job opportunities for better-educated young women are encouraging parents to be more open to schooling.

Employment

Development policy makers harbor the hope that education will open up more employment opportunities for women and that the ability to earn an income will improve their bargaining positions and decision-making power within the family, which will in turn lead to lower fertility. Employment opportunities for women in Bangladesh are limited, however, and what opportunities are available are not deemed desirable by all women or their families. Following pressure from the World Bank to adopt an export-led strategy, Shelley Feldman points out that the Ershad government's 1982 industrial policy enthusiastically encouraged foreign investment by highlighting the "competitive wages and docile labour of Bangladeshi women during a time when quotas had begun to restrict imports from Korea and the Newly Industrialized Countries" (2001b: 221–222). She describes the immediate dramatic changes on the streets of Dhaka: "In the course of little over a year, between 1982 and 1983, women were living in hostels that previously had been limited to university students, going to the cinema, shopping in the markets that surrounded the emerging manufacturing sites, waiting for buses, and walking arm in arm along the road (222). In the past two decades, thousands of women in Bangladesh have entered the formal and visible labor force, with most of them working in the export-oriented garment factories in Dhaka and Chittagong. Between 1979 and 1985, the number of garment factories in Bangladesh jumped from zero to seven hundred; some closed down following the short-lived imposition of U.S. and European quotas on Bangladeshi exports (Crook 1989: 46). Between 1980 and 1989, the number of female garment workers increased from 50,000 to 225,000, creating "a first-generation female industrial work-force" (N. Kabeer 1994b: 181). It is estimated that by 2003 1.5 million women (and 300,000 men) were working in 3,480 export garment factories (N. Kabeer 2004: 15). The Multifibre

Agreement, which since 1974 had guaranteed Bangladeshi ready-made garments access to the U.S. and Canadian markets, expired in January 2005. While it is too soon to gauge the full impact of quota-free competition on the garment industry in Bangladesh, early studies (such as Yang and Mlachila 2007) suggest that major structural reforms are needed to allow the Bangladeshi garment industry to remain competitive.

Factory work, of course, is not an option for all women. As was the case with the first generation of female factory workers elsewhere in the world—for example, in eighteenth- and nineteenth-century New York City—many in Bangladesh regard these workers as "loose" and "immoral" and inappropriate role models for other young women (Stansell 1986; N. Kabeer 2000). Basic literacy requirements by many employers have also tended to exclude a large part of the female population (N. Kabeer 1994: 169–170). Lack of adequate child-care facilities and supervisors' lack of respect contribute to dissatisfaction among female workers and no doubt serve to keep some women away from factory work all together. Naila Kabeer's research demonstrates that while working conditions in such factories "are not as dire as anti-sweatshop campaigners claim, they nonetheless leave much room for improvements" (2000: 17–18).

To explain women workers' willingness to remain in these jobs, Kabeer and other researchers point to the lack of alternatives as well as to the actual benefits women gain from working in factories (Kibria 1995; Siddiqi 1996b; N. Kabeer 2000; Salway, Jesmin, and Rahman 2005). Naila Kabeer finds that "women valued the satisfaction of a 'proper' job in contrast to the casualized forms of employment that had previously been their only options. Their ability to earn on a regular basis gave them a sense of self-reliance, of standing on their own two feet. They also valued their access to new social networks on the factory floor, which replaced their previous isolation within the home; the greater voice they exercised in household decision-making because of their economic contribution; their enhanced sense of self-worth; and in some cases, greater personal freedom and autonomy" (2004: 18). Similarly, Sania Sultan Ahmed and Sally Bould (2004) find that women employed in garment factories increasingly value not being dependent on the male members of their families, and this leads them to make independent choices and decisions. Most dramatically, they "challenge the patriarchal necessity for sons." One married respondent, mother of two girls, reported that she resisted pressure from her husband to have more children in order to try to have a son. With her family dependent on r income from her work in the factory, she told her husband that she wanted to devote their meager resources to educating the girls: "I told him that there is no difference between sons and daughters these days. I want my daughters to be educated and have a better life than I did. One able daughter is better than 10 illiterate sons" (1335).

In rural areas that generally have few options for stable paid employment—unless the village happens to border on an export-processing zone—millions of women have flocked to take advantage of microcredit opportunities. Today, Bangladesh is synonymous in international development circles with microcredit and the Grameen, or Rural, Bank. Dr. Muhammad Yunus, a U.S.-trained Bangladeshi economics professor who pioneered and popularized microcredit and continues to head the vast Grameen Bank, was awarded the Nobel Peace Prize in 2006, as was the Grameen Bank itself. Microcredit has been hailed as the solution to both mass poverty and the population problem (Bruck 2006). In March 2004 panelists at the roundtable "Democratic Reform and the Role of Women in the Muslim World," convened by the National Committee on American Foreign Policy, agreed on the necessity of economic empowerment of women through microcredit to effect "change in the situation of women in the Muslim world" (Hoveyda 2004: 288). The United Nations declared 2005 the International Year of Microcredit, while Irshad Manji, controversial Canadian author of *The Trouble with Islam*, identified microfinance as "a God-conscious, female-fueled capitalism [that] might be the way to start Islam's liberal reformation" (2004: 159). At the international level, even the World Bank, traditionally more interested in funding big dams, bridges, and roads, turned its attention to these tiny loans to individual men and women without collateral, not only in Bangladesh but throughout the world.

Microcredit is now an integral part of the development programs of both the Bangladesh government and most NGOs in the country, large and small. It is estimated that NGOs provide two-thirds of total institutional credit in rural areas (Karim 2004: 301). Studies have found that, despite some significant problems, microcredit gives the rural poor in Bangladesh, especially women, whose mobility is socially circumscribed, the opportunity to earn an income from within the confines of their homesteads (e.g., N. Kabeer 2001; Pitt, Khandker, and Cartwright 2003). The Grameen Bank's recent inroads in the mobile phone industry through its Village Phone scheme have also garnered praise for the opportunities the program offers village women in terms of both income and access to communication (Aminuzzaman, Baldersheim, and Jamil 2003).[23] Indeed, many women involved in such programs were grateful for the direct financial benefits but also for the disruption in their daily schedule offered by NGO activities and the new social networks created through membership. These same networks, of course, can turn nasty when a woman fails to repay her loans, and it is with the inflexible, bureaucratic approach of field-workers that many skeptics of such programs begin their criticisms.

Critics of the microcredit enterprise would make strange bedfellows indeed. Feminists, for instance, argue that microcredit programs tend to restrict women to low-yield enterprises such as making handicrafts or raising poultry rather than encourage them to engage in alternative modes of income generation, and they do not believe that microcredit alone can help women improve their lives. Women who receive these loans do not always maintain control over them; sometimes male relatives seize the money from them and use it for personal or family needs, while at other times the women themselves choose to hand the money to their male kin to invest in more profitable ventures than those open to them as women (e.g., Goetz and Sen Gupta 1996; Develtere and Huybrechts 2005). Shelley Feldman astutely observes that the emphasis on microcredit as "the panacea for poverty alleviation," even as "a central feature of national development, . . . represented a dramatic move away from employment generations that held private forms and the government responsible for expanding productive capacity" (2003: 16). Critics further charge that by facilitating the entry of individuals into the capitalist nexus and focusing on individual profit, microcredit prevents the development of class consciousness necessary to bring about much-needed major structural changes; in other words, the situation of a few individuals may improve somewhat, but the lives of the majority remain unchanged, if they do not actually deteriorate. Aminur Rahman (1999a) and Lamia Karim (2001, 2004) have documented the very real opportunities for humiliation of and violence against women created by microcredit providers working with ideas of development and individual empowerment that do not sit well with local norms (see also Mallick 2002).

While Islamists, for their part, approve of microloans because they enable women to work within the home, within purdah, they point out that charging interest is contrary to Islam and propose the provision of interest-free loans. They also object to the fact that in order to receive NGO loans, women have to attend weekly meetings, chant slogans, and often do physical drills, all under the supervision of predominantly male NGO officers—and in violation of the Islamist understanding of purdah. Many also object to the training in legal and other rights mandated by some NGOs alongside their microcredit programs.

Village men and women voiced similar concerns. Some asked why organizations like the Grameen Bank preferred to give loans to women when, given the incidence of poverty, it would make more sense to invest in male borrowers. According to one religious leader in Sarail interviewed by S. M. Nurul Alam's study team in 1995, "If a man asks for a loan, [NGOs] show indifference. There are millions of unemployed youths that deserve credit but on the contrary they give these to women. When men are capable to work [sic], there is no justification to advance [sic] loans to women" (15). Others were less interested in the greater economic return that male borrowers would ensure than in the appropriateness of women's involvement with NGOs. One madrasa teacher complained, "Our women are going out of the house at the instigation of NGOs. They are doing whatever they like. They are going to town for training. We must stop all these objectionable acts in the country" (S. M. N. Alam 1995: 20).

On the subject of women's employment more generally, Jamaat members constantly point out that Islam has spared women the burden of earning a livelihood and providing for their families; women's primary responsibilities lie elsewhere, as wives and mothers. They hasten to add that this does not mean, of course, that women could not or should not work: they are free to pursue professional careers—within "the bounds of the sharia" (Women for Women 1995: 30). In other contexts too Jamaat leaders are quick to explicate that they are not opposed to women's employment, and their manifesto attests to this. What they do not like is that the present system permits, even encourages, women to dress immodestly, forsake religion, and work in close quarters with men, be they male factory supervisors or NGO staff members. Today the Jamaat clearly recognizes that economic realities are compelling increasing numbers of women into the workforce, while improved access to education is permitting larger numbers of them to take better jobs. In an interview conducted a few weeks before the June 1996 elections, Muhammad Kamaruzzaman, assistant general-secretary of the Jamaat, clarified the party's position on women's employment: "Many think that if we come to power, women will be put away in a box and never be seen again. That is not at all correct. We want women to study to the full extent of their abilities and also to work. However, we want them to dress in the manner prescribed in the Holy Quran."[24]

Many women's apprehension regarding the Jamaat's position on women's employment is manifest in a question posed to Saidi during one of his waaz sessions with women: "Half of the nation's workforce is women, yet the Jamaat's position on women is not very clear. Also, as a result of much propaganda, women have reservations and some anxiety regarding the Jamaat. Is the Jamaat taking any steps to allay these fears? If not, why not?"[25] Saidi responded that women have nothing to worry about, that if an Islamic state were established, "a quota certainly would be reserved for women in employment, in parliament, in the mosques, in business," and their rights would be supported in every sector.[26] The Jamaat has assured women that it wants to set up gender-segregated jobs where women would interact only with women, for example, women tellers for women bank customers. Unfortunately, the Jamaat has been unable to offer any concrete proposals that can meet the needs of the vast majority of women, other than interest-free loans for home-based enterprises and a committee called "Al Hejab" to teach women income-generating skills such as sewing (Women for Women 1995: 30).

NGOS AND CONFLICT AT THE VILLAGE LEVEL

Although some local suspicion is inevitable every time outsiders, be they from Dhaka, Washington, D.C., or Oslo, arrive in a new area and try to initiate change, the widespread violent outburst against NGOs in the 1990s was unprecedented. Because local religious leaders were involved and used fatwas as a weapon in many of the incidents, observers quickly characterized these episodes as the outcome of conflict between the backwardness of Islam and the progressive nature of NGO-led development. While objections were almost always framed in terms of Islam, they were in fact informed by both material and religious concerns. Many involved in the attacks no doubt sincerely believed that, in defending the status quo and traditional hierarchies, they were defending Islam, unaware that other interpretations of the religion were possible and that many of these cherished traditions actually had little to do with Islam. Whatever the actual impact of NGOs, factories, and the government on poor women's living standards, the very focus on these women poses a threat to the traditional class system as well as to gender hierarchies within the family and community. Attitudes and power relations in the countryside are being transformed by the incursion of alien ideas through NGOs seeking to conscientize rural women, by government initiatives to improve female literacy, by satellite stations broadcasting risqué films from Bombay, by export-oriented factories seeking cheap female labor, and by an improved infrastructure bringing in more visitors than ever before. Wealthier villagers, for example, now constantly bemoan the increasing difficulty of "finding good help these days," as young women from families that have supplied domestic servants for generations take advantage of self-employment opportunities provided by various NGOs. Those who do not join NGOs can bargain for higher wages. Local religious leaders, for their part, complain of a decline in the female clientele that used to beat a path to their door to purchase *tabiz* (amulets), *pani-pora* (blessed water), and special prayers for sick children or ailing animals. Not surprisingly, these same leaders also speak out against the health-care services and medical information some NGOs provide for a nominal fee, sometimes even for free (Shehabuddin 1999b).

Despite Islamist campaigns declaring that foreign- and/or Christian-funded NGOs are secretly stripping Muslim women of their faith, millions of women have become and remain NGO members. NGO members we interviewed in 1996 told us that local people had tried to dissuade them from joining in the first place by telling them that they would lose their religion and become Christian, lose all their money, be forced to raise pigs, or be denied a *janaja* (Muslim funeral). Their neighbors also threatened that they would not allow their husbands in the mosque and would expel their families from the *samaj* (community). Omisa recalls, "The village *munshis* [scribes; teachers], my husband, everyone said that women were going to sell the country [to the foreigners]; why do women need to work? They are now without *hadith*." The village murob-bis (elders) warned Azizan that "NGOs were giving out *haram* [unlawful in Islam] money and I shouldn't touch it."

The women, however, did not meekly sit back and accept these obstacles. Ayesha, for example, patiently explained to her husband what NGOs wanted to accomplish and then, over time, showed him what could be done with a loan. "Now," she added proudly, "along with my husband, I am raising poultry, fish, and a cow to meet household expenses." Rahima told us, "I didn't believe what they had to say. They just talk. They never help us. So I went ahead and joined the shomiti [committee or cooperative]." Similarly, Omisa described how, despite all criticisms, she bravely went ahead: "I explained to everyone what I was really doing. I've been able to do something for my village. I now have a business that I started with a loan. [Our village] has received sanitary latrines and violence against women has gone down." Morjina also refused to pay attention to the objections around her because, in her words, "I wanted to become independent." Somirunnessa explained that she had to ignore local disapproval because "I had to think of saving my stomach. . . . [Since joining,] I've formed a shomiti and am earning a living from sewing and embroidery." Fatima too was glad that she had paid no attention to detractors; through NGO involvement, she had been able to buy a cow and some land and even build a small house. In the district of Chittagong, Farida had been subjected to criticism and was furious: "People said a lot of things when we first took money from the Grameen Bank—that we were becoming Christian, that we were losing our religion. If we are, then we must. When have *they* ever lent us ten takas? We must do what we can to survive. Sometimes they say these things because they are afraid that the poor will become rich!"[27] From her study of female garment workers, Naila Kabeer reports similar findings: "the overwhelming majority appeared to have taken the initiative themselves to enter the garment factories. In many cases, this entailed overcoming the initial resistance of male guardians" (1994b: 168).

Women who have joined NGOs say that they have benefited not only financially but also from the general experience; for instance, they admit that they are more articulate and self-confident as a result of having to participate in and even run meetings, speak with strangers, and manage their small businesses. NGOs provide a variety of services, ranging from microcredit, adult literacy classes, legal awareness programs, conscientization, and preventive health education to training in income-generating skills such as poultry and livestock raising. NGOs run or staffed predominantly by women also show village men and women what women can accomplish. This came across very clearly in a comparison of two legal aid NGOs in southwestern Bangladesh, the Madaripur Legal Aid Association (MLAA) in Madaripur and Banchte Shekha (Learning to Survive) in Jessore. In addition to legal services, both NGOs also provide microcredit and skills training. At MLAA, the director, Fazlul Huq, and the majority of the staff are male, while at Banchte Shekha, the director, Angela Gomes, and most of the staff are female. In interviews we conducted in 1996 there emerged a clear difference in the responses of poor women from the two coverage areas. Eighty-seven percent of the women interviewed in Banchte Shekha's service area said they would prefer dealing with a female NGO worker if they had a legal problem. Among the reasons they gave were that Angela Apa (referring to Angela Gomes; "Apa," literally "older sister," is a term of respect for an older woman) was very good, that women could speak more openly to women NGO workers, and that women better understand women's problems and sorrows. In the MLAA's service area, just under 8 percent said they would prefer dealing with a female NGO worker in the event of a legal problem. The MLAA group expressed greater confidence in the ability of male workers to work on their behalf, a sentiment that was scarcely visible in the Banchte Shekha area. In the end, the majority of NGOs operating in Bangladesh today and certainly the two largest organizations are staffed overwhelmingly by men. Brooke Ackerly has calculated that BRAC and Grameen Bank staff are 10 and 9 percent women, respectively (1995: 66, cited in Mallick 2002: 155). This has implications for the effectiveness of an organization's programs as well as its very credibility among both the local populations and the foreign donors. As Ainoon Naher observes, given that "many NGOs themselves (Grameen Bank in particular) are mostly run by men, it certainly makes no sense to tell the rural people that *their* women need to be empowered" (1996: 39).

Of course, despite the overwhelming poverty of rural Bangladesh and the limited alternatives available to women, large numbers of poor rural women have not joined NGOs. Conventional wisdom would claim they have stayed away for fear of violating Islamic injunctions, but this actually explains the decisions of only some women, not all. In interviews, the women who were reluctant to join NGOs turned out to be in the category known as "the poorest of the poor."[28] And their decision to steer clear of NGOs was influenced less by local or national fatwas against NGO involvement and more by the direct opposition of their families and husbands and by fears that they would be unable to repay the loan through weekly installments. Although many lending organizations such as the Grameen Bank claim to target the "poorest of the poor," they are not always successful. The poorest are afraid to take out loans because they may be unable to repay them, unlike a slightly better-off neighbor who can use funds from an additional source of income or from another working member of the family to make regular payments (e.g., Westergaard 1996; N. Kabeer 2001). As Asya in Chittagong explained, "I have no husband, no son. On whose strength can I take a loan?"[29] Tohura, a widow in Dinajpur, said she didn't join because "I don't have enough money to join a shomiti." Similarly, Parveen in Sylhet explained, "I don't have the means to pay the kisti [loan repayment installments]." Women like these are also often deliberately excluded by their peers and NGO field-workers because they are seen as bad credit risks. Mokbul Ahmad cites an NGO field-worker who described the pressure from above to ensure high repayment rates among borrowers: "I tell them that if you die without repaying my loan I will kick on your grave four times because you have not repaid the money" (Ahmad 2003: 71). Juliet Hunt and Nalini Kasynathan report that "fieldworkers responsible for approving loans explicitly assumed that husbands would be using and controlling the credit, and questioned women, before approving the loan, about whether husbands would be able to provide for repayments." They then cite a telling comment from a field-worker: "Women don't know what to do with this money, they cannot understand how to use it, so of course they give it to their husbands" (2001: 44). Given the pressure from the field-worker and the risk of ostracism and even violence from their neighbors, the poorest and most vulnerable women hesitate to take out loans. Clearly, then, it is not the poorest women in the village who actually take advantage of credit opportunities, and it is not religion but their socioeconomic condition that determines their decision or ability to join an NGO.

By contrast, women who do not join but explain their refusal as appropriate Islamic behavior are usually financially better off, even if not members of the traditional rural elite, and can afford to observe rigid purdah—either by never venturing outside their homesteads or by wearing a burka when they do go out. Halima thus explained her position when Grameen Bank first began work in her village: "I have not fallen so low that I would degrade myself by parading in front of strangers from other districts, doing physical drills, and loudly chanting slogans about Grameen Bank" (Shehabuddin 1992: 131). Because they have access to other income through usually male breadwinners, these women can forgo NGO opportunities and aspire to a higher social status by advocating and practicing purdah, like the women of elite families who do not need to go out to work.

Between these two groups lie the millions who have joined NGOs and taken out microloans because they enjoy a financial security that ensures their ability to repay the loans or have a male relative who can help them make effective use of the loans. In addition to handing the loan money over to their husbands or sons, however, there are other ways in which women borrowers do not abide by the official conditions set by the lending institutions. As Najma describes: "The women take money from the Grameen Bank and then 'eat it up' [spend it all]. Then they run around like crazy trying desperately to get money from [the wealthy widow of the village]. Sometimes, they come and 'borrow' [the wealthy widow's] cow to show the bank worker, pretending they bought it with their loan money. Sometimes they point to somebody else's house and claim that they built it with their house-building loan."[30] Women in one village recounted the story of one woman whose husband actively encouraged her to join the Grameen Bank; when she brought the money home, he would take it from her but leave her with the responsibility of the weekly payments. Finally, the woman decided that she had had enough and refused to take any more loans from the bank. She arrived at the next meeting battered and bruised: her husband had sent her to collect her new loan.[31]

As the discussion above describes, then, it is possible to identify three categories of poor rural women, each with a different relationship to NGOs. At the very bottom of the economic ladder lie the "poorest of the poor," those who are ostensibly the targets of NGOs but who consider themselves too poor even to join an NGO. Next come those who are somewhat better off and are confident enough of their ability to pay off loans (usually with the assistance of a male breadwinner in the family) that they are willing to risk initial social censure. Finally, there are those like Halima who have sufficient income not even to need to consider joining an NGO. While they certainly cannot compete in wealth and status with the local landowner, the importance women in this last group attach to purdah and their eagerness to question the morality of those who are unable to uphold social norms of seclusion belie a desire for acceptance by the rural elite as one of them.

Interestingly, very few rural women see themselves as not observing purdah, comments and criticisms from neighbors and the village elite notwithstanding. For many women, purdah is a matter of personal feeling; for others, it requires adherence to strict behavioral codes such as not being seen by male strangers, covering one's head with the end of a sari, and wearing a burka when out in public. The burka, so favored by Islamists and wealthier women, is simply beyond the financial reach of most poor women, and only a few men and women (15 percent) cited it as an indication of purdah. Similarly, in her study of a village in Sylhet, Katy Gardner (1998) found that it was families with members in England or the Middle East who tended to espouse more purist interpretations of Islam. Foreign remittances enabled them to engage in higher-status activities, such as performing hajj and offering sacrifices on religious occasions, and the money absolved the women from having to go out in search of employment.[32]

NGO women counter the objections of Islamist groups by pointing out that they feel they do observe purdah in their own way, even though they cannot afford to buy the burka that many Islamists believe demonstrates true adherence to purdah. While they cannot afford to ignore the opportunities offered by NGOs, at least by working in their homes, they minimize contact with *achena purush* (male strangers); they are certainly less exposed than they would be on a factory floor. Contrary to the expectations of secularist development workers and policy makers, many women in fact use their new incomes to buy burkas or adopt other forms of purdah, even though, as mentioned earlier, many dismiss the significance of this item of clothing when they are unable to afford it. The ability of a family to keep its women in purdah has long been a sign of status in South Asia, the message being that the family can afford not to have its women work. Given this, it should not come as a total surprise that many women spend their newfound income on demonstrating their new status in society, much the way that, contrary to expectations, many women use their autonomy not to limit their fertility but to have more children (Shehabuddin 2004). Evidence suggests that most women take advantage of what limited opportunities are available to them, yet, contrary to the expectations of secular-oriented development workers or Islamists, they do not do so as dupes of the other side.

Although fatwas issued against NGO-provided health care did not initially prevent most pregnant women from receiving prenatal treatment, they did lead several resourceful women to seek out an alternative fatwa—the way one might pursue a second medical opinion—stating that treatment provided by NGO-run clinics was not contrary to Islam; thus armed, they clandestinely resumed their prenatal treatment (M.R. Khan 1996: 34). Mariam, similarly, resumed her tuberculosis medication quietly. Rumena Begum was compelled to repent her past work as a midwife so that local religious leaders would perform her husband's last rites; soon after the funeral, however, financial considerations forced her to rejoin the local NGO. When the imams found out, they boycotted her husband's *milad*, a prayer gathering that occurs a few days after the funeral (38).

In the end, for all their accomplishments, NGOs cannot stand in for the state at a national level. While I have argued that the state in Bangladesh has shown itself to be ineffective in many ways, it is also clear that NGOs should not constitute a parallel state or that the state should be privatized to the extent that NGOs would become responsible for the delivery of all public services (with the possible exception of external affairs and defense). Such a scenario is both unlikely and undesirable. First, despite the vast numbers of NGOs in the country, their operations are not well coordinated; there is considerable inefficiency and replication of services (Fruttero and Gauri 2005). Thus some parts of the country, particularly those within easy driving distance of a major metropolitan area, host several NGOs, all offering roughly the same services, while some more remote corners remain untouched by NGO activity or interest. Second, the experience of the last two decades has shown that NGO interest in any issue is limited by donor interest in that issue. For this reason, NGO provision cannot be substituted for long-term planning in an area as crucial as, for example, education. Third, while successive governments in Bangladesh have been less than accountable to the citizens, NGOs are even less so; a society run by NGOs would not necessarily be characterized by greater participation. In the foreseeable future, then, the two must coexist and supplement one another's efforts. For all their external funding, NGOs remain dependent on the state's goodwill to continue to function; their activities after all are subject to the oversight of the NGO Affairs Bureau. The Bangladeshi state, for its part, given its own location in global hierarchies and networks, has found itself increasingly compelled to acknowledge the role played by NGOs and the influential support they enjoy. As I mentioned earlier, it was indigenous NGOs like BRAC and Grameen Bank that drew Hillary Clinton to Bangladesh in 1995. Over the past decade, international summits have showered praise on Bangladesh's NGOs, and government attempts to regulate NGOs and violent attacks on NGOs from local opponents have prompted immediate statements of concern from powerful donors. Moreover, the state itself remains heavily dependent on foreign aid, and donors too are increasingly requiring greater cooperation between the government and NGOs.

In this chapter I have tried to show that different understandings of development and modernity coexist in rural Bangladesh today, especially in matters pertaining to women: broadly speaking, the first is the hegemonic model espoused by the major international donors like the World Bank and the UN and the states and NGOs, including women's rights NGOs, that they fund; the second is that proposed by Islamist organizations like the Jamaat and premised on a very different conception of gender roles in society; finally, a third is the perspective of poor women themselves and how they understand the policies and programs currently targeting them and the Islamist critiques of these programs. I have argued that poor women try to take the best of the options offered to them, and contrary to the complaints and expectations of both secularist and Islamist elites, they are not constantly pawns of one side or the other. I cite an important example to do with purdah—when women join an NGO, many do so in the face of objections that they are violating purdah and will lose their religion, yet when they have saved up some money, many of these same women will spend it on buying a nicer, fancier burka—that confounds both Islamist claims that NGOs are ruining the tradition of purdah and secularist hopes that women involved with NGOs will shake off the shackles of traditions like purdah and embrace a secularist understanding of modernity.

In the end, it appears that neither the secularists nor the Islamists truly take into account the realities, needs, and concerns of the poor women they claim to represent. While the former incorrectly assume that women would limit their fertility or discard purdah if given a choice, the latter wish to impose on women an interpretation of Islam that limits the options available to them. Secularist women's rights NGOs have become increasingly attractive to donors largely because they are correctly seen as working more intimately and effectively with disprivileged women than do larger organizations like Grameen Bank and BRAC, yet even their policies and projects are often designed on the basis of secularist assumptions that may not always accurately reflect the views of the people for whom these programs are intended. The preoccupation with purdah, as in the Saptagram textbooks, for example, is a case in point. In *Seeing Like a State*, James C. Scott explores the disastrous consequences of massive projects undertaken by highly interventionist modern states without consideration for local complexities and practical knowledge, or "metis" (1999: 313). In contrast, the situation I explore is dominated by NGOs, not the state, at least as far as rural women are concerned. In the next chapter, I show how poor women's perceptions of the state's role in development influence their understanding of secularist and Islamist elites' debates and bear on their attempts to advance their interests by voting in parliamentary elections.

5

DEMOCRACY ON THE GROUND

I traveled from Dhaka to Jessore in southern Bangladesh early on the morning of June 10, 1996, just two days before the elections. My companions on the short flight down included a team from the Asia Foundation—a representative from the Dhaka office and eight observers from Cambodia—and their escort, a junior officer from the Bangladesh Foreign Office. After breakfast in the canteen of the local NGO, Banchte Shekha (Learning to Survive), we headed to the Jessore district commissioner's office, located in an old building dating back to the British period. In a large room upstairs with noisy fans whirring overhead, the local election officials showed us detailed maps of the different constituencies in the area and long lists of registered voters; they also enthusiastically described to us the elaborate procedures they would follow to collect and tally the election results. Next we visited a Banchte Shekha women's center in a nearby village to learn a little about the voters themselves. There, as in numerous other villages in the area, Banchte Shekha had conducted a strenuous voter education program over the past four months (partly with funding from the Asia Foundation, hence this visit by the foundation's staff to see results). The head of the Cambodian delegation posed various questions about voting and elections to the women who had gathered in an open outdoor space in the village. The women had

FIGURE 5.1 Asia Foundation staff meeting with Banchte Shekha women, Jessore.

learned their lessons well, and several repeated the memorable statement continually broadcast throughout the country in the preceding months: "Amar bhot ami debo, jakey khushi takey debo" (I will cast my own vote, and I will cast it for whomever I wish). They also performed a song they had learned from Banchte Shekha about the importance of selecting a candidate who was honest and patriotic.

The Asia Foundation team returned to Dhaka that same afternoon while I stayed on in Jessore to watch Banchte Shekha at work and, of course, to observe the elections. On the morning of June 12, 1996, Election Day, I set out with some Banchte Shekha workers to witness democracy unfold at the grassroots. We found a rickshaw van that could accommodate us all and asked the driver to follow a route along the main road so that we would be able to see voters on their way to and from the polling centers. Throughout the day, we watched men and women, many of them with their children, rushing along the country roads to their assigned centers, seemingly eager to exercise their democratic right, many for the first time. I wondered how much thought they had given to the votes they were about to cast. How exactly did they understand the concepts of democracy and democratic rights? How had they decided

FIGURE 5.2 At the polls on Election Day, July 12, 1996, in Jessore.

FIGURE 5.3 Banchte Shekha founder Angela Gomes in line to vote on Election Day, July 12, 1996, in Jessore.

which candidate or party to support? What role, if any, did religion play in their decisions? In previous chapters, I have examined different ways in which the state, Islamists, and secularists have professed to promote women's interests through legislation and development projects. In this chapter, I show how women's perceptions of the state, and its limits, have direct implications for the extent and nature of their participation in formal politics.

Following the Jamaat's dismal performance in the 1996 elections—it won only three seats out of a total of three hundred, compared to eighteen in 1991—both the Jamaat and its avowed adversaries claimed that the latter had successfully turned voters, particularly millions of NGO-mobilized rural women, against the Jamaat. Secularist groups had undertaken a nationwide campaign before the 1996 elections to publicize the Jamaat's collaboration with West Pakistani forces during the 1971 War of Liberation, its plans to implement regressive laws, and its opposition to women's involvement with NGOs. It emerged, however, that the assumptions of secularist and Islamist elites were only partly correct. It was neither horror at the Jamaat's conduct in 1971 nor dread of Islamic laws as such but the perception that the party presented a threat to the employment and educational opportunities afforded rural women by NGOs that had turned most impoverished women against the Jamaat. Despite loud proclamations by Jamaat *kormi* (workers, activists) that a bed of fire awaited them in the afterlife for not supporting the Jamaat in this one, most rural women—although they saw themselves as good Muslims—did not support the party they believed would take away the little freedom they did have. At the same time, when most of them voted for one of the other parties, the Awami League, the Bangladesh Nationalist Party, or the Jatiyo Party, it was not because those parties' agendas for reform struck a chord among them—after all, there was very little to distinguish the platforms of the three parties—but usually because one of those parties had recently benefited them in a direct and tangible manner. Given the use of Islamic symbols by all four main parties, it was not religion that determined the outcome of the elections. Rather, it was impoverished women's own experiences and encounters with the state and the different political parties that shaped their political awareness and, specifically, their responses to democratic politics, to female political leadership, and to the overtures of parties and movements across the religious-secular spectrum. Interestingly, despite being under no illusions regarding most of the promises made during the election campaign and undeterred by threats of violence on Election Day or warnings from some quarters about the inappropriateness of Muslim women voting, millions of women voted in recent elections. This remarkable turnout was due largely to the efforts of the caretaker government and, for most voters, the novelty of the very act of voting, regardless of the outcome, and faith in the grand purpose of democracy, if not in individual parties or leaders.

GETTING THE VOTE OUT

Although a small group of women in British India had received the right to vote under the Government of India Act of 1935, universal adult franchise was not granted throughout the subcontinent until the British left in 1947.[1] The 1972 constitution of the newly independent Bangladesh affirmed the political equality between men and women and their equal right to contest and vote in elections; nonetheless, extended periods of military rule both before and since Bangladesh gained independence meant that most Bangladeshis, men and women, had little opportunity to exercise democratic rights. This changed dramatically in 1990 with the overthrow of military rule through a mass uprising. While Bangladesh was one of several countries that underwent the transition from authoritarian rule to democracy in the last decades of the twentieth century, a striking feature of the Bangladeshi experience has been the nature of the national leadership since that transition: two Muslim women, Khaleda Zia of the BNP and Sheikh Hasina of the AL, have alternated as prime minister—in 1991, 1996, and 2001—and ordinary women have shown increasing interest in the democratic process, if we are to judge by the high rate of female voter turnout and the number of women interested in running for elected office (see F. Chowdhury 1999a, 1999b).

In the months preceding the 1996 elections, the government bureaucracy and several NGOs launched voter education campaigns, targeting women in particular, that proved extremely successful. In accordance with the dictates of the thirteenth amendment to the constitution, passed in March 1996, the elections of June 1996 (and, later, October 2001) were preceded by three months under a neutral caretaker government led by a retired chief justice (see N. Ahmed 2003: 59). While this provision clearly arose from a mutual lack of trust among the political parties, it contributed to a general perception of fairness in the elections, accompanied by an international seal of approval, later accusations of rigging by the losing parties notwithstanding. Without a mandate to pursue major policy changes during its three months in office, the caretaker government channeled its energies into preparing for the elections and encouraging voter turnout. In both 1996 and 2001 voter turnout was an impressive 75 percent, of which women were responsible for roughly half.

One of the more effective strategies employed by the 1996 caretaker administration, as a member of the interim cabinet later informed me, was to declare Election Day a national holiday and promote a festive atmosphere, akin to Eid al-Fitr, by encouraging men and women to dress up in their finest and go out and enjoy the day.[2] Also very helpful in encouraging women's participation were repeated assurances by the government that there would be no violence on Election Day—understandably, an issue of great concern to voters. The significance of personal security to voters became clear in a program on Bangladesh Television broadcast in May shortly before the 1996 elections, during which women's rights activists and ordinary village women discussed the problems that women voters had faced in past elections. Since elections have very often been accompanied by sudden outbreaks of violence, many expressed concern about being in and around voting centers. One village woman, Najma, described what had happened on an earlier occasion when she had tried to vote: "We set out for the center to go vote. As we approached the center, we saw a great deal of fighting. We told them to let us pass. We went in, but there was also fighting inside [the center], so we turned back and ended up not voting that day." Women were also clearly worried about the location of the center: How long would it take them to get there? Would the route be safe? Who would take care of their children while they went to vote? They voiced a desire for "an end to violence and oppression and a society free of dowry. That will make this a better country." Some women were also concerned about law and order: "We need security. We now walk around with large sums of money, ten to twenty thousand takas, loans for our projects. We need our country to be safe." Others articulated widely felt needs for more educational facilities for female students and electricity in their homes.

During the same discussion, Farida Akhter, a prominent women's rights activist, pointed out important social considerations that determined whether a young girl would be permitted to vote. She had found that many parents were unwilling to let their young daughters vote because they did not wish them to be marked as being over eighteen. Given that birth and death records scarcely exist in rural Bangladesh, it is very difficult to know a person's age with any degree of certainty, but parents worried that if it became known that a daughter had voted, it would be immediately assumed that she was at least eighteen; this would jeopardize her marriage prospects and lead to demands for a larger dowry. Even though eighteen is also the minimum age at which women can marry, as noted in chapter 3, most young girls marry at a much younger age; thus, by a strange twist, it is quite likely that a girl married at, say, fifteen would be registered to vote because she would have claimed to be eighteen on the marriage registration form.[3]

The notion of a "festival of democracy" obscured the fact that hundreds, maybe thousands, of people who wished to vote were not permitted to do so.[4] In many parts of the country, religious minorities—particularly Hindus, who have traditionally supported the historically secularist AL—were prevented from reaching their polling centers.[5] In a few areas, fatwas were issued to deter women from asserting their right to vote on the grounds that it would be contrary to Islam and tradition (Shehabuddin 1999b). Tragic though these incidents are, ultimately they should not detract from the greater achievement of the elections: that millions of men and women did vote under generally free and fair conditions.

As mentioned earlier, the caretaker government and NGOs were very active in their voter education efforts in the months leading up to the elections. Anyone with access to a TV or radio had undoubtedly heard the oft-repeated "Amar bhot ami debo, jakey khushi takey debo!" (I will cast my own vote, and I will cast it for whomever I wish). But what exactly did the women and men of rural Bangladesh understand this to mean? When we asked them why they had voted, most of the men and women interviewed responded that they voted because it was their "right" to do so, because everyone else around them voted, or because it was "necessary" to vote. As Zinnat Begum, a mother of three in the northern district of Dinajpur, put it, "Everyone was going to vote; if you didn't go, you felt bad. That's why I voted." Bokul, who ran her own small business with NGO assistance, also in Dinajpur, was adamant about one's democratic responsibilities: "If you live in this country, you have to vote. Voting is my right as a citizen. It is wrong to not vote." She was also very clear on what she expected the elections to accomplish: "We voted so that we could elect a minister to whom we can make our demands." Several men and women saw a connection between voting and the "good of the country." Ali, a day laborer in Sylhet, shared with us his high hopes that the government would "bring about unnoti [positive change, improvement] in the country and help the poor."

On the Bangladesh Television program mentioned earlier, rural women spoke eloquently about their resolve to vote wisely and independently of all peer, family, and party pressure. One woman described the recent changes in women's attitudes: "There was a time when we couldn't speak clearly, get our thoughts across. Our husbands or someone else would tell us whom to vote for and we would vote that way. Now that we've learned about voting, we won't do that anymore. We won't vote where someone tells us to vote, but where we think is right. And whom I vote for is my business. Amar bhot ami debo, jakey khushi takey debo!" Another woman agreed: "We used to do as men told us. Now we understand that as women we have rights. We understand bhalo-mondo [good and bad]. Just because someone tells us that something is good, we won't assume that it is." The women also seemed aware of the demands they could make on an elected official as opposed to the village matbor: "The matbor often refuses to help us. We want to able to go directly to our MP with our problems." One woman elaborated on her priorities: "We have to think of our children's education, we have to think of safety for women . . . opportunities for women . . . we will think of who will deal with these concerns and vote accordingly." Several women were adamant that no amount of money would affect their voting decision: "If I think about a candidate— yes, that's the sort of person who could do the country some good, then I'd vote for [that person]. For example, I have a daughter I need to get married. And I need ten thousand or fifteen thousand or twenty thousand takas to get her married. If someone says to me, 'I'll give you twenty thousand takas if you vote for me,' I still won't vote for [that person]. We will vote so that there is peace in the country."

The voter awareness campaigns of the government and various NGOs proved effective in bringing new voters, especially women, to the polls and in encouraging them to think about the issues at stake and the integrity of candidates. As I show later in this chapter, NGOs engaged in specifically anti-Islamist campaigning were successful in discouraging support for the Jamaat but more when they told women that the Jamaat would outlaw all NGOs and prevent women from working outside the home than when they focused on the Jamaat's atrocities in 1971.

ELECTING WOMEN

Many rural women were also drawn to the polls by the prospect of electing women candidates. An overwhelming majority of the women we surveyed in 1996 expressed a preference for women politicians in office because, in the words of Anwara Begum of Jessore, "Only a woman can understand a woman's sorrows." Eighty-two percent of women thought that only women leaders could help ordinary women; the corresponding figure for male respondents was 55 percent. Other than the two women leaders of the AL and BNP, however, few women are able to run for office and even fewer are actually elected. The following statement by Shakuntala in a Chittagong village reflected a widespread resignation to most women candidates' inability to compete with men: "Women don't stand for election because there are too many men who stand. Why would people vote for women when there are so many men to choose from?"[6]

Along with the right to vote, democratic rights include the right to contest elections and run for office. Yet, despite a long history of universal suffrage in what is today Bangladesh and a noteworthy record of female leadership at the highest level of government since the restoration of democracy in 1991, women politicians generally have not had easy access to party nominations or campaign funds. Indeed, recent debates over women's presence in parliament suggest little interest in changing the situation. An affirmative action policy that was begun in a limited manner in British India and implemented at the parliamentary level by the government of united Pakistan (1947–1971) has been corrupted over the years and today serves, in effect, to restrict the number of women in parliament to those seats—plus a few prominent women politicians who successfully compete for general seats; what was meant to ensure a minimum representation of women now serves to impose a near maximum.[7] The Pakistani government reserved a number of seats for women to be filled by the indirect election of women by the legislature; the framers of the Bangladeshi constitution retained that provision, recognizing that women "were not in a position to compete successfully with male politicians for territorial constituencies" (Najma Chowdhury 1994: 98). Understandably, the women who occupied these seats felt at a disadvantage vis-à-vis the regular MPs for a number of reasons, chief among them that they were entirely dependent for their nomination and election on the ruling party and its directly elected, predominantly male MPs. Because they were not directly elected by a constituency, the women felt that they lacked both a mandate and a power base, though, as I mentioned in chapter 3, indirectly elected female MPs such as Farida Rahman occasionally did attempt to push through legislation meant to help women.

The actual number of seats reserved for women in parliament has fluctuated over the years. The tenth amendment to the constitution, passed in 1990, declared that there would be 30 reserved seats for women until the year 2000 (out of a total of 330). This amendment was passed not through a democratic process but following a discussion between then First Lady Roushan Ershad and two factions of the ruling JP; "there were no opinion polls [or] public discussions and no women's organizations were consulted" on the matter (Choudhury 1995: 9). Come April 2001, with the then-opposition engaged in a lengthy boycott of parliament, the provision was allowed simply to lapse, and the parliament elected in the October 2001 elections did not include any reserved seats for women. Women's rights activists were hopeful, however, that when the matter was brought up again in parliament the ruling party would fulfill an earlier promise not simply to renew the existing provision but to increase the number of seats reserved for women and open them up for direct election. There was certainly popular support for such a move: in polls undertaken by the Fair Election Monitoring Alliance (FEMA) in the late 1990s, citizens had expressed a strong preference for direct election to seats reserved for women (Islam 2000a). Despite hunger strikes and massive protests by women's rights activists demanding directly elected seats, however, in early 2004 the cabinet agreed to propose a constitutional amendment increasing the number of reserved seats from 30 to 45; as before, these seats would be filled by indirect election, distributed "among political parties based on their respective strengths in Parliament" (Majumdar 2004). The amendment, finally passed in parliament on May 16, 2004, was strongly condemned by women's rights activists. Ayesha Khanam of Mohila Porishad, for instance, declared that it would "undermine women's political role" and was "insulting" (*Times of India*, May 16, 2004).

While prominent female politicians such as former prime ministers Sheikh Hasina and Khaleda Zia and former minister for agriculture Motia Chowdhury all entered parliament by winning general seats, the percentage of women candidates nominated for such seats has been extremely low in all national elections since independence (Matin 2002:

224). Concerned that women candidates cannot be as successful as male candidates in gaining or even retaining parliamentary seats, parties have been unwilling to risk general seats by nominating women. And the few women who receive nominations routinely encounter obstacles in the course of their campaigns, though, of course, such difficulties are by no means unique to the Bangladeshi political scene.[8] Conversations with women parliamentary candidates in Bangladesh revealed that general economic dependence on men combined with accepted notions of appropriate social behavior restricted women's ability to raise funds for their campaigns. According to Hazera Sultana, a candidate from the Workers' Party: "It is extremely difficult for us to raise funds. Even for money we have to depend on men. We have to go to our husbands or brothers, since most of us do not have the means to finance ourselves. Getting donations, something which is very normal for a male candidate, is almost impossible for a woman candidate.... I cannot go to a businessman's office every day and sit there for hours as a male candidate can. People will get other ideas and I cannot compromise my self-respect." Several women candidates agreed that concerns about their security and reputation prevented them from campaigning as effectively as men can, whether it was a matter of going into the more remote parts of their constituency or just working late into the evening. One woman pointed out, "I cannot go to a tea stall to talk to voters, so I have to go to households, which takes a lot more time" (A. M. Amin 1996: 6). And once elected, women politicians find that their conduct remains under scrutiny in a manner that does not extend to the behavior of their male colleagues. Indeed, even discussions within parliament itself have touched on the personal conduct of female MPs, the most flagrant incident involving no lesser personages than the prime minister and the leader of the opposition in 1999. As Dilara Choudhury noted at the time:

> Bangladesh has been taken aback by the recent unfortunate, inde-
> cent and vilifying remarks of Prime Minister Sheikh Hasina about
> the personal conduct of the leader of the opposition on the floor
> of the Parliament. Her insinuations about Begum Zia's character
> (because she spent a night in Hotel Purbani during the anti-Ershad
> movement in 1987) do not in any way fall within the operating
> guidelines of a parliamentary government.... If a woman of [the]
> opposition leader's stature is liable to lose public respect if she stays

out of her own residence, and that too for political reasons, whereas a man in her place is free to do so, what then would be [the] fate and reputations of hundreds of Bangladeshi women who are out on the streets to make a living? How about the women in politics who would need to stay out late at night for party activities?

(Choudhury 1999)

The Local Government (Union Parishad) Second Amendment Act of 1997 marked a commendable attempt to increase women's access to elected office, calling for three seats to be reserved for women members in each union parishad (UP) and for these seats to be filled by direct election.[9] (In the past, women's seats had been filled by women nominated by those who had already won the "general seats, as continues to be the case in parliament.) The passage of the act clearly reflected an effort to realize certain aspects of the recently announced Beijing Platform for Action, which the BNP government of Khaleda Zia had adopted without reservations (Siddiqi 2006b; S. Akhter 2002). The December 1997 union elections were the first to be held under the new act. Just under thirteen thousand women were elected as union parishad members in both 1997 and 2003. A small number were even elected to general seats and a few as chairpersons. According to an estimate by the Association of Development Agencies in Bangladesh (ADAB), at least 90 percent of the female candidates in the 1997 elections were members of NGOs (*Dhaka Courier*, November 27, 1998). This was in marked contrast to the situation a decade earlier when, according to a 1987 study on local government, most nominated women members belonged to the rural elite and among the most important considerations in granting nomination were kinship and status while "education, experience of corporate activity in a cooperative society or in an income-earning occupation or involvement in village welfare activities were hardly taken into consideration" (Qadir 1994: 8).[10]

Perhaps not surprisingly, the integration of women into local government has not been smooth. At a convention of union parishad members and chairpersons in early June 1998, one female member claimed that male colleagues "always ignore us, both in policy making and implementing decisions" (N. Kabir 1998). Another woman demanded to know, "If Prime Minister Sheikh Hasina can run the government successfully why should we not be able to manage a union ward?" (*Daily Star*, July 3, 1998). Journalists learned that women members' opinions were not sought at

FIGURE 5.4 Rally during upazila women leaders' meeting in Rangpur, organized by Nagorik Uddyog in March 2007. (Courtesy of Nagorik Uddyog.)

union parishad meetings, even on matters pertaining to women. Women members were also generally excluded from committees responsible for development projects or any matters involving money. When asked about such discrimination, a chairman explained that the government had provided no instructions regarding the responsibilities of women members; clearly, he expected the women union parishad members to have specific responsibilities distinct from those of male union parishad members. Another chairman said that women needed to learn the job before they could be given "serious" responsibilities (*Dhaka Courier*, November 27, 1998).[11] The situation has not improved in the years since. In March 2005 Meher Afroz, a member from the Kishoreganj district, complained that the chairman and other union members did not invite women to important meetings "or if they invite us, the meeting will obviously be scheduled for [an] odd time like night. This is mischievously done so that we cannot join" (*New Age*, March 18, 2005).[12]

That the political parties recognized women faced problems in campaigning and were at a distinct disadvantage to men in raising funds became clear in discussions organized in 1995 by the Dhaka-based women's research group Women for Women to explore the different parties' positions on women and gender in society, politics, and the economy. The three parties that have been in power since independence—the Awami League (AL), the Bangladesh Nationalist Party (BNP), and the Jatiyo or National Party (JP)—can be categorized as generally centrist, with the AL slightly to the left of center and the BNP and the JP to the right. The Workers' Party (WP) and the Communist Party of Bangladesh (CPB) fall to the left of the AL while the Jamaat-i Islami and the Islami Oikyo Jote or Islamic Unity Alliance (IUA) fall on the far right. All the parties generally supported the increased presence of women in parliament; however, the Jamaat members voiced practical concerns about women's ability to contest the general seats successfully, pointing out, for instance, that it was difficult for women candidates to campaign door-to-door the way men did. For the Jamaat, this was reason enough not to pursue the nomination of women rather than a problem to be addressed precisely so that women might be able to campaign safely in the future. In a clear departure from at least the formal rhetoric of the other parties, the Jamaat representatives insisted that "where there are both men and women, men should take the leadership position. It is the responsibility of men to provide leadership in the parliament and the government" because, after all, women's primary responsibility was to look after the family and the home (Women for Women 1995: 31–32).

According to one Jamaat representative, "if women got the opportunity to look after their children in a peaceful, disciplined and ideal home environment and could produce honest sincere, ideal and personable citizens of character, women's contribution to society and economy would be higher than what they could give by participation in activities in the public domain [while] leaving the house and children unattended." Some conceded they saw no reason that a woman could not be involved in electoral politics once her children reached maturity and no longer needed her attention (Women for Women 1995: 31–32). A high-ranking man in the Chittagong branch of the Jamaat echoed these sentiments in an interview with me: "We follow what is in the Quran and hadith. And it is said there that women can do everything that men can—except lead. That is because of their physical and psychological weakness, particularly during their time of the month. Thus, women cannot be judges—because they do not think clearly for a few days every month. How can you claim equality if you require maternity leaves every few years and a few days off every month? Men do not take time off for such things." He added that since men could not become pregnant, "it would not be fair to ask a woman to do a man's job when a man can never do her job of bearing children. Women cannot be responsible for everything." As a result, he concluded, a sexual division of labor was the only solution.[13] At the root of the Jamaat's gender ideology, which is based on the interpretation of Quranic precepts by its founder, Maulana Maududi, is the idea that men and women are equal and complementary. In other words, although men and women have the same status in the eyes of God, there is a distinct difference in their spheres of work, given the difference in their physical abilities and emotional strengths: "Man's life and civilization on the earth stand as much in need of coarseness, vehemence and aggressiveness as of tenderness, softness and plasticity. Good generals, good statesmen, and good administrators are as necessary as good mothers, good wives, and good housekeepers" (Maududi 1972: 120–121). A particular notion of what we might think of as "Muslim Motherhood"—akin to "Republican Motherhood" in France and the United States in the eighteenth and nineteenth centuries and with similar attendant biases of class and gender—thus traditionally anchored the Jamaat position on women.[14]

The profound ambiguity in the Jamaat's views on female political leaders became quite apparent in the earliest days of Bangladesh's current democratic era. In 1991, the year the BNP won the parliamentary elections and Begum Khaleda Zia became prime minister, the Jamaat's publication house, the Bangladesh Islamic Centre, published a pamphlet entitled *Female Leadership in the Sight of Islam*. In this small, inexpensive, widely circulated pamphlet, which was reprinted in 1994, M. Ruhul Amin declared that God created man to be women's protectors. Given that God had not deemed women fit to be in charge within the home, he argued, surely women were not meant to be responsible for millions of households by taking charge of an entire state (1994: 2). Indeed, while no political party has fielded more than a handful of women candidates for direct election in any of the recent elections, the Jamaat was the only major party to put forward no women candidates at all. Yet, after both the 1991 and the 2001 elections, the Jamaat did agree to support the BNP and its woman chief, Khaleda Zia, giving the BNP a majority in parliament. Moreover, following this tactical alliance with the BNP, the Jamaat accepted two of the thirty reserved women's seats in 1991 and two cabinet posts in 2001.

THE POLITICS OF PIETY AND THE PIETY OF POLITICIANS

Following an elaborate empirical study of the relationship between Islam and authoritarianism, M. Steven Fish questioned the validity of the "commonly embraced but rarely scrutinized argument [that] holds that religious and secular authority are joined in Islamic societies, both in the popular imagination and in institutional practice, and that this fusion helps explain the democratic deficit." As examples of this view, Fish cites the work of Jamal al-Suwaidi and Samuel Huntington (2002: 20).[15] In his remarks about the findings of an opinion survey undertaken in the United Arab Emirates, al-Suwaidi observes, "Secularism and the privatization of religion are alien to the Muslim conception. Muslims have continued to assume that only a 'religious leader' can provide good government for the Muslim community and that the main function of an Islamic government is to ensure obedience to God's law as explained in the Quran . . . and the sunnah" (1995: 87). Similarly, according to Huntington, "God and Caesar, church and state, spiritual and temporal authority, have been a prevailing dualism in western culture," whereas "in Islam God is Caesar" (1996: 70, cited in Fish 2002: 20). Even a quick glance at the history of predominantly Muslim countries, from Albania to Indonesia, including Bangladesh, reveals that there has been no greater deference to religious authority in the political arena than in non-Muslim countries. Rather, much as in many non-Muslim countries, there is a general expectation of some degree of religiosity in candidates for office. As Fish points out, "What are the chances of a self-proclaimed atheist becoming president of Costa Rica, the Philippines, or the United States? Social scientists in predominantly Christian societies may ignore candidates' religion; much of the electorate does not" (2002: 22).

In Bangladesh, the public piety of the candidates—rather than any expectations of formal religious authority—has indeed been a factor in all three elections since the restoration of democracy. In election campaigns, all the major parties have tried to outdo one another in highlighting the piety of their own candidates while attempting to discredit their opponents with charges of impiety and impropriety. Women and gender—and their nexus with religion or at least "Muslimness"—emerged as an important issue early in the 1996 campaign season. One of the more starkly visual examples of this was the intense focus on the religiosity of the two main contenders for the prime minister's post, both of them women. Given the BNP's emphasis from its earliest days on the nation's Muslim identity, Khaleda Zia's close association with the Jamaat and her party's use of religious symbols came as no surprise to most observers. What was unexpected to many, however, was Sheikh Hasina's public display of her own Islamic credentials to the voting public. Her visit to Mecca for hajj a few months before the elections was well publicized; she returned to Bangladesh wearing a snug black scarf on her head beneath the *anchol* (end of her sari) that had been her sole head covering in recent years. As the June 1996 elections approached, both the AL and the BNP rushed to distribute posters throughout the country with pictures that depicted the female leader of the rival party engaging in such inappropriate, un-Islamic activities as shaking hands with a male foreign dignitary or raising a wineglass for a toast at a state function while on an official trip overseas.

Studies of the political use of Islam at the national level—in the contexts of Egypt, Indonesia, Pakistan, and Bangladesh, for example—have focused on leaders' use of Islamic symbols to legitimize their hold on power; the basic argument is that forceful expressions of support for Islam on the part of an unpopular ruler help obscure other sins, such as an undemocratic seizure of power or ineffectual policies. Such arguments assume the populace's automatic attraction to Islamic symbols, but surely this should be a matter for investigation rather than assumption? Are religious symbols indeed of such importance to the majority of the population? Are Muslim voters necessarily drawn to Islamic symbols? In the 1996 ASK survey, we asked men and women if they believed that a person must be religious in order to be a good leader.[16] An overwhelming 76 percent of the 384 rural men and women who responded to this question said yes; 22.5 percent felt it was not important, while the rest responded that they did not know. Of the 291 men and women who did consider religiosity to be an important requisite for good leadership, a quarter believed that a religious person would work for the good of the country, while just under 10 percent felt that a religious person naturally would be honest and of good character. Of the 87 men and women who felt that a person does not have to be religious in order to be a good leader, 59 percent believed that it was more important that a leader be of good character than visibly pious, while 23 percent were skeptical because there were simply "too many *ghalad* (problems)" in religion.

From the perspective of the rural poor, what markers of religiosity serve as evidence of a political leader's personal piety? Almost half of those who selected Hasina said they could tell she was religious because she had performed hajj, observed purdah, and conducted herself modestly. Those who thought Khaleda Zia was the most religious of the four main party leaders pointed to her attention to the poor and needy while in office. Ghulam Azam's piety was said to be evident from the fact that he was known to fast and pray, wore a prayer cap, had a beard, and headed a religion-based party, the Jamaat-i Islami. The supporters of Ershad, head of the Jatiyo Party, pointed to such public displays of piety as his attendance at mass prayer gatherings when he was in office in the 1980s, his 1982 decision to declare Friday the weekly holiday in place of Sunday, in keeping with other Muslim countries, and his close association with a number of *pirs* (holy men).

Gendered differences emerged quickly in the responses. It was clear that the signifiers for male and female piety were distinct. In the Bangladeshi context, male leaders such as Ershad and Ghulam Azam could display their piety by participating in public prayers; Ershad is remembered well for doing that while president.[17] Muslim women in South Asia tend to pray at home rather than in the mosque; thus women leaders offer proof of their religiosity by observing some degree of purdah and making frequent trips to Mecca, whether for the annual hajj or the *umrah*, the lesser pilgrimage that can be performed at any time of the year. According to a male union parishad member from Sylhet, "Women cannot propagate religion as well [as men can]."

While the rural poor focused on different markers of religiosity depending on whether a politician was male or female, as a group, their notions of Islamic or religious leadership differed significantly from those of both secularist and Islamist elites. For instance, impoverished village women and men alike were impressed that Sheikh Hasina had performed hajj (some were even aware that she had done so twice) and covered her hair with a black scarf; for them, these were indisputable indications of her piety, her certification as a good Muslim woman, and proof of her suitability for leadership. The elites were far more cynical. According to Lubna, an urban professional woman who saw herself very much in the secularist camp, "The BNP is clearly pro-Pakistani. Look at the way Khaleda Zia wears a separate chiffon *dupatta* (scarf) on her head. Sheikh Hasina [before her recent hajj, that is] simply pulled her *anchol* over her head. Khaleda, on the other hand, wears a separate *orna* [scarf]—that's very Pakistani."[18] And, according to many secularists, following Pakistani customs automatically implied support for parties like the Jamaat, which opposed the breakup of Pakistan and the creation of Bangladesh in 1971. Neaz, a Dhaka-based, openly secular professional man demanded, "Why is Sheikh Hasina all covered up now after the hajj? She wasn't *im*modest before. Why is she doing this? I'll tell you why—she's trying to shed the [AL's] pro-India and secularist image."[19] While it is not uncommon for men and women who have performed hajj to adopt new outward signs of piety after returning from Mecca—women tend to dress more modestly while men often grow beards—skeptics commented that Sheikh Hasina's decision to wear the scarf had more to do with the fact that it was an election year; moreover, this was the second time she had performed hajj, so why the greater show of piety now? they asked.

Skepticism about the women leaders' modest attire was not limited to secularist elites. High-ranking Islamist women were similarly contemptuous during our discussions on the subject. One Jamaat woman I interviewed some months after the elections insisted that she could see right through such hypocrisy. She vehemently condemned both Khaleda Zia and Sheikh Hasina for setting a bad example for the nation's women and failing to provide true Islamic leadership: "Tell me, aren't Hasina and Khaleda Muslim women? So why do they not tell all women to observe purdah? Isn't that their duty?"[20] Her neighbor, also a member of the Jamaat, added scornfully: "It is said that if one *haram* [illegally earned] penny is used to cover hajj expenses, then that hajj is not valid. These people can perform hajj as many times as they want—it will never be valid. When my father, who was a great maulana, went on hajj, he had to sell all his land. As for that black scarf, [Hasina] started out with it right here, covering her brows, but it has been rising gradually over the last few months so that it now barely covers her hairline."[21]

Perhaps not surprisingly for female politicians in a male-dominated political context, the women heads of the BNP and AL made little attempt to draw attention to the fact that they were women or to promise special attention to women's problems while they were in office; instead, they continually referred to their relationship with famous, slain men (Sheikh Hasina is the daughter of Sheikh Mujibur Rahman and Khaleda Zia is Ziaur Rahman's widow). During campaigns, it was their piety on which they chose to focus—much like male leaders—undoubtedly in an effort to legitimize their incursion into and dominating presence in the male sphere of politics.

On the face of it, the candidates' displays of piety were important to voters. It was not at all clear, however, that a voter supported a particular candidate simply because that person was the most religious. More often than not, people described the leader of whichever party they already supported—be it the BNP (Khaleda Zia), the AL (Sheikh Hasina), the JP (Hussain M. Ershad), or the Jamaat (Ghulam Azam)—as a good, religious person, while an overwhelming majority (79 percent) of those who identified Azam as the most religious of the four leaders said that they did not vote for the Jamaat. Rural men and women were equally skeptical of the use of religious symbols by the different parties, all of which—not only the Islamist ones—were eager to imply that the party most favored by God would be the most effective in solving the nation's multitude of problems. The Jamaat went so far as to claim that a vote in its favor was no more and no less than a vote for God and Islam.

GOD ON THE CAMPAIGN TRAIL

Some months after the 1996 elections, I asked a cabinet member from the newly elected AL about his party's evolving relationship with religion. He was quite adamant that the party was "as secular as ever" but added quickly, "By secularism, we do not mean that we are *anti*-religion, rather that we are opposed to the *political* use of religion. You must understand that the majority of the population is Muslim. It therefore makes sense for a political party to use symbols that will appeal to that majority. Political parties throughout the world do this. There is nothing wrong in that."[22]

While the use of Islamic symbols became prevalent during the authoritarian period, the practice survived—indeed, flourished—in the democratic era in Bangladesh, with political parties repeatedly invoking God and the Prophet on the campaign trail. In 1991, for instance, the BNP used a variation on the Muslim statement of faith, the first *kalimah*, as one of their campaign slogans: "La ilaha illallah; dhaner shishey bismillah" (There is no god but God; [vote for] the sheaf of rice [BNP ballot symbol] in the name of God). The Freedom Party, a small party in favor of an expanded role for Islam in Bangladesh, brought the Prophet into their slogan: "Bhot diley kuraley khushi hobey Rasuley" (The Prophet will be pleased if you vote for the axe [Freedom Party ballot symbol])

(S. Kabir 1995: 44). The Jamaat for its part announced that a vote in its favor would bring the voter a step closer to heaven, while opposing the party would be tantamount to rejecting Islam. One of its more popular slogans was "Bhot diley pallay, khushi hobey Allah" (God will be pleased if you vote for the scales [Jamaat's ballot symbol]). Not to be outdone, even the AL took pains to stress its Islamic credentials through "La ilaha illallah; naukar malik tui Allah" (There is no god but God [and] you, God, are the master of the boat [AL ballot symbol]) (see also Riaz 2004: 39).

Having decided to support women's right to vote, the Jamaat set out to sway the direction their voting took through carefully calculated and eloquently crafted appeals. Just a few months before the June 1996 elections, the popular Jamaat speaker Delawar Hossain Saidi advised a large gathering of women listeners about the importance of voting—and of carefully selecting the right candidate:

> From the standpoint of Islam, you must vote for those who support Islam. The vote is an indication of support, a verdict. In whose favor are you casting your support? During the elections, the nationalists will come to you, the capitalists will come to you, the socialists will come to you—and those who wish to establish Islam will also come to you. Now whom will you support? That is the question. As a Muslim, you must support someone who wants to establish Islam, someone who is active in a movement for Islam. This is the sort of person for whom you should vote—someone who, once in power, will establish God's religion.
>
> This is why, in order to establish Islam, it is extremely important that women vote. Because of your one vote [against him], an Islamic candidate might "fail." At the same time, an Islamic candidate might "pass" because of your one vote [for him]. This is why it is imperative that you vote. *It is actually wrong to stay away from the polls.*[23]

To bolster his point, Saidi cited the example of Asya, the pharaoh's wife who "even as the wife of an unbeliever . . . *voted* for God's prophet [Moses]. For that, God will grant her heaven" (emphasis added). As an example to be eschewed, he pointed to the wife of the prophet Lot, who "cast her *vote* . . . in favor of the misled established society of the time. Therefore, while Lot will certainly go to heaven, his wife, even though the wife of a prophet, will go to hell. This is clearly stated in the Quran" (emphasis added).[24] This waaz mahfil was recorded and widely distributed on inexpensive audiocassettes, taking Saidi's message far beyond the women physically present that day.[25]

Political parties eager for votes were not alone in assuming the seductiveness of religious symbols for the masses. As I show in the next section, secularist groups and organizations fearful of religious rule were sufficiently concerned about people's attraction to such language that they organized a vehement campaign against the more Islamically oriented parties in the run-up to the elections.

ANTI-ISLAMIST CAMPAIGNING

Voter education efforts by the government and NGOs were supposed to be nonpartisan. As the elections approached, however, many of the NGOs and citizen groups began to worry about the actual outcome of the election and launched a nationwide campaign to draw attention to the dangers of supporting the avowedly Islamist parties, the Jamaat-i Islami and the Islami Oikyo Jote or Islamic Unity Alliance (IUA), and, in some cases, even the Islam-friendly BNP and JP. In particular, opponents of the Jamaat and the political deployment of religion undertook intensive anti-Jamaat campaigns, focusing in particular on those areas where the Jamaat had won parliamentary seats in the 1991 elections. Since 1996 coincided with the twenty-fifth anniversary of Bangladesh's independence, the secularist nationalist groups took every opportunity to hark back to the country's founding moment. Time and again, secularist groups and individuals reminded the electorate that only one party (clearly implying the AL) was committed to upholding the spirit and ideals of 1971, while others (not explicitly mentioning the Jamaat) had collaborated with the Pakistani army and government rather than side with the movement for an independent Bangladesh during the 1971 War of Independence.

On May 23, 1996, just a few weeks before the elections, I traveled to Roumari near the northernmost tip of Bangladesh with some prominent NGO and feminist activists to attend a celebration of the twenty-fifth anniversary of the War of Independence. By the time we arrived, several hundred people had gathered in a field for the outdoor celebrations. We were late, but since we were traveling with one of the chief guests, the program had not yet begun. The evening started with very moving speeches by local freedom fighters, including the recently rediscovered

FIGURE 5.5 Taramon Bibi with her family and Khushi Kabir at the twenty-fifth anniversary celebration of Muktijuddho, Roumari.

and celebrated woman freedom fighter Taramon Bibi. They spoke of their activities in 1971 and their disillusionment with the nation that they had helped to found. The speeches were followed by a series of short skits by landless men trained by the NGO Nijera Kori (We Do It Ourselves), which was well known for its use of puppets and theater to raise awareness about various issues among its target population. That evening, the skits revolved around the recent history of East Pakistan/Bangladesh, especially events of and since 1971. One skit satirized the different political parties currently competing for state power. The character representing the Jamaat was particularly colorful, and his statements were clearly intended as a warning to the audience of the dangers of supporting the Islamists in the upcoming elections. Bearded, of course, and dressed in a *panjabi* (local long shirt) and prayer cap, he began by confessing his opposition to the independence movement in 1971:

I was not wrong to oppose independence in 1971. This country will become Pakistan once again. The moon and star flag [of Pakistan and a few other Muslim countries] will once again be unfurled in these skies. Have you not seen how much better organized we have become in the last twenty-five years? ... Do you not hear? We can now shout "Pakistan Zindabad" [Long live Pakistan!] in our rallies. That is how far we have come in the last twenty-five years! The war criminals of the Second World War are still being pursued, yet at my leader's command, hundreds of thousands of people were killed and thousands of women raped [in 1971], but have your people and your leaders been able to do anything to my leader [Ghulam Azam]? ... That day is not far when the slogan "Joi Bangla" ["Victory to Bengal!" the slogan of the independence movement] will be declared illegal.

At the other end of the country, the southwestern constituency of Satkkhira, a longtime Jamaat stronghold, was the site of much Jamaat as well as anti-Jamaat campaigning and a good example of the campaign wars being fought elsewhere. Local Nirmul supporters traveled around the area giving speeches and putting up posters supplied by the central office. One of the posters juxtaposed verses from the Quran with quotations from the writings of Maududi, the founder and main ideologue of the Jamaat, in order to show that Maududi had willfully distorted the Quran. Another poster drew attention to war crimes committed by various members of the Jamaat. A local journalist I interviewed insisted that the Nirmul Committee was committed not to the AL but rather simply to persuading people to vote for any party other than the Jamaat.[26]

WOMEN'S ISSUES

In public forums, all the major parties made some effort to demonstrate publicly their commitment to women's issues, but little in these statements was concrete or distinct. In the 1995 Women for Women group discussions mentioned earlier, BNP representatives pointed out that their party has supported the concept of "women in development" from its earliest days and that BNP founder Ziaur Rahman had established the first ministry for women's affairs. They felt that the greatest obstacle to women's participation in politics was the "misinterpretation of the principles of religion by motivated men upholding patriarchal social norms" and called for women's organized resistance to fundamentalist activity seeking to hinder "women's progress and development." The representatives from the AL declared that their party was in favor of "gender equity in all spheres of life" and pointed out that "the opposing forces that operate in this society hinder women's development and progress and create obstacles in establishing gender equity in social, economic and political spheres." All three centrist parties—AL, BNP, and JP—generally agreed that among the barriers to gender equity in Bangladeshi society were the low level of education among women and the limited opportunities available to women generally (Women for Women 1995: 17–23; see also Guhathakurta 1994: 52). For instance, like the BNP, the AL did not perceive a need to effect "changes in the social structure to enable women to enjoy equal rights with men in all spheres of life" (Women for Women 1995: 25). Candidates from the parties on the Left were more willing to identify patriarchy rather than simply poverty as the main source of women's oppression in Bangladesh; like the centrist parties, however, their manifestos lacked any lucid proposals for change, and in practice they channeled their energies into mobilizing female factory workers (Guhathakurta 1994: 55).

The centrist parties were also vague on how exactly the country's laws might be reformed to enhance women's rights. Although the BNP members condemned polygamy, they foresaw problems in abolishing the practice. Similarly, they expected problems in any attempt to pass the Uniform Family Code, but said that "if people belonging to all the religions accept it, [they] would not stand in the way" (Women for Women 1995: 21). The AL was more overtly opposed to religion-based politics and more supportive of the Uniform Family Code than were the BNP representatives.[27] Again, on the Left, Workers' Party members stood apart in that they took a much stronger position on the matter of inheritance, insisting that there should be "no discrimination between men and women on the question of inheritance of family property" (Women for Women 1995: 27). They were also very much in favor of the Uniform Family Code.

The Jamaat representatives, for their part, spoke with greater clarity about their party's position on women's issues. On the subject of legal reform, they insisted that only the enforcement of true Islamic law would properly protect women's interests. Thus polygamy should not be outlawed; the Quran had sanctioned it precisely in order to provide for women who had no male support. They were strongly opposed to the Uniform Family Code because they believed that the Quran, rather than a man-made law, should govern all aspects of life. The Jamaat's support for women's voting rights was evident from Jamaat leader Saidi's use of his waaz, cited earlier, to ask women directly to support the party of Islam and God. In fact, by organizing a waaz and question-and-answer session devoted exclusively to women and arranging for the distribution and sale of the recorded lecture, Saidi and his party had taken a bold step that revealed a growing awareness on their part of women as a significant presence in society and politics and of the need to target women as women. There were no similar grand efforts to court women's votes on the part of the other parties, perhaps because they did not feel they needed to fight as hard for these votes. Feminist activist and scholar Roushan Jahan observed even before the 1996 elections that the Jamaat had the most clearly articulated position on gender of all the political parties in the early 1990s (1995: 104). Its election manifesto of June 1996 provides a succinct statement of the party's views on gender in society (Jamaat-i Islami 1996):

1. Employment will be provided in accordance with women's intelligence, qualifications, and needs.
2. Violence against women within and outside the home will be thoroughly suppressed.
3. Appropriate measures will be taken to put an end to the practice of dowry.
4. Appropriate measures will be taken to protect women's inheritance rights.
5. Seats will be reserved for women on trains, steamers, planes, and buses, and separate bus service will be provided for women within the city.
6. Strong measures will be taken to safeguard women's possessions, honor, and chastity during travel.
7. Arrangements will be made to rehabilitate destitute, widowed, and homeless women.
8. To realize the honor and status given women by Islam, prostitution will be abolished and steps taken to ensure the social rehabilitation of prostitutes.
9. Family courts will be set up to safeguard women's rights.
10. Arrangements will be made so that women can earn a living from within their home or neighborhood.

11. Women will be granted all opportunities to earn a living and participate in the task of nation building within the limits prescribed by the shariah.

At public gatherings, during television appearances, and in interviews, Jamaat members have elaborated on the party's position on these matters (Shehabuddin 1999a). Their statements at the Women for Women meeting also closely followed the official party line. According to the Jamaat representatives present, the physical differences between men and women meant that, in accordance with their party's understanding of Islamic law, their roles in society must be different. In their view, the main obstacle to women's enjoying their God-granted rights was their ignorance of religion as well as the absence of a state that fully supported those rights.

RELIGION, GENDER, AND POLITICS ON THE GROUND

Just over 5 percent of the men and women we surveyed said they had voted for the Jamaat in 1996.[28] Before turning to the vast majority of voters who did not support the Jamaat at the polls, it is worth exploring the views and motivations of the small number that did. In the course of my research, it became evident quite quickly that many who supported the Jamaat did so because they believed it was the Islamically correct thing to do; a vote for the Jamaat would help bring about an Islamic society in Bangladesh and help ensure individual salvation in the hereafter. Mohammed Ilyas of the southeastern district of Feni told us that he had voted for the Jamaat in order to support Islam; he was convinced that Islamic rule in Bangladesh would mean an end to all wrongdoing and could not think of any disadvantages that might follow the establishment of Islamic rule in the country. Nurul Islam of Jessore said he supported the Jamaat because "they would run the country in accordance with the Quran.... There would be a decrease in the level of immorality in the country." Jaan Mohammed of Rajshahi felt that under Jamaat rule God's laws would be established in this country and people's characters would improve. Many of the women supporters of the Jamaat were similarly confident that a Jamaat government would mean a more Islamic environment in the country in this life and ensure paradise for the voter in the next. In the words of one elderly woman I spoke with as she was on her way to vote in Jessore on Election Day in 1996, "What I've heard about the Jamaat is, . . . well, I'll be held accountable for all my actions when I die and if I vote for the Jamaat, I'll be able to justify that. Allah will be happy if I vote for the Jamaat."[29] According to Somirunnessa of Jessore, "Boys and girls would not be allowed to walk around holding hands anymore!" Tohura expected that under Islamic rule "everyone would follow the teachings of Islam and God's blessings would fall upon this land." Asked if she thought Islamic rule would be good for Bangladesh, Mosammat Akhlima Khatun of Jessore replied yes, because the "rule of the Quran" would be established. Even Suraiya, who admitted that she knew little about the Jamaat, was convinced that it would be good were it to come to power: "People would pray, fast, maintain *ijjot* [honor]. It would be like the Pakistan days. When women became too fashionable and *beparda* [out of purdah], the army used to stop them on the streets and tell them to cover up. Women were more *pardanashin* [purdah-observing] then. They used to wear long sleeves. All that would come back if the Jamaat were in power."[30] One woman believed that Islamic rule would give women the opportunity "to stay in purdah but be independent at the same time. So we thought that *daripalla* [scales] would be good for us." She added that there had been "no pressure [from local religious leaders], but we know we have to think about *parkal* [the afterlife], so we voted for the Jamaat."[31] Several women surveyed believed that the Jamaat candidates were more honest than candidates from other parties, as well as better qualified to stamp out terrorism and violence. One woman said that the embezzlement of government funds would cease if the Jamaat were to come to power and that women would be able to walk the streets without fear. Abeda of Rajshahi voted for the Jamaat because she was concerned about the fate of her soul, even though, as she herself recognized, the Jamaat might make life harder for impoverished women: "The Jamaat came to us and asked us to vote for them. They said that, this way, we don't have to worry about being weighed [assessed]) upon dying. That's why I voted for them. . . . It's true that it would be difficult for poor women. Now we go out and work, but [under Islamic rule,] we wouldn't be able to do that." Asma Begum in Sylhet followed the example of her entire household in voting the Jamaat: "Our whole *bari* [extended household] voted for the Jamaat. Under Islamic rule, nobody would conduct themselves in violation of God's laws. I don't see any disadvantages to Islamic rule."

While it is not clear whether Asma Begum was pressured to vote for the Jamaat, we did come across a very small number of women who admitted that they had voted for the Jamaat at their husbands' behest: "My husband said, we're all for the Jamaat. . . . Islamic rule would be good for the country, because everyone would pray, women wouldn't go out of the house or go about *beparda* [without purdah]" (Shirifa). "My husband is a *dari-palla* person [someone who supports the "scales" ballot symbol, i.e., the Jamaat]. . . . Under Islamic rule, people would observe purdah and the Jamaat would bring an end to dowry" (Huttunnessa). "My husband told me to vote for the Jamaat. . . . Under Islamic rule, everybody would conduct themselves properly and dowry would be wiped out" (Kadbhanu).

Like Kadbhanu, many supported the Jamaat not simply because of the promise of paradise but because the Jamaat had assured them that Islamic rule would ameliorate many of the more mundane problems plaguing rural life, such as the crushing burden of dowry. And indeed, in various forums, Jamaat leaders had expressed their outrage against the practice of dowry, calling it un-Islamic, in direct opposition to the Islamic rules for marriage. In the same waaz cited earlier, Delawar Hossain Saidi fumed against the practice in front of an all-female audience:

> At the time of marriage, the groom's father demands, "My son is an MA or a BA. Therefore, what should he be given? A radio? Actually, that's no longer enough; it's now at the bottom of the list. . . . A television, a car, hundreds of thousands of takas in cash, a job in Abu Dhabi—these are demanded. Is it really necessary to give all this when you're giving away your own daughter? . . . And if the bride's family fails to provide these things, the marriage is called off. . . . Remember, it is *haram* [prohibited] for the groom's family to demand this of the bride's family. You should refrain from demanding dowry and you should socially boycott those who do not. They are absolutely shameless. If the bride's father wishes to give his son-in-law a present, such as a watch or a shirt, that's different. But to demand this and that of the bride's family . . . can you not earn your own living? Are you a beggar that you should take charity from your in-laws?[32]

Others, like Mohammed Abdur Rahman of Jessore, supported the Jamaat because they were certain that Jamaat rule would mean the end of violence and terrorism and the establishment of basic rights for all. A few supported the Jamaat simply because, unlike the other three main parties, it had never had a chance to run the country and deserved a chance; in the words of a burka-clad woman waiting outside a polling center on Election Day, "Let's see what they can do."[33]

In keeping with national trends, however, the overwhelming majority of our respondents in 1996 did not support the Jamaat. From the responses to our survey, it was clear that those who were opposed to the Jamaat either were not persuaded by the party's brand of Islam or were concerned primarily with material issues they felt the Jamaat did not address adequately in its campaigns. The general lack of support for the Jamaat among poor rural women was naturally the source of much consternation for the Jamaat leadership. A well-educated, elderly Jamaat woman activist I interviewed in her village home lamented village women's lack of support for the Jamaat: "What I do not understand is . . . here is an opportunity for you to cast a vote with God and the Last Day in mind—and yet these women choose not to! Do they not realize that come Judgment Day, there will be no Khaledas or Hasinas. They will be lined up along with the rest of us. The only law will be the rule of God. So why not vote for God right now rather than waste it on a manmade ideology?"[34]

Why did so many women who said they prayed, fasted, read the Quran regularly, conformed to notions of purdah or female modesty, and generally saw themselves as good Muslims object so strongly to the Jamaat when it too insisted on these points? Many men and women told us that they did not vote for the Jamaat because they had longstanding loyalties to other parties. Some women, again, admitted they had voted as they were told by their husbands. A few voters saw no point in voting for the Jamaat because they believed the party stood no chance of winning. Just over a tenth of those who did not vote for the Jamaat simply said they did not like the party or the local candidate. Many others gave more specific reasons for not supporting the Jamaat, and this litany of criticism is worth exploring in some detail.

Many women we spoke with said that they did not support the Jamaat because, as Chandina of Jessore put it, "Mullahs are no good—they always find faults in women." Even though, as shown earlier, Jamaat leaders like Saidi had repeatedly condemned the practice of dowry that had made marriage a very difficult and risky enterprise for most rural women, these leaders had also, at the same time—indeed, often with their next breath—managed to blame women themselves for this phenomenon. Just after the diatribe against dowry quoted above, Saidi went on to say:

> There is a reason why the mohrana situation has reversed like this today. It is this: the attraction that is supposed to exist toward women has been transformed into repulsion. That which is available easily, cheaply, has no value.... God has said ..."Women, stay indoors."... By this, the Quran does not mean that women should be locked up inside the house.... Rather, it means that when you women do go out, you should retain the atmosphere of a home around yourselves. What is the atmosphere of a home? There is a door, there are windows.... What is meant then is that when you go out, wear a burka. The burka has a door and windows, has it not? ... And if you wear a burka, male strangers cannot see you, therefore they will develop attraction towards you. Your value will rise. Your status will increase. And your chastity and your body will be protected.

Rural women were quick to point to statements such as these, which held women responsible for the dowry demands and violence that could ruin their lives, as evidence that Jamaat politicians blamed women for all problems and ultimately were not interested in women's votes. Large numbers of women—and some men—were particularly concerned about the implications of Jamaat rule for women's ability to work outside the home. Qasem Ali, a carpenter in Dinajpur, was fearful that "under Islamic rule, it would be difficult for women to work. In our families, it would be very hard if the women didn't work." Over and over again, women expressed concern that Islamic rule, by the Jamaat or any other party, would lead to the burka being made compulsory and make it difficult for women to move about freely, join NGOs, or work outside the home. From what they knew of the Jamaat from neighbors and relatives, secularist and Jamaat activists, and waaz mahfils, they inferred that the Jamaat was uninterested in the poor, especially in poor women, and would impose codes of conduct and dress that would threaten their survival. Many women were wary of Jamaat rule because they feared they would lose the option of choosing what aspects of Islam to follow and what to ignore as irrelevant. In an Islamic state, religion would no longer be left to an individual's personal judgment but be dictated from above. To quote Sahera of Baruthan,

Chittagong: "The Jamaat? I'd never vote for them! My religion is my business."[35] For about a third of the women interviewed, the primary concern was restrictions they expected a Jamaat government to impose on their ability to work outside the home, as reflected in the following responses from the 1996 ASK survey: "If the Jamaat comes to power, they'll say that I can't leave the house anymore to earn a living. Who's going to feed my children and me then? I'll tell you this: none of those people who are so concerned about purdah now will rush forward to help me then!" (Anwara Begum Anu).[36] "Mullahs cannot tolerate women going out of the house. If the Jamaat established Islamic rule, it would be hard for women to get around" (Reena Khatun). "Women would not be able to work at NGOs; they would have to stay within purdah" (Morjina). "Women would not be allowed to leave their house, but if they cannot work, they will die of starvation!" (Morjina Khatun).

In 1996 a majority of the women interviewed admitted to having heard waazes by Saidi and other speakers, either live or on cassette, and to have learned a great deal about Islam and the Quran. While the women clearly had occasional access to cassettes, they did not listen in as regular or disciplined a manner as the educated urban Egyptian men studied by Charles Hirschkind (2006). Moreover, as the following story recounted to me by a village woman in Chittagong indicates, rural women like herself and her neighbors did not take at face value every word a religious figure uttered, especially when it conflicted with their own interests:

A mullah once issued a fatwa at a waaz mahfil that it is *najayez* [inappropriate; not permitted by Islam] to use fuel sticks made with sun-dried cow dung or use quilts made from women's old clothes. When he came home after the waaz, he found that his wife had not cooked dinner. He got into a huff and went off to sleep hungry, but could not sleep because it was too cold without any coverings. He yelled at his wife. She explained that she had thrown away all the dung sticks—and was thus unable to cook that evening—as well as all their quilts. His response (my interviewee is in a giggling fit at this point) was "You silly woman! That fatwa was meant for those who came to listen, not for me and my family!"[37]

In the end, when free to choose a candidate without pressure from relatives, rural patrons, or local party workers, the vast majority of women made their decision on the basis of self-interest, usually understood broadly to mean the good of the women themselves and their families. The anti-Islamist campaign had been successful in convincing many women that the Islamists were opposed to NGOs and to women working outside the home and might even put an end to such activities were they to come to power. The anti-Islamist campaign, however, had also highlighted the Jamaat's collaboration with the Pakistani army in 1971, its opposition to the independence of Bangladesh, and its direct involvement in the brutal killings and rapes during the nine months of war. Yet the Jamaat's activities in 1971 turned out to be far less significant a factor in the voting decisions of the vast majority of the rural men and women we spoke with all over the country. Indeed, only a few rural teachers and local elected officials—in other words, not the poorest members of rural society—even brought up the Jamaat's activities in 1971.

THE NECESSITIES OF LIFE

The gap between elite assumptions about what mattered to the rural poor and what impoverished rural women themselves saw as their actual concerns is well illustrated in the following account by a high-ranking member of the secularist Nirmul Committee of his own experience while working on voter education before the 1996 elections:

> We started out by urging people to vote for the party and candidate who best represented the spirit of 1971 and would work to achieve those goals. That does point to the Awami League but we didn't want to say that explicitly. However, as we got closer to the elections, we realized that we should be more aggressive and urge people directly to vote for the Awami League.
>
> One time, we were visiting Kulcha.... This is near Chandpur. To get there, we had to park our cars and then walk a mile or so. We called a large group of women together. Since I'm a journalist, I had a cameraman with me, so we have pictures of this. I asked the women to vote for the Awami League, and they were quite outraged!
>
> "Why?" they demanded, "Why should we vote for the Awami League? Have they ever given us anything? The BNP has given us money and we will vote for them."

I tried to explain to them that the one hundred or five hundred takas that they may have received from a political party would only last so long, while a candidate that they elected would be [in office] for five years. I tried to draw their attention to the achievements of the last Awami League MP in that area. I pointed out that it was under him that proper roads had been constructed in their village. A journey that used to take eight to nine hours from Dhaka now took just a few hours.

The women retorted, "We don't need those roads. They're not for us. Those *pucca* roads are for the rich people. We're doing just fine walking on the aisles in the fields."

I couldn't really fight her on that and pointed instead to the tube-wells that they all now use. She insisted that those had been installed by NGOs.[38]

This exchange shows quite clearly the dangers of assuming women's interests rather than actually identifying them. What was assumed by an MP—and by this journalist—to be a marker of progress for the village was clearly not so as far as the local women were concerned. It is quite likely that tradition and purdah kept them off the busy new roads, filled with motor vehicles and strangers, yet, interestingly enough, they dismissed the roads as being meant for "rich people" and not as being for "men," thereby privileging socioeconomic class divisions over those of gender.

What factors, then, helped determine the votes of impoverished rural voters? When selecting a party, these ordinary, illiterate rural voters who professed to being observant Muslims certainly found little to distinguish among the four main parties in terms of religious symbols; all four parties used them throughout their campaigns. Rather, voters tried to pay close attention to party promises on such issues as personal security, health care, and education, but given their past experiences and encounters with the state, they knew better than to rely too heavily on campaign promises. An impoverished woman in rural Bangladesh assessing the different parties' commitment to issues that were important to her could be confident that, no matter who came to power, she would receive some immediate assistance, in the form of food and a sari, in the event of a flood or cyclone. She might even have an opportunity to be photographed receiving her bounty and see her picture in a newspaper the following day with a caption or headline about the munificence of the prime minister. But as she listened to the parties' promises, what could she really count on as far as her daily needs were concerned in the five long years before the next elections? And how might this affect her decision of whom to vote for? From where she stood, there had actually been little cause in past years to be enthusiastic about voting. The much-vaunted distinctions of left wing versus right wing, of Islamist versus secularist, made little sense to her when she looked at the parties' actual actions and accomplishments. Given her past experience with elected officials, she had little reason to believe that any party would deliver on its preelection promises or to trust the quality of whatever services they might provide.

In the 1996 ASK survey, conducted just after Sheikh Hasina replaced Khaleda Zia as prime minister, many women and men acknowledged the former government's efforts to improve girls' access to education, for instance, by providing free education for female pupils up to the eighth grade and implementing a food-for-education program in schools. In-depth interviews, however, revealed a deep sense of disillusionment with what children could be expected to learn and accomplish in state schools, regardless of who was in power. Kamrunnahar Shamsu of Chittagong complained that the teachers at the local government school sat around gossiping all day instead of teaching. Anwara complained: "It's true, our kids don't learn anything in school. . . . The teachers are careful with the kids of wealthier people, those who give them money on the side, send *bhat-nasta* [literally, rice and snacks; gifts, goodies]. When we complain to those wealthier people about the quality of schooling, they just look at us and say, 'Really? Why, *our* children seem to be learning a great deal at school!'" Their neighbor, Rizia, had little faith in their children's prospects even if they managed to complete secondary school: "You see that they have to be a carpenter's apprentice even after the matric exam [national board exams at the end of tenth grade], so you begin to think, what's the point of going to all that trouble to keep them in school?" Rizia's experience with the local health center had also been far from positive. She complained that the local government doctor regularly charged for medicine that he was supposed to dispense for free (or for a nominal fee).[39] Similarly, as I reported in chapter 3, rural women evinced little faith in the ability of the state and its local agents—the police, the courts—to protect the traditionally disadvantaged: women and the poor. Asked what they thought were the duties of the police, many of the women we spoke with suggested catching criminals and the maintenance of law and order. Yet very few poor men, and even fewer poor women, had ever gone to the police for help. Banu said it was because the police always insist on "a little money for tea"—in other words, a bribe.[40] Morjina's complaint that "the police don't help the poor without taking money from them" was echoed by large numbers of women in other parts of the country.

Since impoverished rural women lack both money and powerful influence, it is easy to see why they do not, as individuals, seek out government assistance in times of trouble. Their lack of faith in the state is reaffirmed by their everyday experiences with local state institutions such as local government and police and with local services provided by the state such as medical centers and schools. Despite much public expression of democratic duty, many women seemed resigned to the notion that the state—secular or otherwise—was of little relevance to their daily life. As one woman lamented, "So many governments have come and gone and nothing has changed in my life. The people in Dhaka must be terribly busy with other things" (Shehabuddin 1999a: 157).

Impoverished women's encounters with the state help to explain why they enter the political process with no illusions about what they can expect from any of the political parties and, as a result, clarify some of their choices and actions during elections. Although many women spoke with reverence about the noble exercise of voting in a democratic process, many throughout the country also admitted, basically, to having sold their vote to the highest bidder.[41] It was common knowledge that party workers distributed cash and clothing—saris for the women, *lungis* [saronglike garments] for the men—just before the elections to bribe voters into supporting their respective parties. It was also assumed, by both the political parties and disinterested observers, that the poorest of the poor would respond in gratitude to such gifts. Given the extreme poverty of many of these families, each additional piece of clothing was indeed a luxury; however, the effect was not as direct as has been assumed. It was not that people actually supported the party from which they accepted bribes; rather, they did not expect anything in the long run from any of the parties, even the party that won the election, so they voted for the one that offered them something in the immediate term. As one woman put it, "Since we never hear from any of the parties once they get into office, I decided I might as well go with whichever one is most generous before the elections! Maybe I'll get a new sari before the next elections too!"[42]

No woman described a scenario in which she had made a promise to her husband or a party worker to support a particular party and yet voted for a different party—that of her own choosing—once she found herself alone in the voting booth. Promising one thing and doing another would be an act of *be-imani* (bad faith).[43] It is likely that many of the promises even to husbands were made not simply out of wifely devotion but also because the women did not regard their votes as valuable or powerful enough to warrant defying their husbands' wishes; after all, if a woman's husband were to find out that she had voted for a different candidate, no government elected into office would protect her from the violence of his fury. The indifference of many women voters ultimately is a direct response to the indifference of the political parties to women voters and women's issues. Despite the prominence of Sheikh Hasina and Begum Khaleda Zia, the absence of concrete proposals to ameliorate problems faced by women combined with a dearth of women candidates rendered the electoral process less attractive and less interesting for most women voters.

Not all women of voting age in Bangladesh voted in recent elections. In some cases, like their male neighbors and relatives, they simply had not registered to vote. There were, however, numerous instances where women did not vote or were not permitted to vote precisely because they were women. Some families did not permit women to vote because they did not believe women should do so or because they feared neighbors would then assume the women were over eighteen. In certain parts of the country, women were not permitted to vote following fatwas by local religious leaders that it was un-Islamic for women to vote. Finally, a few women chose not to vote because of the distance to the nearest voting center, out of fear that there might be violence on the road, or because they saw no point in it. In the end, however, women made up nearly half of the 75 percent voter turnout in the last two elections, thus millions of women—around twenty-eight million in 1996 and thirty-six million in 2001[44]—did vote, and it is likely that a large number of them made up their own minds about how to vote and how to assess their own self-interest.

This chapter has sought to examine the factors that influenced the decisions of impoverished rural women who chose to participate in formal politics by voting in recent elections. As it turns out, the secularist-Islamist divide that animated much elite-level discussion of politics was not as relevant as posited. The secularist organizations, such as the Nirmul Committee and NGOs, campaigning against the Jamaat focused a great deal on the Jamaat's war crimes in 1971 and the specter of the Islam-ization of laws. Islamists for their part assumed that assurances of greater honesty in government and easy passage to heaven would be sufficient to win electoral support. Contrary to claims by rival parties that rural women were simply duped by other parties into voting for their candi-dates, women understood the competing messages through the filter of their own knowledge, experiences, and realities. In the end, Bangladesh's elites failed to gauge and respond to the needs of women in rural Ban-gladesh, the majority of whom turned out to be far more concerned with material issues than any of the parties had foreseen and whose decisions were informed less by religion than by their ongoing encounters with the state at both national and local levels and the political parties that con-trolled all the branches of the state machinery.

Contrary to the hopes, expectations, and claims of the country's elites, then, religion was not as significant a factor in the women's decisions as anticipated. Given the prodigious use of Islamic symbols by all four of the main parties, voters found it difficult to discern differences in their relative levels of religious commitment, and in the end rural women cared about religion only to the extent that they required some minimal indications of piety from national leaders—which all the major players were happy to furnish and display. Rural women's rejection of the Jamaat should not be interpreted as a rejection of religion in the public sphere. Neither was it the case that they rejected the Jamaat on the basis of such issues as 1971 and Islamization that have long been of great concern to urban, secular elites. As noted in chapter 3, they were ill equipped to take advantage of the legal system, be it secular, Islamic, or, as currently existed, something in between. Promises to secularize the legal system meant as little to most rural women as did threats to Islamize it; from where they stood, laws had little bearing on their lives. They did not vote for the Jamaat because the Jamaat failed to counter charges that it would put an end to women's involvement with NGOs. At the same time, when they did vote for one of the other three parties—the AL, the BNP, and the JP—it was not because they found its promises credible. Having learned over the years that it was imprudent to count on politicians' fulfilling campaign prom-ises on the issues that mattered to them, they chose instead to act on the basis of immediate short-term gains, such as gifts in cash or kind that were handed to them just before the elections. Thus women ultimately chose to trust a sari in the hand—and, in a few cases, faith in heaven after death—over almost certainly specious campaign promises of shelter, education, jobs, and land. In the end, rural women used the elections for what they knew they could get out of them rather than placing futile hope in campaign promises of dramatic improvements in their lives.

My argument is not that unlettered rural women are not swayed by ideological arguments. Rather, I have shown that despite the plethora of parties on the political scene the range of ideologies represented is rather limited and poor rural women have come to realize that their interests are very different from those of the elites who control the parties, even when these claim to be concerned about the poor, the needy, and women. The story, of course, does not end here, for the lessons of the 1996 elections would prove important to the contenders for power five years later. In the next chapter, I turn to the 2001 elections and the impact of a mobilized female citizenry on the Islamists' approach to politics.

6

BEYOND MUSLIM MOTHERHOOD

With my shalwar pulled halfway up my calves, I followed the two women down a monsoon-drenched path into a large rectangular building. Built primarily of sheets of corrugated tin and lengths of bamboo at some height from the ground to protect it from rising floodwaters, the structure consisted of a single large room. It took my eyes a few moments to adjust to the darkness inside. Then I discerned that the room was furnished sparsely, with two tables, a few chairs, and several benches. The women debated between opening the small windows to allow in some light and air and leaving them shut to keep out prying male eyes. After some deliberation, they compromised by opening the windows only partway. They took their places in the chairs set against a long wall, put their books down on the tables in front of them, and waited patiently.

Women from the neighborhood began to stream in, stepping over the high sill at the door, often with babies and children, often with other adult women. Each woman raised her right hand to her forehead and greeted us with "Assalam wa alaikum" (Peace be upon you). Within fifteen minutes, about seventy women had gathered in the room. Only a handful wore black burkas, while the rest wore their regular brightly colored cotton saris with the anchol or an extra *chador* (large shawl) drawn over their heads. The younger children cried and fussed as their mothers exchanged news of their families and what they had cooked and eaten recently. A few of the early arrivals found space on the benches and the rest sat down on the floor, all of them facing the two women I had accompanied. A couple of women had brought in homemade hand fans that they now used vigorously to stave off the heat and humidity.

It was early afternoon on June 30, 2003, a hot day in the middle of the annual monsoon season. About an hour earlier, just after lunch, I had met Samira Khatun outside her home, and we had proceeded together to the apartment of Maleka Begum, a few miles away. From Maleka's home, we went on foot into the large slum behind her apartment complex. Both women lived in government staff housing because their husbands were government employees, and both were middle-ranking members of the women's wing of the Jamaat-i Islami in Dhaka City. That afternoon, they had graciously agreed to let me accompany them on one of their regular visits to this particular slum. As the room filled, Samira began to speak, opening with "Bismillah" (In the name of God). The gathered women stopped their conversations and turned to face her with rapt attention for the next two hours. She made them recite out loud rhymes they had learned in an earlier session about how to perform the ablutions necessary before praying: what to wash, how many times, and in what order. Then she recited in Arabic Surah Fatihah, the opening chapter of the Quran. For about an hour, she went through this short but important sura of just seven verses, translating and discussing each verse at length. In the course of these elaborations, she managed to emphasize the importance of purdah, prayer, and group work. She ended the meeting by reading out a letter from the male head of the Dhaka City chapter of the Jamaat, translating into colloquial Bengali any words she felt this particular group might have difficulty understanding. This letter, which began "Dear brothers and sisters," reminded the listeners of the important work being done by the Jamaat in the service of God, Islam, and the nation and ended by urging them all to vote for the Jamaat in future elections.

A deep conviction that it is their religious duty to bring a correct Islam to the impoverished illiterate women of the country is leading large numbers of well-educated Islamist women to take up activism in unfamiliar neighborhoods; concerned about their interests in this world as well as the next, large numbers of the poorest women in society are making an effort to heed the Islamist message. In this chapter, I explore the nature of the interaction between the Jamaat and impoverished women in the context of a democratic polity and the implications of this relationship for our understanding of the transformative potential of and within Islamist politics. Arguing that the Jamaat's dismal results in 1996 compelled the party to rethink its strategies and rhetoric in order to broaden its support base, I show how it intensified its efforts in the run-up to the 2001 elections.

It is a truism that political parties concerned with survival and power adapt their ideology over time in order to appeal to newly emerging and ever-changing groups of voters. In a democratic setting, sufficiently mobilized women voters possess the power to shape and moderate the ideology even of groups who claim to be fully committed to ideas elaborated over a millennium ago. The interesting question is to what extent Islamist parties, which point to the Quran as the sole source of their ideology and seek a return to a putative golden age in Islamic history, can transform themselves in response to the exigencies of current political and social realities, in particular, the increasing involvement of women in formal politics. In this chapter, I seek to go beyond the questions of whether Muslim countries can be democracies or whether Islamists are willing to participate in democratic elections. Recent research demonstrates clearly that several predominantly Muslim countries are indeed electoral democracies and Islamists in many of these, as well as other less free, Muslim countries have participated in a succession of parliamentary elections (Clark 2004; Clark and Schwedler 2003; Hefner 2000; Karatnycky 2002; G. Robinson 1997; Shehabuddin 1999a; Stepan 2003; Stepan and Robertson 2004; Taraki 1995, 1996; J. White 2002; Wiktorowicz 2001).[1] As Vickie Langohr reminds us, however, the "ultimate value [of democracy] lies in its pledge, however short it may fall in reality—to value the rights of all citizens equally" (2001: 592). By this argument, a party that does not recognize the equality of Muslims and non-Muslims, of men and women, cannot really be accepted as democratic. It would seem, then, that a more useful way of investigating an Islamist party's democratic credentials would be to examine its relationship to women or non-Muslims and its assertions about their rights. From his study of the relationship between Islam and authoritarianism, which I cited earlier, M. Steven Fish concludes that "Muslim societies are distinct in a manner that may affect politics: the treatment and status of girls" and offers some tentative ideas on how "the status and treatment of women and girls affects political regime," using sociological, psychological, and demographic explanations (2002: 24, 29–30). While he recognizes the tentative nature of his conclusions, Fish expresses "skepticism regarding the chances for robust democracy" even in the countries generally "seen as the Islamic world's leading candidates for thoroughgoing, lasting democratization," namely, Bangladesh, Pakistan, Nigeria, and Turkey, precisely given their unbalanced sex ratios and the large gender gaps in literacy and participation in high office (33).[2] While such links are certainly cause for concern and caution, a look at the situation on the ground in these countries and the interaction among local, national, and international actors shows a less dismal picture.

Competition for votes in a democratic context has led the Jamaat-i Islami to seek out new supporters over the years; the female population of Bangladesh—long enfranchised but only recently mobilized, even galvanized, by democratic politics and the activities of NGOs—is the most recent and most dramatically visible of these groups. Such women pose a special challenge to the Jamaat because the curriculum that is the very cornerstone of the Jamaat's recruitment strategy was designed with an elite, male readership in mind. In this chapter, I focus on some specific ways in which the Jamaat has been trying to work around this particular problem in an effort to reach out to and win the support of poor, illiterate women in order to make them, if not card-carrying members, then at least part of what Carrie Wickham calls a "supportive public" (2002: 165). I begin by examining some of the specific strategies the Jamaat has undertaken to court mobilized women voters. I follow this with a discussion of how poor women themselves have thus far received and understood the Jamaat's message. I conclude by considering the implications of these developments for our understanding of Islamist political activism, both in Bangladesh and globally.

ELECTORAL COMPETITION AND THE JAMAAT

Since the restoration of democracy in Bangladesh seventeen years ago, the Jamaat has become a key player in national politics, though primarily so far as a crucial electoral coalition partner rather than as a viable independent contender for state power. The vast majority of official Jamaat members, men and women, are middle class, well educated (primarily Western educated), and urban based, in other words, essentially identical to the core supporters of most Islamist movements in other parts of the world—and indeed very much like the secular elites of Bangladesh.

Unlike Islamist parties in many other Muslim countries, especially in the Arab world, but like the Jamaat-e-Islami in Pakistan, the Felicity Party in Turkey, the Islamist Prosperous Justice Party (Partai Keadilan Sejahtera, PKS) in Indonesia, and the Islamic Party (Parti Islam SeMalaysia, commonly referred to as PAS) in Malaysia, the Jamaat in Bangladesh regularly contests democratic elections. The "opportunities and demands created by the ballot box" have led the party to woo ever-new constituencies (Nasr 2005: 14–15; see also Stark 2005). Thus in the years since its founding, the Jamaat has slowly and cautiously opened its doors first to educated men and then to working-class men and educated women. The massive mobilization of impoverished, unlettered Bangladeshi women in recent years by international and indigenous development organizations serves to distinguish the political dynamics in Bangladesh from those of other democratic Muslim countries. Domestically, these women have become a force that can no longer be ignored. Today, the Jamaat appears to have come to the realization that it cannot expect to win national power by relying exclusively on an educated support base in the midst of mass illiteracy and without addressing the needs of the increasing numbers of poor women who demand educational and employment opportunities.

The 1996 parliamentary elections in Bangladesh, the second in the current democratic era, marked a turning point in the Jamaat's relationship to the electorate (see Kabir and Begum 2005). The historically secularist AL won a majority of parliamentary seats and returned to power after twenty-one years while the Jamaat emerged with only three seats in a parliament of three hundred. Following the elections, both the Jamaat and its opponents came to the conclusion that the unprecedented mobilization of poor women voters by NGOs and anti-Islamists has been almost single-handedly responsible for the Jamaat's poor performance at the polls. The Jamaat has lamented—and its critics have celebrated—the success of the anti-Jamaat campaign in persuading poor women that the Jamaat is opposed to their attempts to improve their lives through wage labor or NGO assistance. Shortly after the 1996 elections, Dr. Yunus, the founder and managing director of Grameen Bank, described the election results as a signal and historic victory of poor women against Islamist politics, against a worldview that was critical of women's empowerment (Shehabuddin 1999a).

The claims of secularist groups and NGOs were not unfounded. According to the Jamaat's own statements in interviews with me, in media appearances, and in its publications, the main solution it long proposed to the problems facing the women of Bangladesh was the establishment of an Islamic state. The Jamaat argued that Bangladeshi women had been denied the rights granted to them in the Quran over fourteen hundred years ago—rights that only a proper Islamic state could guarantee, an Islamic state that only the Jamaat could implement. A gender ideology grounded on the notion that men and women are equal and complementary and thus subject to a strict sexual division of labor led the Jamaat to be critical of NGOs that in recent years had been targeting women specifically.

Over the last decade, the Jamaat in Bangladesh periodically denounced NGOs as being the reincarnations of nineteenth-century Christian missionaries who operated in British India under the protection of the colonial state. It criticized NGOs and their international donors for explicitly targeting women in literacy, income-generation, and microcredit programs, pointing out that large numbers of uneducated and unemployed men also needed assistance, that in fact they needed more because it was a man's duty to provide for his family. This position, of course, ignored the fact that the number of female-headed households had been rising steadily over recent decades and that these households were among the poorest in the country (Mannan 2000). And the similarity between nineteenth-century missionaries and today's NGOs clearly did not lie in their position on women; the missionaries, after all, strongly advocated the notions of domesticity for women that were then prevalent in their home countries. The similarity lay instead in both groups being seen as agents of Western imperialists. Given the Jamaat's strident attacks on NGOs, it was not very difficult for those who were opposed to the Jamaat to portray it as anti-NGO and, by extension, anti-women and to hail the secularist groups as the true champions of women's rights (Shehabuddin 1999b). As I discussed in chapter 5, many poor rural women were indeed persuaded that they would not be allowed to work outside the home were the Jamaat to come to power and hence made a point of voting against it. It is widely believed that this contributed to the Jamaat's winning only three seats in 1996. Many women and men we spoke with after the 1996 elections also explained that they had not been approached by Jamaat workers and so did not really know the party: "We don't hear about them. People from the other parties come to our homes and tell us about themselves, about their meetings. When we can, we go to these meetings. The

Jamaat? They never came to us. I know they have an office around here but we never hear about their meetings."[3] Thus, while NGOs concerned with their own survival undoubtedly encouraged notions that the Jamaat was opposed to women working outside the home, the conspicuous absence of the Jamaat in most of rural Bangladesh meant that the rural poor did not have access to counterarguments.

Even before the 1996 elections, Jamaat leaders appeared aware that they were at a disadvantage vis-à-vis other parties in their ability to attract women voters:"The problem is that, because of household responsibilities, our wives cannot spare as much time as we [men] can to go out and talk to prospective women followers."[4] The underlying assumptions seemed to be that women workers were more effective at recruiting women sup- porters than were men and that women workers in other parties could afford to delegate household tasks to domestic servants. Primarily, how- ever, Jamaat leaders attributed their party's poor performance at the polls to the anti-Jamaat campaign launched by some NGOs and groups as well as to the liberal distribution of money among the voters just before the elections. In a meeting in her office just ten days after the 1996 elections, I asked a high-ranking member of the women's wing for her analysis of the election results. She was adamant that the presence of dirty money and a corrupt administration had cheated the Jamaat of its rightful share of votes. She expressed concern that the people of Bangladesh were not yet ready for true democracy; they wanted Islamic rule, but they were still too easily influenced by money and misinformation. Thus they were quite likely to vote for any party that offered them money, a sari, or a lungi. She said that she herself had come across fraud at numerous poll- ing centers and pointed out that the candidates put up by the other par- ties in several constituencies were known to be corrupt and dishonest. At that point, one of her colleagues at work, a fellow Jamaat member who until then had been sitting quietly and listening to our conversa- tion, brought up the issue of fraudulent voter lists. She alleged that at least two men-only university residences at Dhaka University, Salimullah Muslim Hall and Jagannath Hall, were found to have about thirty and one thousand registered women voters respectively.[5] Other Jamaat men and women expressed similar views in subsequent interviews. Some also cited the persistence of patron-client ties: the poor tended to be wary of voting for the Jamaat in areas where local elites clearly supported one of the other parties.[6]

In an interview about six months after the elections, a senior rural-based Jamaat woman posited that there had been a nationwide (and foreign-funded) secularist plot to detract Muslim voters from their "natural," "faith-motivated" inclination to vote for the Jamaat: "There was a conspiracy here by an NGO called Proshika. They went around telling people not to vote for us, saying, 'How is dari-palla [scales, ballot symbol of the Jamaat] going to help you? You should all vote for *dhaner shish* [sheaf of rice, ballot symbol of the BNP]. If you vote for rice, you will never again go without rice.' Also, the BNP distributed a great deal of money among the villagers. And, of course, who won? The BNP! . . . [The local Jamaat candidate], on the other hand, did not have a single penny to give the villagers." She added quickly that winning elections was not the party's primary objective. It was simply a means to the end they really desired: they wanted state power in order to Islamize society and were willing to wait for that time to come. "We are not concerned about winning or losing elections. The Jamaat-i Islami of Bangladesh is much more than a political party. We want all Muslims to be *true* Muslims. We tell them that this world does not matter, that it is the next one that counts, that goes on forever. And if you do not behave as you should here, you will have to pay the price when you face God on the Last Day. Does a mother not reprimand an unruly child? Similarly, God punishes those who break His rules. In hell, one is made to lie down on a bed of fire and then is covered with a blanket of fire. One cries out for it to end, but one does not die there. This continues forever."

I knew that this woman and her neighbor, also a Jamaat worker, had both worked hard to try to persuade the poorer women of the village to support the Jamaat in the 1996 elections. I inquired how they had gone about this work. They explained that they tried to inform the less educated women around them about the importance of thanking God for the blessings they have:

> If a car is without a driver, can it maintain a straight course? Does the car know where to go and how? Similarly, everything around us is there for a reason and there is a driver directing the slightest detail. Why does the sun always rise in the east and set in the west? Because a grand director has decided that that is how it should happen. It is all part of a grand plan. All this free air and water we enjoy—shouldn't we be thankful for these? It is because it is free

that we don't think about it. But if we had to buy bottled air and water in order to survive, wouldn't we be willing to pay the price?

All God asks of us is that we be thankful for bounties, that we pray and fast. . . . Yet we don't. It is said that . . .[a majority] of this country is Muslim. But they are Muslim only in name. It used to be that 40 percent were true Muslims who prayed, etc. . . . Now that figure is down to 25 percent. Only those people are thanking God for all he had given us. . . . We want all Muslims to be true Muslims.

The following statement, cited earlier, clarified that, from the Jamaat's perspective, one way to show one's gratitude to God was to vote for the Jamaat: "What I do not understand is: when you are alone inside the voting booth, you are free to vote as you please. Your husband, your father, or the party worker who gave you a sari in exchange for a vote, aren't there with you. Here is an opportunity for you to cast a vote with God and the Last Day in mind—and yet these women choose not to! Do they not realize that come Judgment Day, they will be lined up along with the rest of us. The only law will be the rule of God. So why not vote for God right now rather than waste it on a manmade ideology?"

When I asked how the poor women had responded to such appeals, one woman shook her head and lamented, "The village women usually sit at our meetings and nod in agreement with everything we say. But then they leave and forget it all!"[7]

Clearly, the Jamaat failed to communicate to the majority of the nation's women with any degree of success in 1996. Most voters' personal piety did not automatically translate into support for the Society of Islam. In some cases, the voters simply had not had any interaction with the Jamaat; in others, they had not liked what they had heard. By the time of the next parliamentary elections in October 2001, the Jamaat appeared to have rethought both the content of its message as directed to impoverished women and its modes of communication.

WOOING WOMEN

Elections aside, the Jamaat has traditionally reached out to prospective supporters through written literature, direct personal contact, and large public lectures (waaz mahfil). Prospective and existing members of the Jamaat—both men and women—are required to maintain a written daily log of certain required activities: for example, reading the Quran, hadith (the traditions of the Prophet), and prescribed Islamic literature; praying in a group; extending the message of the Jamaat to new individuals; recruiting new members and maintaining close contact with existing workers; distributing Jamaat publications; donating money to the Jamaat; and engaging in introspection. In her pamphlet on women's responsibilities in the Islamic movement, senior Jamaat member Begum Rokeya Ansar discusses in detail the necessity of women's active participation in the Islamic movement in order to help establish a true Islamic society. She begins by explaining why it is necessary to have an Islamic state. Without an Islamic state that makes prayer, fasting, purdah, and so on compulsory, Muslims only pray, fast, and observe purdah as, when, and if they want. Such irregular observance of the Islamic requirements has contributed to the sorry state of society today, to "the prevalence of theft, robbery, kidnapping, murder, violence against women, disorder, instability, usury and corruption" (1991: 7–8).

Like the Jamaat woman cited earlier who faulted Khaleda Zia and Sheikh Hasina for not mandating the observance of purdah by the women of the country, Ansar reserves particular fury for the state's failure to force women to maintain purdah and attributes acts of violence against women to women's unwillingness to observe it (9–10). To counter this decline in society, she calls on women to organize because they can work far more effectively as part of an organization than they can as individuals. She identifies as "our greatest misfortune today" the well-organized nature of "our mothers and sisters who believe in Western civilization and follow the path of godlessness.... By forming various committees, organizing all sorts of meetings and gatherings, they have created much disorder in society in the name of women's emancipation, freedom, and conscientization. Indeed they have gone so far as to criticize various Islamic laws including the marriage and inheritance laws and demand changes in these laws in the name of women's rights" (44–45). She calls on women who are concerned about the future of their society, families, and children to organize themselves to confront these Westernized women and to work to establish a different kind of society. She warns them against assuming that participation in the movement is only a man's job: "Islam has given woman appropriate rights. She is not seen as a part of a man. So women are not expected to behave just as men tell them to.... Just as men are responsible for their faith, for attaining knowledge about Islam, and to follow Islam with sincerity, so are women. Men and women will be liable for their respective deeds. . . . On the Day of Judgment, no woman can expect to be excused by God on the grounds that her husband was an important leader or a conscientious worker in the Islamic movement. Nor will she be excused on the grounds that her husband did not encourage her or even allow her to participate in the Islamic movement" (15, 17).

Ansar informs her readers that the most effective means of organizing is by joining "any organization that believes in the Islamic ideals as directed by God and demonstrated by the Prophet" and by doing so "without any further delay." The next step is to "win over the countless women in our society to the path of Islam." For literate women, this Islamic reeducation is conducted through the dissemination of books intended to serve as an introduction to Jamaat ideology; the books should be selected on the basis of "the woman's mindset and level of education" (46). She reminds readers of the importance of reading in the nurturing and development of the Islamic character and advises current members to exercise judgment and discretion when recruiting: "When spreading the message, remember that you must never behave as though you know more than they do and that you are proud of it. The woman worker must always say little and listen closely to the other person. During your discussions, you will learn about her problems, her intelligence, her weaknesses, and her thoughts. . . . At no point should you become involved in a dispute with her, and you should be careful not to hurt by anything you say or do. To remove weaknesses in her thought, give her suitable books and pamphlets" (52–53). Prospective and established members are expected to meet regularly in study circles to discuss what they have read on their own and to sharpen their understanding of Jamaat ideology and Islam.

WOOING UNLETTERED WOMEN

Clearly, a different strategy is necessary when working with illiterate women and men—an entirely oral form of pedagogy—and Ansar's little book does not really address the issue of outreach to the unlettered. Speaking with me in 1996, however, another senior Jamaat woman explained how the party's message was spread among the predominantly illiterate population in rural areas: "We target those who read a little, tell them about the Quran and hadith and tell them to take the message to others, to explain our goals." When I asked if this could be done orally, she did not hesitate to remind me, "Yes, just the way Islam was originally preached!"[8]

While accompanying senior Jamaat women on their missions into poor homes and neighborhoods, it struck me that, ironically, some of the techniques they were using bore an uncanny resemblance to those used with great success by explicitly secular NGOs; these un- even anti-Islamist organizations have long used verbal communication and rote learning to teach their illiterate members about social and health issues, from the evils of dowry to the importance of having a vegetable garden of one's own. The Grameen Bank's Sixteen Decisions, which Grameen members are required to recite from memory at the beginning of every weekly meeting and implement in their own lives, are a famous example of this method at work.[9]

JAMAAT WOMEN AT WORK

While in the past, Jamaat women were expected to impart Islamic teaching only to the poor and uneducated in their immediate vicinity, such as servants in their homes, they now find themselves venturing into unfamiliar slums, overcrowded shantytowns, and distant villages, where large numbers of impoverished women live. Senior Jamaat women leaders concede that this is far from easy work, since these sites have little possibility for privacy, hygiene, and what they consider a suitable Islamic space. Yet dedicated party workers persevere, insisting that it is their religious duty to propagate the Jamaat's message.[10]

In the summer of 2001 I accompanied senior Jamaat leader Jamila Akhtar on her visit to a shantytown in Chittagong. Near the edge of the impoverished neighborhood, we stopped to pick up another Jamaat woman, Nahar, whom Jamila credited with having transformed the faith and practices of the women who lived in that area. Although the Jamaat's central command had declared the project of gonoshikkha (mass education) a priority, Jamila pointed out that the extent of progress ultimately depended entirely on the initiative and dedication of local individuals: "The order is there but different areas have made different degrees of progress.... If there is someone who can take the initiative and do the work, then we do well." A small, middle-aged woman, Nahar had been educated in both religious and secular curricula and earned a master's degree along the way. She had begun working in these slums some ten years earlier, "just before the big cyclone of 1991." Her husband, a senior government employee, had joined the Jamaat following her example, rather than the reverse. Recalling the importance attached to women's domestic obligations by official Jamaat ideology, I asked Nahar how she managed to balance her household responsibilities with her work for the Jamaat in the *bosti* (slums). She responded that she had simply "made time in [her] day for this." She elaborated:

> I take care of my home at the same time.... I wake up at 3 A.M. to say my *tahajjud* prayers.[11] I read the Quran, I say my *fajr* ([early morning] prayers ... and in accordance with the Quran and hadith, I spend the day seeking God. I want to bring about an Islamic society in Bangladesh in keeping with God's dictates, the Prophet's (peace be upon him) dictates, as I understand them from reading the thirty *para*s of the Quran.... The Quran that God has given us, I want to bring it alive. Our Prophet (peace be upon him) said, as long as you hold God's Quran, the Prophet's (peace be upon him) *sunna*, close to your heart, you cannot be led astray. So today, if we don't educate ourselves ... we are not being true to this.... I want to work with sincerity to fulfill our responsibilities for Judgment Day.[12]

Nahar explained that she had chosen to focus on the poor because both the Prophet and his daughter, Fatima, were poor; she realized that "it is through the poor that I must fulfill my religious obligations. It is my *faraj* [obligation]. I must love them." She told me that she was dismissive of those who were surprised that a woman of her social standing worked in the slums: "Many people say to me, how can you, the wife of [a senior government employee], work in the slums like this? I reply, certainly, but of course, I must do this work. Certainly, I must appear in front of God on Judgment Day. I will not remain [here] forever as the wife of [a senior government employee]. I must die one day and go to my grave and be held accountable on the Day of Judgment.... That is why, as a matter of practice, I have descended into the field to do this work for Islam."[13]

By working closely with impoverished women over the years, Nahar had developed an appreciation of their particular hardships and had modulated her expectations accordingly. She explained that there was a smaller turnout than usual that afternoon because most women were busy watching the weekly Friday afternoon Bengali film on TV: "We have to let them do that. We have to work with a calm head if we want to accomplish anything." She spoke of the dire poverty in the neighborhood and the difficulties this posed for her work: "I can't take away their need and poverty. They are really very needy. They have trouble getting medication, education, having a burka made, having even an orna made. . . . I cannot make up for these things. . . . That is why I always say, we need more money. These women don't have food in their belly. They don't have water. Their tube well doesn't work. If I tell them to perform the *wadu* [ablutions], to say their prayers, they won't listen. They will not listen to anything we say. If I try to tell them about the Quran, they will say, 'Go away. I have no food in my belly, I can't take my child to the doctor's. How can I read the Quran now?'"

Nahar pleaded with Jamila Akhtar for more money to meet the women's basic needs, so that they might then find time to serve God, but Jamila simply responded by urging Nahar and the poor women to be patient: "If someone works hard, God will see. Ask God for help. . . . They have to be taught to be patient."

Some of the other Jamaat women present explained that these meetings in the slums were usually organized twice a month. One complained of the difficulty of carving out an Islamic environment in the midst of such dense human habitation and population. There was little space to accommodate everyone inside any of the homes so they usually met outside; of course, this was not possible if it rained. That afternoon, we sat outside in one part of the slum, in a large open space between two rows of shacks, protected from the unwelcome gaze of passersby by large bedsheets hung along the perimeter of the meeting area. In another area, the senior Jamaat women and I sat on the bed of one of the wealthier women in the neighborhood, while well over a hundred local women sat on chairs and on the floor around us, spilling out through the open doorway into the courtyard outside. In a third neighborhood, we sat on chairs at a table in the gated front yard of a house, the local women on the ground in front of us.

Another worker described to me the nature and content of the typical meeting: "We start with a reading of the Quran. We then talk to the women about heaven and hell, about praying, about the fear of the afterlife, about covering their head. . . . We explain everything in easy language." The Jamaat workers regularly reminded the women that the Prophet himself had been poor and that Islam had first spread among the poor.

As one worker told us, "I tell them, my poor sisters, if Islam must spread again, then I say, it will spread through you. Rich people have never been here and will never come. It will spread through you, if you can live in accordance with your faith. Only then will Islam thrive in this country."

While educated recruits were expected to read the Quran and Maududi's interpretations of it with utmost diligence and then meet to discuss what they had read, the unlettered women worked with cassettes of speeches and Quranic discussions sold to them by the Jamaat workers. Jamila Akhtar elaborated:

> Just as you can understand a song when you listen to it, you can listen to and understand a speech. Then [the workers] announce there will be a program where *iman* [faith] will be discussed. At the meeting, iman is discussed and explained orally with quotations from the Quran and hadith. We then turn to talk about how this life on earth is not our real life, that we have eternity ahead of us, that death lies ahead. There are many deaths all around us now. So they come to believe in death, that life does not end with death. If it were such, if it said in the Quran-hadith that there was nothing after death, then that would be the end, and we could do as we wished. But there is a God and we will have to account for everything. All this is described in various verses.[14]

Jamaat men were doing similar work among the illiterate men in the community. As one Jamaat woman pointed out, "We cannot expect to get anywhere if we don't involve the men." Jamila Akhtar explained further the importance of involving men, "They will say we're breaking up the family, but we have to take the family unit as a base and work from there. Relations between husband and wife should be under control. If there are problems, there is a *bichar*-shalish [arbitration, mediation]. They should get along well! If we ruin the family base, then we cannot proceed with this work." As I noted in chapter 4, the NGOs' almost exclusive focus on women has been the source of much domestic and community conflict. Given the centrality of the family in their view of society, the Islamists currently appear to be more sensitive to the potential for problems.[15]

According to the senior and elite Jamaat women, regular attendance at such meetings granted the impoverished women a new understanding of Islam, which in turn led to greater honesty, as well as dramatic changes in speech and dress. (Here, they betrayed, of course, their own class bias.) To quote Jamila Akhtar, "The situation here is quite bad. If you suddenly visit any place here, you'll see that they don't even know about having to cover their head. The way they live . . . !" She spoke at length and with great passion about the changes wrought among the women who had been exposed to the Jamaat's efforts:

> If we teach them all this, it even happens that many [better-off] women say to us, "What are you teaching our *kajer beti, kajer meye* [domestic servants, maids]? These days, they return not simply hundred-taka notes, but even five hundred–taka notes, telling us, 'No it would be wrong to take this.'"

In the past they would've just stolen it. In the past, they might've helped themselves to the food, picked up an onion here, some garlic there. Now because they receive training, they no longer do such things. Even if people don't see you, such as the owner of the house, God can see you. It is because they now have this fear of God. We say that . . . if the people from this slum are such that they are *imandaar* [have faith] and fear God, then God will shower this slum with more blessings, with improvement, more than any other slum. . . . God will open up the heavens and shower this slum with blessings. . . .

When people here understand that by giving to others, theirs will also increase—and they see this in practice—and we too see that if we give on one side, we get it back on another. . . . By continuing to donate [*amol kora*] and discuss the Quran-hadith, this is how they end up. And, of course, the matter of interest does not even enter into this because God has said, Satan will put the fear of poverty into you in order to make you do indecent things . . . and God talks to you about *maghferat*, about forgiveness. There is an example: do you not get many stalks from each grain of rice you plant? If you donate to others, yours will increase in a similar manner. Kindness and consideration, love, helping others in trouble, showing patience—these all set a good example and there is reciprocity. Say one person is in trouble and asks the other person to show patience, and the other person shows patience. In this manner, a society based on the teachings of the Quran is a truly established society. As for the help from NGOs, they "eat" crores of takas themselves and give crores of takas, but they will never get results because they charge interest. Those of us who try to provide uplift to these women, if our lives are a certain way, then we can hope that with God's *rahmat* [blessings] theirs will be like that too.

Addressing the large crowd that had gathered, Jamila Akhtar emphasized the importance of women's participation in the movement to rid society of un-Islamic influences:

Just think about how God has given us life on this planet.... No man can ever understand that in the way that each and every mother can begin to comprehend it, don't you agree? Mothers understand better than fathers. It amazes me how what is written in the Quran exactly matches my own experiences of childbearing. How that child emerges from that tiny beginning, God has described everything in the Quran. And I saw that everything I experienced while I was carrying my child, what it did while inside, it matches exactly the descriptions in the Quran. You will see, mothers will understand what a person's life means.... What we love most and value most is our child. And how can that child stay well, if you look at today's society, if you aren't good? We are a large organization. If we are not good, if we don't leave a good environment for our children, then just think about what will happen? Even five or ten years ago, our parents' lives, our lives, were one way. I mean, they were not so difficult. But in the future it will become even more difficult. For just one reason ... we do not live in accordance with God's Quran and hadith.

Nahar complained about the absence of meaningful religious education in the public school curricula: "there is no Quran-hadith in these schools anymore." She saw it as the responsibility of the Jamaat and its workers to keep the "Quran-hadith alongside everything else, fulfilling our responsibilities for the Day of Judgment." The primary means of ensuring that the younger generation received this education was through their mothers. As I showed in chapter 5, much like the idealized Republican Mother in the early days of the American and French republics, the Jamaat's ideal Muslim woman is expected to fulfill her responsibilities to God and society by inculcating her children with the correct ideals, in this case, Islamic ideals as defined by the Jamaat. In recent years, however, the Jamaat has expanded these responsibilities to include activism and voting and extended its reach to the vast illiterate majority of women.

GENDER AND POLITICS IN THE WAAZ

In addition to direct contact with prospective supporters, the Jamaat has long used the forum of the public lecture, or waaz mahfil. As I mentioned in chapter 5, in the 1990s renowned Jamaat leaders like Saidi began to organize waaz mahfils specifically targeting women. While thousands of men and women attend the waazes of the most charismatic speakers, millions more hear the lectures through widely available audiocassettes. These religious lectures, which often last several days and nights, are neither new nor unique to the Jamaat. What was interesting is that Jamaat leaders began to use the waazes to appeal to women directly, as a distinct and independent audience. During special women's sessions, Saidi spoke and answered questions about women's specific responsibilities within the home but also about their equal responsibilities to men in their relationship to God—and in the election booth. In April 2003, as a further sign of the Jamaat's recognition of women as both a constituency and a market, approximately six hundred of these questions from women and Saidi's detailed responses to them were compiled and published in two hardcover volumes. The questions selected for publication ranged from queries about women's participation in electoral politics to questions about one's duties towards one's non-Muslim neighbors (Saidi 2003).

In the months preceding the 2001 elections, several cassettes of recent lectures by Saidi were again released on the market. While he did address strictly religious topics in these lectures, such as the importance of praying and fasting, he devoted much more time to attacks on the incumbent AL. Whenever possible, Saidi connected religion and politics, for instance, by repeatedly stressing that Islam could not thrive in Bangladesh while the AL was in charge of the country. He warned listeners that if the Awami League—"enemies of Islam" he called them, much as the Jamaat had referred to the freedom fighters in 1971—were allowed to return to power, Bangladesh would "face the fate of Turkey." In Turkey, he revealed, his voice hoarse with horror, men were not permitted to grow beards or women to observe purdah. He repeatedly called on his audience to ensure that the Awami League did not win a majority in the upcoming elections.[16]

Turning to the five years of Awami League rule between 1996 and 2001, Saidi claimed that over forty thousand women had been raped in that period. Not only had the AL government failed to protect the honor of the women of the country, he pointed out, but in fact AL workers were very often the perpetrators. Far from being "a government of the *awami* [people]," the AL, he charged, had become "a government of *dharshan* [rape]." He supported this charge by referring to a particularly appalling incident when a university student, a member of the youth wing of the AL, had held a party to celebrate his one-hundredth rape or, as the student is alleged to have bragged, "a century of rapes" (see, for example, Farooq 2002). The student was suspended from the university, but no criminal charges were brought against him. Saidi assured his listeners that under a government with which the Jamaat was affiliated, a government that was more favorably inclined toward Islamic principles and values, such criminals would be dealt with severely; moreover, strict observance of purdah by all women would prevent such acts from occurring in the first place.

It is likely that the Jamaat focused on AL workers' alleged involvement in these rapes as a way to counter, even invert, allegations of its own involvement in mass rapes during the war in 1971, a charge that secularists and feminists have kept alive for the last three decades through demands for a war crimes tribunal and a formal apology from the government of Pakistan.[17] It would also be naive to jump to the conclusion that the Jamaat drew special attention to the issue of rape only as a special gesture to women. In a context where a rape is often perceived as a violation of family and male honor, the crime is of great import to men too. Nonetheless, I believe it is significant that the issue of violent assaults on women has only recently begun to appear in election campaigns and that the Jamaat is framing its discussion of the subject in the language of Islamic respect for women (Benford and Snow 2000). Even if the Jamaat has broached the topic in order to appeal to men, it is important to keep in mind that women voters are mobilized, listening, and eager for a more secure environment as they go to work, to schools, and to polling centers. In the process, the Jamaat is effectively seeking to delink rape from the historical 1971 context and connecting it, in the minds of women who work outside the home and of their concerned relatives, to the very current issue of women's safety on the streets.

THE 2001 ELECTION CAMPAIGN AT THE LOCAL LEVEL

Individual candidates campaigning in their constituencies reproduced, with locally appropriate modifications, the debates under way at the national level. For example, in speeches in his home constituency of Piro-jpur, Saidi made a point of reminding his listeners that they must use democratic means to achieve their desired government and demanded that they promise to vote for the Jamaat: "Raise both your hands high. Looking up at the heavens, say, 'God, I swear on your sacred name . . . that on October 1 with these two hands I will cast a vote for no symbol but the dari-palla. . . . Amen.' Now lower your hands." He also took a few minutes to explain why it was essential that women vote and how this could be accomplished without violating rules of gender segregation:

> First, women must be brought to the voting centers. Otherwise it will be a disaster. The Awami League's people will put a burka on a woman and get her to cast multiple illegal votes. If you have an elderly eighty-year-old mother in your home, carry her on your shoulders for two miles if necessary to get her to a voting center so that she can cast her vote.
>
> Second, women must be done with going to the voting centers to cast their votes by 10 A.M. Then from 11 A.M. to 3 P.M., the men will cast their votes. . . .
>
> Third, each of you must go home today and say your prayers and plead with God for the Jamaat's victory.[18]

He concluded his meetings by leading the gathering in a prayer for the Jamaat's success in the upcoming elections.[19]

In nearby Satkkhira, which I had visited in 1996, support for the Jamaat was still strong in 2001. This was the source of much consterna-tion for the AL candidate, M. Nazrul Islam, who had gone out of his way to help the survivors of the devastating 1998 floods while the Jamaat MP had made no special effort.[20] He seemed frankly stunned that the Jamaat candidate, Maulana Abdul Malek Mandol, was so easily able to attract supporters without spending any money. In his 2001 campaign speeches, Islam reminded his listeners of the AL's accomplishments over the previ-ous five years, notably that "nobody had starved to death" during the 1998 floods thanks to the AL government's relief efforts. He called his Jamaat opponent a razakar, accusing him of having fought against Bangladesh's liberation in 1971. Moreover, in an effort to discredit his opponent's Islamic credentials, he distributed flyers revealing that Maulana Abdul Malek Mandol's father was called Lal Chand Mandol, clearly a Hindu name.[21] Maulana Mandol, for his part, vehemently denied all charges the AL candidate had leveled against him, including the accusation that he was of such recent Hindu stock. He retorted by calling the AL prime minister "Killer Hasina" and describing the five years of AL rule as characterized by disorder, corruption, and rapes. He pointed out that Sheikh Hasina had worn *shindoor* (vermilion) during her visit to India and permitted the Venezuelan president to kiss her hand—acts he expected his listeners to recognize immediately as being completely contrary to the teachings of Islam.

Just days before the elections, on September 25, 2001, Matiur Rahman Nizami, now the Jamaat's amir, arrived to campaign for the local Jamaat candidate. Speaking to a large gathering in the playing field of the local government secondary school, Nizami promised that if the Jamaat were to come to power, the country's name would be changed to the Islamic Republic of Bangladesh and Bangladesh would be transformed into an Islamic state in which the entire legal system would be in line with the shariah. He expressed profound concern that Bangladesh would be turned into a colony of India's if the AL were permitted to return to power and urged his listeners to keep that party out of office. During this campaign speech, he also made a point of emphasizing the importance of women's observing purdah.

In an interview, a local Jamaat leader spoke of the importance of courting women voters, who constituted about half the voting population. He said it was essential that women workers be engaged in efforts to explain the party's philosophy to women voters and win their support; as long as they dressed properly, he saw no problem in women's engaging in such campaign work on behalf of the party. The Jamaat workers urged the women they visited to vote for the candidate who was honest and qualified and for a party that would stand firm against the "nakedness" and "shamelessness" that NGOs were currently propagating and ensure that women enjoyed the rights that Islam had granted them.

Local women described how burka-clad Jamaat workers had visited them in their homes before the elections and pleaded with them to vote for the Jamaat.[22] Apparently, the Jamaat women had clutched the hands of the women they were visiting to their own chests and made them promise to vote for the Jamaat's symbol, dari-palla. On their way out, the Jamaat women had informed the women that they had a small Quran under their burkas and that therefore the women had actually—and unknowingly—sworn on the Quran. This had the effect, the local women complained, of compelling many of them to vote for the Jamaat out of fear of the torment of hell for breaking an oath taken on the Quran. In any case, several people with different political affinities admitted that the other parties (BNP, AL, and JP) had made no special effort at all to reach out to women voters in this area, certainly nothing as systematic and organized as the Jamaat. Efforts to campaign on behalf of the AL by local branches of NGOs such as BRAC, Proshika, and Uttaran had led to clashes with Jamaat supporters; for instance, according to a local journalist, Jamaat workers had smashed the motorbike of an Uttaran worker.

THE HEARTS, MINDS, AND VOTES OF POOR WOMEN

Senior Jamaat activist Jamila Akhtar forcefully asserted to me in 2001 that she discerned a new political awareness among women in Bangladesh: "This revolutionary thinking and awareness, this political consciousness among the ordinary women of our country . . . this is new. Women today are much more aware of politics . . . [and] seem better informed than their men. It used to be different, women used to stay at home and cook and clean. . . . No longer. Today, Bangladeshi women are teaching their husbands about politics!"[23] As this quotation illustrates, the Jamaat has become increasingly aware in recent years that its past strategy for reaching out to nonelite women would not help it to win the support of this sizable voting constituency, and it has implemented certain changes to correct its reputation as uninterested in their very basic needs and concerns. While it is not my argument that the Jamaat turned its attention to poor women only after the debacle of 1996, it is clear is that since then it has intensified its efforts and reconsidered its methods with electoral outcomes in mind. In this section, I examine how women of Bangladesh have responded to the overtures from the Society of Islam since 1996.

To a small group of the nation's women, the Jamaat does offer a promising future, in this world and the next. Destitute slum women I interviewed in Chittagong just before the 2001 elections insisted that through their involvement with the Jamaat they now knew how to pray properly and understood the importance of purdah, fasting, and the meaning and interpretation behind many of the Arabic Quranic prayers they used to memorize and recite routinely. Here is a sampling of the responses I received when when I asked women about their religious practices before their encounter with the Jamaat: "We knew some, not much." "We only knew what the hujurs taught us when we were little." "The way we understand purdah now, we didn't understand it then. We didn't fear non-kin men then, the way we do now. We didn't observe purdah then." "We knew about praying. Our parents told us to pray, so when it was time to pray, we prayed, but we didn't attach as much importance to it then as we do now. We didn't prepare and plan for prayers. The fear that we must pray, we didn't have that before." They had learned there were many supposedly incorrect Islams, corrupted over the centuries by local customs and practices, and only one correct Islam: that propagated by the Jamaat. These poor unlettered women thus attended the Jamaat's meetings, attempted to live by its teachings, and no doubt voted for it at election time because they believed these actions would help safeguard their passage to heaven. Taking their faith and belief in the afterlife seriously, one can argue that the motivation behind their support of the Jamaat was self-interest, albeit intangible and unverifiable.

The women had also gained a valuable lesson in how they could use the democratic process to achieve the kind of government they believed they wanted. That the Jamaat workers had discussed voting and elections in some detail with the slum's inhabitants became evident from the poor women's responses to my questions regarding their plans for the upcoming elections of October 2001. One woman I spoke with expressed hope that the current prevalence of violence against women would come to an end under an Islamic government that required women to observe purdah:

People throw water and acid at them from small plastic bags. They spit at them. They throw color[ed liquids and powder] at the girls. What we want to say is that there are many problems in our country....

What we say is that if our country were an Islamic state, if we had a truly Muslim government, then that government would announce that all women must wear the burka. Then all women would have to wear the burka. If the government said that women couldn't go out without a burka, then they certainly couldn't go out without one.[24]

She had not been persuaded by detractors who had warned her that a Jamaat government might prevent her daughters from working outside the home: "People say that if we vote for the Jamaat, the garment factories will be shut down. Why should they be shut down? Men and women will simply have separate garments factories! People tell garments workers that they will lose their jobs if they vote for the Jamaat. Why should that happen? There should just be separate factories for men and women! Can't it be that way? Why should we lose our jobs if we vote for the Jamaat?... It's only if we work with men that men can see us... if we don't, then they can't see us."

She also believed that an Islamic government would be able to ensure the piety of its citizens by mandating breaks for prayers.

All offices and workplaces would close down following the *azan* [call to prayer]. Yes, everyone would certainly stand in line to pray then.... We also say that if the government said that garments factories must provide a space for *namaj* [prayer] so that the girls could pray five times a day, then they would have to. This cannot happen unless the government orders it. Now, if my daughters want to pray at the garments factories, you know what [their supervisors] say? They ask, "Is this your father's home that you want to pray here?! What's this about praying here? Can't you pray at home?" My daughters tell them, "Sir, it takes a long time to say the *kaja* [makeup] prayers at home afterward. That's why we'd rather say our prayers [on time] at work." But the supervisors insist, "There will be no prayers here. You can pray at home. If you want to pray, then don't get a job, just stay home. If you want to pray, why do you work in a garments factory?" So you see, if the government ordered that all garments factories, schools, colleges, madrasas must provide time and space for prayer, if the government required it, would they not have to? Would the government listen to the public, to me? If you were the government, would you listen to me? But if the government were honest [*shat*], everyone would listen to the government.

In the end, she felt strongly that the Jamaat—as real Muslims—deserved a chance to run the country: "If we go to anyone, they don't listen to us, they say we are *shibir*.[25] That's what they say if any of them [Jamaat members] stand for election. But this is a Muslim country, why not see what happens if we vote for Muslims? You have brought the Awami League to power once, you have brought the BNP to power once, you have brought the plough [JP] to power once . . . why not vote for the Jamaat once and see what happens?"

The perception among many women that the Jamaat is absolutely honest and above the corruption that plagues politicians everywhere is also of enormous importance. Even critics of the party concede that Jamaat candidates have long enjoyed a greater reputation for honesty than have other candidates. Indeed, a background check of all electoral candidates by the election commission in 1996 found that the Jamaat was the only major party with no bank loan defaulters on its slate. By the personal example of its members as well as the formal party rhetoric of religiosity and honesty, the Jamaat poses an alternative to the corruption and patronage that have long characterized the political scene, under both authoritarian and democratic rule.

In early 2007, Jamaat individuals were charged with corruption in the caretaker government's anticorruption drive, but it is too early to assess what the long-term implications will be for the Jamaat's reputation (*Daily Star*, May 23, 2007). In addition, it will prove hard for the Jamaat to avoid being tainted by its tacit support for the clearly greater corruption of its alliance partner, the BNP.

There are, of course, certain limits to the Jamaat's overtures to a distinct female constituency, and this reluctance continues to cost them dearly at the polls. Even in 2001, after all its direct appeals to women voters and its participation in a four-party alliance led by the victorious Bangladesh Nationalist Party, the Jamaat won only seventeen seats. I contend that this is in part because the Jamaat continues to cast women in a subordinate role in society, despite its talk of spiritual equality between men and women, despite a recognition that women today want and need to work outside the home, and despite an acknowledgment that Muslim women, mothers or not, already have suffrage. It continues to insist on a strict form of purdah as the most important marker of authentic Islam and opposes women working alongside men in garment factories and NGOs, the two largest and most visible employers of Bangladeshi women in recent decades; it adopts male-biased positions on issues with immediate implications for women such as family law; and finally, it refuses to field female candidates for parliament. This last point, the refusal to field female candidates for parliament, for example, illustrates perfectly the contradiction inherent in the Jamaat's support of democratic rights for women and perhaps an explanation why all women, especially poor, illiterate women, do not flock to support the party.

Although Jamaat members have publicly supported the increased presence of women in parliament, accepted parliamentary seats from the women's quota (of indirectly elected seats), and indeed been part of a coalition under a woman prime minister twice, in 1991 and 2001, the party still refuses to nominate women candidates for direct election to parliament. There are, of course, impoverished women who actively support the Jamaat and have no problem with the Jamaat's refusal to field women candidates. Exactly in line with the Jamaat position, they too voiced strong opposition to female politicians. One woman I interviewed was quite adamant that no self-respecting Muslim woman would even want to run for public office: "Why should they when there are men who can run?" She insisted that if elected to parliament women are expected to shake hands with random men, walk on the streets in the midst of strangers, and get their hair cut in short bobs, conduct she felt was highly inappropriate for any God-fearing Muslim woman. One young woman sitting nearby chimed in, "There can be no question of there being a female prime minister when there are plenty of men around to do the job."[26]

My research clearly shows, however, that the vast majority of poor women are beginning to think otherwise, that many women have developed an interest in politics recently precisely because of the presence of women prime ministers and the growing number of NGO-supported women in local elected office. In many areas, rural women have also had the opportunity to interact with powerful women in the form of heads of NGOs and important NGO workers. For many ordinary women, these are all clear indications that, as many said to me, "Women can now do anything!" These women are left dissatisfied by the Jamaat's view of women as what Linda Kerber calls "deferential citizens" or voters "who freely chose their social superiors to office rather than exercise a claim on office themselves" (1976: 203).[27]

THE 2001 ELECTIONS

The results of the October 2001 parliamentary elections in Bangladesh caused great anxiety in secularist and progressive circles. In addition to the centrist BNP and JP, the victorious alliance included the Jamaat and the Islamic Unity Alliance (IUA), both of which have repeatedly called for the establishment of an Islamic state in Bangladesh (Schaffer 2002). The election results immediately prompted fears of the "Talibanization" of Bangladesh (Roy 2001; Baldwin 2002). Indeed, as many had dreaded, the weeks and months around the October 2001 elections were marked by large-scale systematic attacks on members of minority communities, especially Hindus (Riaz 2004: 51–60). In the midst of American plans to bomb Afghanistan following the 9/11 attacks in the United States, media reports and scholarly work focused on statements by politicians such as the IUA leader, Fazlul Huq Amini, who declared, "We consider an attack on one Muslim country to be an attack on all Muslim countries." It would be naive to ignore the dangerous role played by such leaders and their followers in the violence that engulfed Bangladesh in 2001; at the same time, it would be simplistic to equate all expressions of anti-Americanism with support for the Taliban and al-Qaeda. The truth probably lies somewhere in between.

Vali Nasr draws a distinction between Islamists and "Muslim Democrats" based on his analysis of recent generally free and fair elections in Bangladesh, Indonesia, Malaysia, Pakistan, and Turkey, with a focus on the last two countries: "Islamists view democracy not as something deeply legitimate, but at best as a tool or tactic that may be useful in gaining the power to build an Islamic state. Muslim Democrats, by contrast, do not seek to enshrine Islam in politics, though they do wish to harness its potential to help them win votes" (2005: 13–14). Nasr concludes that "it is clear that the sheer competitive logic inherent in open politics is driving Muslim Democracy forward. . . . Muslim Democracy offers the Muslim world the promise of moderation. As Islamists find themselves facing—or caught up in—the Muslim Democratic dynamic, they will find themselves increasingly facing the hard choice of changing or suffering marginalization" (26).[28]

While the necessities of democratic participation have certainly led the Jamaat in Bangladesh to pay attention to enfranchised groups that it had initially ignored, such as workers, unlettered men, and now unlettered women, the mobilization of millions of impoverished uneducated women who are increasingly vocal about their specific needs is compelling the party to make changes to its rhetoric and strategies. Armed with the right to vote and a growing awareness of the power of the vote, these women are slowly, gradually, prompting the Jamaat to rethink its position on issues of crucial interest to women as well as to revise how it interacts with potential voters who are beyond the reach of its traditional written materials. Clearly, the Jamaat has made a special effort in recent years to reach out to the unlettered majority, and women in particular, by modifying its campaign strategy. While the Jamaat may have begun such overtures to poor women simply to get more votes, the recognition that they are a real constituency has led the party to give sincere attention to new nonreligious, worldly policy areas of particular concern to women. Thus one discerns a shift in emphasis on very secular issues that the Jamaat recognizes are of interest to most women today, such as employment, education, and voting rights. For instance, in contrast to the now infamous Taliban, the party has repeatedly stressed that it is very much in favor of women's right to vote, work, and go to school and university. And indeed the Jamaat has succeeded in winning over many women whose husbands and fathers are not Jamaat supporters. The party does continue to insist on a rigid interpretation of purdah and to condemn what it sees as inappropriate mixing of the sexes, but this is not necessarily an obstacle to its popularity given that even women who have never attended a Jamaat meeting are hesitant about joining NGOs or working in garments factories because they too worry about such things. It is precisely because poor, working women have not completely embraced secular notions of the modern woman that the Jamaat has had an opportunity to court their support. Of course, it remains to be seen whether the party can outline concrete measures for providing the sex-segregated educational and work environments it advocates at every opportunity. With just the right mix of religion and politics, with statements of genuine concern not only for women's souls in the afterlife but also their empowerment in this world, the Jamaat may actually gain ground in the battle against more secular forces vying for women's votes.

Rural Bangladesh has changed dramatically in recent years as various NGOs have entered villages, drawn nonelite women into new networks, and thereby affected their relationships with neighbors, local landed elites, religious leaders, moneylenders, the state, and, of course, members of their families. NGOs have not always attained their stated objectives, such as reaching the poorest of the poor, but they have certainly disrupted rural life, in ways expected and unexpected. What has been of particular interest to me in this book is how impoverished rural women, who struggle to improve their lives within formidable social and economic constraints, negotiate the competing attempts of secularist and Islamist elites, political parties, and NGOs to win their hearts, minds, and votes.

In investigating the allegedly primordial pull of religion and the role of gender in development and democracy in a very specific context, I found that Islam and modernity (the second usually seen as concomitant with democracy, rights for women, and Westernization) are not the antithetical categories they are often made out to be. Many of these categories, binaries about tradition and progress, were established in the nineteenth century, in South Asia and elsewhere, and still inform influential elite perspectives in Bangladesh. By overplaying the role of religion—in this case, Islam—as the villain behind the subordination of women (Kadioglu 1994), secularists, including many feminists, in Bangladesh find themselves aligned with Western critics of Islam whom, in any other context, they would dismiss as voices of imperialism. This response to Islamism emerges directly out of the specific history of what is now Bangladesh, in particular the Pakistan era and the role of Islamists in the Muktijuddho. As a result, secularists and feminists in Bangladesh have been wary of measures that would bring them into conversation with more Islamically oriented individuals and groups, as has happened in Indonesia and Malaysia (see, for example, Adamson 2007).

As I have shown, the rivalry between secularist and Islamist visions regarding the future of state and society has been particularly intense and visible in the arenas of legal reform, development, and formal politics. In these arenas, impoverished rural women behave in ways that may appear contradictory at first glance but can be explained by a close examination of their everyday lives. Contrary to popular as well as some scholarly notions about the role of Islam in the lives of Muslims, in the context of rural Bangladesh, religion was not the sole determinant of women's behavior. It was indeed important to the women we spoke with in the sense that they strove to pray, fast, be modest, and be good Muslims. Most visibly pious women, however, were unwilling to support the Jamaat with actual votes. At the same time, women who joined NGOs did not stop observing purdah. Some simply redefined what counted as modesty and purdah, while others actually planned to use their hard-earned money to buy burkas.

A more significant influence on their conduct was their experience and knowledge of the state. On the basis of their daily encounters with the disaggregated state, they developed an assessment of its ability to help them improve their lives. For the most part, rural women in Bangladesh find themselves neglected by an aid-dependent state that has shown itself unable to protect its most vulnerable citizens or provide necessary services like education and health care. Because many women sincerely believe that changes at the very top have little bearing on their lives, they see no harm in voting for whichever party offers them cash or presents just before the elections or in voting in accordance with the advice or orders of their male relatives. While continuing such behavior can only be detrimental to democracy in the long run—in that these women do not hold elected governments accountable for what they do while in power but simply use the elections for their immediate benefit—the solution is not to stop holding elections but to restore people's faith in the state's ability to provide for its poor and marginalized.

Through individual, public acts such as joining NGOs, poor rural women are helping to transform gender relations within their communities and the wider society by changing norms of appropriate female behavior and gender roles generally. Values among the rural poor have indeed changed over time: what would have been unthinkable even a few decades ago and warranted much malicious gossip—such as women leaving their homesteads to attend NGO meetings—today, in most places, raises only a few eyebrows. People tolerate these changes because they recognize that they are necessary. Such changes, however, have been less acceptable to those who for generations have relied on the rural poor as a source of cheap labor—namely, the rural elite, the landowners. Many of the latter have responded by monetizing relations that in the past would have been better characterized as falling within a "moral economy" framework (Scott 1976; Leve 2007). As Shamsu, a landless woman from Baruthan, Chittagong, explained, "In the past, at least some people used to lend us money without charging interest. Now they say, 'If you can pay interest to Grameen Bank, you can pay us interest too.' So when we borrow money from them to pay our Grameen Bank *kisti* [weekly installment of loan repayment], we have to pay interest. As a result, we're permanently in debt."[1]

Over time, one can only hope that poor women's increased visibility in rural areas—as they troop to NGO offices to attend weekly meetings or line up in front of polling centers to vote on Election Day—will attract the serious attention of policy makers and vote seekers. Although they are at the center of much international and domestic attention today, poor rural women's needs and interests have very rarely been taken into consideration in planning future projects; their choices and decisions are readily dismissed as uninformed and they themselves as illiterate and powerless beyond their ability to attract donor aid and investment. A closer look at their everyday lives permits us to see beyond the stereotyped images and identify possibilities for change.

In a sense, some important changes are already under way, for instance, in the response of Islamists to the largely secular mobilization of poor women by NGOs and in the manner in which the Jamaat-i Islami is casting itself as a champion of women's rights (albeit within the framework of its own interpretation of Islam). This is reflected in the party's campaigns for the votes of women, when it urges them to vote even against the wishes of their husbands if necessary. The Jamaat's very willingness to begin making important shifts in rhetoric and strategies should lead us to rethink common assumptions about Islam and Islamist politics and the role of gender in shaping these categories. Forced to compete against NGOs that have long worked to meet poor women's needs for education and income, the Jamaat has had to move beyond typical Islamist assumptions of Muslim motherhood and separate spheres for men and women and beyond its emphasis on the burka when women do enter the public sphere. Traditionally secular women's rights organizations are also paying more attention to religion in their activism: for example, the Bangladesh National Women Lawyers' Association recently cosponsored the seminar "Ensuring Women's Rights Within an Islamic Framework" with the Asia Foundation (*Daily Star*, February 4, 2007).

These shifts in emphasis should make us reconsider the implications, and indeed the appropriateness, of the usual dichotomies between Islam and the veil, on the one hand, and modernization, Westernization, and women's rights, on the other, that are often bandied about, at times with greater sophistication and subtlety than at others. To the extent that gender and women have been part of recent discussions about the democratic deficit in the Muslim world, the situation of women in Muslim countries has been seen as both an explanation for and a reflection of undemocratic attitudes in these countries. Muslim women's own views about Islam, development, and democracy generally have not been taken into consideration.

As this book goes to press, the future of democracy in Bangladesh is unclear. The caretaker government meant to oversee the 2007 elections has indefinitely postponed elections, is relying heavily on the support of the military, and has suspended all political activities. Poor rural women, in the meantime, will no doubt continue to choose the course of action that they believe best serves their interests, mediating between competing needs to make ends meet in this life and to reach *jannat* (heaven) in the next. Because most secularist and development organizations have hesitated to acknowledge and meet the population's spiritual needs, there has remained a role for more religiously oriented groups in the public arena. And that is why, at least thus far, the mobilization of women by NGOs over the last twenty-five years has led not to the defeat of Islamism, as many asserted following the 1996 elections, but to its gradual refashioning. By compelling a party like the Jamaat to concede publicly the importance of women's access to education, employment, and the voting booth, impoverished rural women in Bangladesh are redefining the very characteristics of what constitutes a good Muslim woman in the public sphere.

Unless otherwise noted, all translations are my own.

1. GENDER, ISLAM, AND POLITICS IN BANGLADESH

1. Given the extensive coverage of this incident in both the Bengali and English press in Bangladesh, I have been able to refer to a large number of reports that appeared between January 1993, when the incident occurred, and February 1994, when the men responsible were finally sentenced. I list only a few here: M. M. Khan 1993; M. Begum 1993; and *Ittefaq*, February 23, 1994, and February 27, 1994. See also Hashmi 2000, Pereira 2000, and Siddiqi 2006b.

2. Literally, "imam" means "leader"; the term is commonly used for the man who leads congregational prayers in a mosque. "*Maulana*" is a term of address for one known to be learned in religious matters.

3. A *shalish* is a traditional village council, usually presided over by local elite and religious leaders. Other local terms for the council are "*panchayat*" and "*darbar*" (Siddiqi 2006b: n. 22).

4. The most recent figures available estimate that about 83 percent of the country's population of just over 150 million is Muslim, 16 percent Hindu, and the remaining 1 percent Buddhist, Christian, and others (CIA 2007).

5. In that sense, my findings correspond very closely to those of Farida Shaheed, who undertook a similar nationwide study in Pakistan (1998).

6. The word "*sarkar*" translates as both "state" and "government," but I have used only "state" throughout the book since most of the people we spoke with used the term to refer to the state and its bureaucracy generally rather than the administration of a particular party.

7. The very term "female-headed household" is problematic because of its

underlying assumption that a household has a female head only when and because there is no male earner. The term "lone mother" has been used as an alternative (see Albelda 2005), but "female-headed household" remains the more prevalent term in scholarly work. For an interesting interrogation of the conventional assumption that female-headed households are necessarily the poorest of the poor, see Chant 2003.

8. Khaleda Zia is the widow of Bangladesh's first military ruler, Ziaur Rahman, who was assassinated in 1981. Sheikh Hasina is the daughter of Sheikh Mujibur Rahman, who led the 1971 independence movement for Bangladesh. He was assassinated in August 1975, along with his entire family, with the exception of Hasina and her younger sister, Rehana.

9. Already by the mid-1990s, the Grameen Bank's work with women had been the subject of numerous network television programs including *60 Minutes* and the WGBH (Boston) series *Local Heroes, Global Change*. NGOs targeting rural women in Bangladesh featured prominently at the United Nations Social Summit in Copenhagen and the Beijing Conference on Women, both in 1995, the International Micro-Credit Summit in Washington, D.C., in February 1996, and subsequent similar gatherings.

10. The innovations of the Grameen Bank have spawned a large body of generally celebratory literature, including H. Hossain 1984; Shehabuddin 1992; Counts 1996; Yunus 2001; Bernasek 2003; and Bruck 2006.

11. For Nasrin's own account of the fatwa against her, see, for example, Nasrin 2000.

12. Of Persian origin, the term "purdah" literally means "curtain" but refers to a range of practices such as female seclusion, designated male and female spheres both within and outside the home, and the use of clothing to cover various parts of a woman's body. Anita Weiss defines the term as "the practical as well as figurative curtain separating the everyday worlds of women and men" (1998: 125). In Bengali, the word is pronounced "porda," but I use the more familiar spelling "purdah" in this book. See Rozario 1992 and 1998 for a thoughtful discussion of the relationship among seclusion, purity, and honor in the Bangladeshi context. See also Papanek 1971, 1973; and Adnan 1993.

13. For a nuanced and sophisticated discussion of the construction of an alternative Islamic modernity by Shia women in a Beirut suburb, see Deeb 2006.

14. The two sides are likely to agree, however, on the need for a free market economy, which many argue is a defining characteristic of modernity. See, for example, Kasper 2005.

15. The prevalence of corruption at all levels of Bangladeshi society has been amply documented by Transparency International. See www.ti-bangladesh.org for recent reports.

16. Of course, this trend is more recent within political science than in the other social sciences. As Diane Singerman has pointed out, it is "anthropologists, historians, and sociologists who have told us about the politics of the com-

mon people while the 'high politics' of the elite (including interest group politics) remained the domain of political scientists" (1995: 5).

17. For example, as Lila Abu-Lughod (2005) observes about melodramas in Egypt, satellite TV projects throughout Bangladesh images of upper- and middle-class urban life in Bangladesh as well as Hollywood and Bollywood lifestyles that are beyond the reach of much of the country's population. Moreover, while television offers access to positive educational messages about women's role in society and the importance of voting and education, it also increases exposure to commercial advertising and promotes demands for consumer goods that have contributed to escalating dowry demands.

18. See Singerman 1995 and Sullivan 1994 for discussions of how many poor Muslims in Egypt are initiating private alternatives to the state-sponsored financial system that they feel has failed them.

19. The modernization approach, which posits an evolutionary model of development, has recently resurfaced after decades of critiques. Recent restatements include Pye 1990, Huntington 1991, and Diamond 1992.

20. Exceptions in the Anglo-American academy include McCarthy 1993, Gardner 1998, and S. White 1992.

21. As I discuss below, the research project that resulted in Shehabuddin 1997 was initiated by external donors.

22. While there have appeared useful articles and book chapters on gender and Islam in Bangladesh, the only monograph devoted entirely to the subject is Hashmi 2000, which investigates whether patriarchy or Islam is to blame for women's oppression in Bangladesh—a very different question from my own.

23. In late spring 1996, I was approached by Salma Sobhan and Hameeda Hossain, cofounders of Ain o Salish Kendra, with which I had been loosely affiliated for several months while conducting dissertation research. They asked if I would be willing to direct a research project on poor rural women's legal awareness and attempts by NGOs to increase women's involvement in community-based dispute resolution, that is, in the institution of the shalish. The project would be funded by the Asia Foundation. I agreed on condition that I would be able to ask questions also about other aspects of women's public behavior that were of interest to me, such as their decision-making process in the June general elections, their understanding of gender relations within the family and the community, and their views regarding the role of NGOs. They agreed without hesitation and several members of the ASK staff worked with me to design a list of questions that would help us all better understand different areas of rural women's lives. While the report was submitted but never published, I have tried to make our findings available to a wider readership by drawing on them in my own publications. Unless otherwise indicated, all quotations from interviews in this book were drawn from this 1996 ASK survey.

24. These two surveys also received outside funding but as a result of grant proposals I submitted with Nagorik Uddyog (Citizens' Initiative) staff: in 1996

I wrote a proposal with Mirza Hassan, and we received funds from Grameen Poverty Research at Grameen Trust in Dhaka; in 2001 I wrote a proposal with Zakir Hossain and received funds from the Social Science Research Council in New York.

2. GENDER AND SOCIAL REFORM

1. Not only do debates about the relationship among gender, religion, and the nation date back to the colonial era in South Asia, but they also have parallels in reform movements in the nineteenth-century Ottoman empire (e.g., L. Ahmed 1992; Sonbol 1996; Abu-Lughod 1998; Tucker 1998).

2. The Tebagha uprising of 1946–1947 is one prominent example of such protest (Custers 1987). There have been many others, of course, some of which we know about, and others that are lost to the historical record. See also Basu 1992 and Calman 1985.

3. We should keep in mind, of course, that poor women have always had to work outside their homes, but seldom for cash, while until recently education has been the privilege of a few elite women.

4. In 1853 Macaulay, along with Sir Charles Trevelyan, went on to establish the Indian Civil Service.

5. As I show later in this book, twenty-first-century Islamists in Bangladesh are once again reviving and reshaping the *waaz mahfil* to target the poor and illiterate.

6. Traditionally, there have been four schools of Sunni jurisprudence: Hanafi, Maliki, Hanbali, and Shafii. Distinctions among them, however, have become increasingly blurred as states have borrowed at will from different schools in formulating legislation.

7. Outraged Indian leaders and reformers dismissed Mayo's account as unwarranted and "scurrilous"; Gandhi, for example, called it a "Drain Inspector's Report" (Jayawardena 1995: 97–98).

8. Just over a half-century later, the Shah Bano case would prompt the Muslim community to put forward multiple and contradictory demands to the Indian state.

9. The following details about Rokeya Hossain are drawn from Roushan Jahan 1988; see also S.N. Amin (1996: 155–159; 2001) and Mitra 2006. See Aftab 2005 for a discussion of a historic feminist address to Syed Ahmed Khan in Gurdaspur by an organization of Punjabi women. In this address, women demanded access to education and other opportunities for women, all "grounded and legitimized in the framework of early Islam" (89).

10. The American Charlotte Perkins Gilman's utopic story *Herland* would appear a decade later, in 1915.

11. On her return from an international feminist meeting in Rome in the

spring of 1923, Huda Shaarawi and Saiza Nabarawi stepped onto the platform at a Cairo train station and removed their veils to uncover their faces (Shaarawi 1987: 7).

12. A long, coatlike garment that conceals the entire body, head, and, if wished, even the face, the burka has been described as "portable seclusion" (Papanek 1971: 520).

13. For the multiple motives informing women's decisions to take up the veil in different contexts today, see, for example, MacLeod 1992, Odeh 1993, El Guindi 1999, Mahmood 2005, Deeb 2006, Smith-Hefner 2007.

14. As I show in chapter 4, this argument continues to be used today in debates about impoverished women in Bangladesh: that once they know their rights, whether granted by the Quran or by a secularist international charter, they will be full citizens and autonomous beings.

15. Unless otherwise indicated, details about Maududi's life in the following paragraphs are drawn from Rafiuddin Ahmed 1994 and Nasr 1994, 1996.

16. Under the 1962 constitution, six seats were reserved for women in the 156-member national assembly: three for representatives from East Pakistan and three for representatives from West Pakistan. A woman candidate was, of course, also free to contest any general seat. The constitution also reserved five seats for women in each of the two provincial assemblies (Mumtaz and Shaheed 1987: 69).

17. The UFWR, created in 1955, was the only organization to focus exclusively on women's rights. This did not last long beyond the 1961 ordinance, however, especially given the undemocratic political environment of Ayub Khan's military rule (Mumtaz and Shaheed 1987: 55).

18. Lamia Shehadeh identifies similar contradictions in the writings and actions of several other twentieth-century ideologues. For example, Khomeini declared women's suffrage "un-Islamic" in 1963 yet described the vote as "a religious, Islamic, and divine duty" and actively sought women's votes for the Islamic Republic (2003: 235).

19. In 1951 East Bengal had 168 Bengali and 5 Urdu newspapers and journals. As Tazeen Murshid remarks, clearly "even among the literati, knowledge of Urdu was limited to a few" (1996: 298).

20. The muhajjir-Punjabi elite's lack of interest in framing a constitution is suggested by the fact that between 1948 and 1954 the Constituent Assembly met for about sixteen days a year to discuss the constitution and each meeting was attended, on average, by only forty-six members (Aziz 1976: 86, 89).

21. According to Rehman Sobhan, a member of Bangladesh's first planning commission, "The struggle for self-rule by the Bengalis of Eastern Bengal was predicated on the belief that the relative deprivation of the region derived from the fact that the Bengalis were denied the power to forge their own economic destiny" (1993: 76).

22. See Rahim 2001 for a biographical sketch of Ghulam Azam and the early history of the Jamaat in East Pakistan.

23. For a useful, concise discussion of Ghulam Azam's role in Bangladeshi politics, see Hossain and Siddiquee 2004.

24. The example of the Indian constitution cannot be overlooked here; it too begins with references to a "sovereign socialist secular democratic republic." The phrase was amended in 1976 to read "sovereign democratic republic" (Government of India 1983: 1). See Jacobsohn 2005 for an excellent comparative analysis of the Indian polity's understanding and implementation of the constitutional principle of secularism.

25. The commission's findings were published in 1974.

26. Betsy Hartmann and Jim Boyce report that when they first arrived in 1974 in the Bangladeshi village in which they would live for two years, many villagers suspected that they had come to investigate the "missing blankets": they had heard that, after the war, the United States had sent ninety million blankets (for a population of seventy-five million), yet they only knew of one person who had received one: the local landlord (1983: 6).

27. Rice is the staple in Bengal, but during times of famine and hardship most families could afford only *ata*, the whole-wheat flour used to make chapatis.

3. "A LITTLE MONEY FOR TEA"

1. See Siddiqi 2006b for a critical analysis of *Eclipse*.

2. The logic of majority-minority community relations in the South Asian subcontinent has meant that Muslim personal laws have undergone some reform in predominantly Muslim Pakistan and Bangladesh, as have Hindu personal laws in predominantly Hindu India. The Indian state has left the Muslim family code largely unchanged, however, for fear of being perceived as attacking the Muslim minority, and similar concerns have hindered changes in Hindu law in the other two countries. For a historical discussion of the actual codification and subsequent reforms of family laws in British India and then Pakistan, see Anderson 1976 and Esposito 1982.

3. Interview, Chittagong, March 16, 1996.

4. The full text of the convention is available at www.un.org/womenwatch/daw/cedaw/.

5. It withdrew these reservations quietly, without any publicity. According to Najma Chowdhury, adviser under the interim caretaker government in Bangladesh in 1996 and professor of political science and women's studies at Dhaka University, "A kind of politics of silence was used to appease forces that might not welcome such inroads into issues which might be seen as ensuing from compromises with the women's movement" (2001: 225–226).

6. ASK meeting, Syedpur, Sitakundo, July 18, 1996.

7. See chap. 1, n. 23.

8. Among those who have sought police assistance, their reasons for having done so include the following: with the assistance of the local legal aid organization, one woman filed charges against her husband when he denied their marriage and later took him to court; one woman had her younger sister's husband arrested after he threw her sister out of their house; another woman filed charges against her husband because he would neither divorce her nor pay her maintenance; one woman sought assistance in tracking down an errant son-in-law; others simply visited relatives in jail.

9. Disillusionment with the police was by no means limited to the rural poor. The following comment from an educated, upper-middle-class urban man reflected a sentiment widespread among those who, while not among the most vulnerable, are also not among the wealthiest and most powerful in society: "The only reason that people can walk on the streets, that we can sit in a tea stall and chat is that there is *gonopituni* (mob policing). Not every woman who walks outside wearing a necklace will have it snatched because the potential criminals are terrified. Of whom? Certainly not of the police, who are on their payroll. What they are scared of is *gonopituni*. It's up to the people to protect themselves. The police won't. The state won't" (interview, Dhaka, May 12, 1996).

10. Interview, Chittagong, March 2, 1996.

11. Interview, Dhaka, May 18, 1996.

12. Given the importance of alternative forms of dispute resolution to marginalized groups throughout the world, Golub 2007 calls on the development community to devote resources to legal empowerment strategies "from below" as well as to formal, state-centered justice systems.

13. ASK meeting, Syedpur, Sitakundo, July 18, 1996. As I noted in chapter 1, some of these matters may be related: investigation after Nurjahan's death indicated that her accusers had been involved in a property dispute with her second husband, Mutalib, and charged the couple with adultery in order to teach him a lesson.

14. In early 1998 the government had 1,335 qazis, each serving no more than three city wards or unions, thus at most 4,005 unions. There are 4,451 unions in Bangladesh.

15. It ought to be kept in mind that "grown daughter" generally implies a young girl who has reached puberty; she may be very young in actual age.

16. ASK meeting, Syedpur, Sitakundo, July 18, 1996.

17. "Delawar Hussain Saidi on Purdah and Women's Rights in Islam," audio-cassette recording, (Dhaka: Spondon Audio-Visual Centre, n.d.).

18. It is precisely for this reason that some feminists object to the dower.

19. ASK meeting, Syedpur, Sitakundo, July 18, 1996.

20. Ibid.

21. This naturally begs the question, if a woman's family can be expected to

sell everything to pay her dowry, why can the husband not somehow come up with the money for the mohrana he agreed to at the time of the marriage?

22. ASK meeting, Syedpur, Sitakundo, July 18, 1996.

23. Group discussion with Banchte Shekha members, Banchte Shekha Center, Dogachhia, Jessore, June 13, 1996.

24. Ibid.

25. Bangladesh Television, *Sobinoye Jante Chay* (If you please, we'd like to know), June 4, 1996

26. Ibid.

27. Interview, Chittagong, March 16, 1996.

28. It is, of course, a much older practice in Hindu households, and there is much disagreement among scholars and activists on how or when the practice entered the Muslim mainstream in Bangladesh in the form it assumes today.

29. "Delawar Hussain Saidi on Purdah and Women's Rights in Islam."

30. The Quran calls for flogging as the punishment for adultery (24:2); however, during the reign of the second caliph 'Umar (634–644), stoning rather than flogging became codified (L. Ahmed 1992: 60) on the basis of certain hadith in favor of stoning.

31. Today, *zina* generally refers to any sexual activity other than that between husband and wife, for example, adultery and (nonmarital) rape. In her classic text *Women and Gender in Islam*, Leila Ahmed muses that the term "zina" may have originally, in early Islam, "referred to other types of marriage, including polyandrous ones, and to forms of 'temporary' marriage also practiced in the Jahilia, which Islam would outlaw" (1992: 44–45).

32. In a culture where long thick hair is considered a highly prized asset for any woman, the humiliation implicit in cutting Rokeya's hair in this manner would be not be lost on the spectators.

33. Recognizing the limited reach of the state—which I demonstrate in this book—the judgment not only declared the practice of issuing fatwas illegal but also outlined specific steps to curb its prevalence in rural Bangladesh by directing local imams and madrasas to become better versed in the details of the MFLO (S. Hossain 2001 [2002]).

34. Gender issues workshop, Banchte Shekha Office, Jessore, June 15, 1996.

35. Ibid.

36. Ibid.

37. Ibid. This tragic phenomenon is not restricted to the rural poor; one often reads in the papers about the mysterious deaths of young brides in middle- and upper-middle-class urban households. In India, the crime has been labeled "dowry death" or "dowry murder." See, for example, Teays 1991, on the phenomenon of the "burning bride" in the Indian context, and, for an important historical perspective, Oldenburg 2002.

38. If marital rape is not recognized by the law, neither do local custom and tradition come out against it, although Islamic tradition discourages husbands from extracting sexual favors from an unwilling wife. This, of course, refers only to the occasional lack of interest; a wife who is always unwilling is not to be tolerated.

39. For reports of similar incidents in Pakistan under the Hudood Ordinance, see Mumtaz and Shaheed 1987.

40. Interview, Chittagong, March 16, 1996.

41. Interview, Dhaka, May 18, 1996.

42. This account of the Nurjahan-Fazlu incident is taken from M.R. Khan 1996: 53–67.

43. Under some schools of Islamic law, a divorced couple that wishes to remarry must undergo hilla, that is, the wife must marry and divorce a second husband before she can remarry her original husband. Many religious scholars believe that this requirement of an intervening marriage is designed precisely to deter husbands from divorcing their wives on a whim. Although the 1961 MFLO had outlawed hilla, recent incidents such as these compelled the high court division of the Bangladesh Supreme Court to reconfirm that hilla is unlawful (*Daily Star*, January 7, 2001).

44. See Mir-Hosseini 1994 for a discussion of the "three distinct constructions of what constitutes a legitimate marital union" in the Iranian and Moroccan contexts (55).

45. Interview, Ayeshakandha, Tangail, June 20, 1996,

4. CONTESTING DEVELOPMENT

1. As Anne Marie Goetz points out, while the Ugandan state's WID/GAD (Women in Development/Gender and Development, consecutive paradigms used by the global development community) unit shares institutional space with youth and culture, in Bangladesh, one ministry is responsible for both women and children's affairs (1998: 59).

2. "Summary of National Action Plans and Strategies for Implementation of the Platform for Action." Available at www.un.org/womenwatch/daw/country/national/asiasum.htm. Accessed June 2005.

3. According to a 1995 government estimate, there were approximately six million landless and functionally landless (a half acre of land or less) households in Bangladesh (GoB 1995a: 21). Since May 2002 BRAC has also been working in Afghanistan as a foreign NGO, helping to rebuild that country's war-ravaged economy and human resources (BRAC 2004: 44).

4. See, e.g., Lazreg 1994 for a description of a ceremonial unveiling of Algerian women by French generals.

5. Rashid has publicly admitted to being one of the ringleaders of the group

of army officers who assassinated Sheikh Mujib and fifteen members of his family in August 1975. A formal trial on the murder case did not begin until after Mujib's daughter became prime minister at the helm of the party he had led, the AL, in 1996. It would not be until April 2001 that a final verdict would be pronounced. Rashid and eleven others were given the death sentence, and three were acquitted. Only four of those convicted are currently in custody, however. Following a change in government in October 2001, technicalities have held up the appeal process.

6. Taslima Nasrin is the physician and writer who was dubbed the "female Rushdie" by the international press after an Islamist group in Bangladesh issued a fatwa in 1993 demanding she be killed for her writings and public statements about women and Islam (see chapter 1). Farida Rahman was a BNP member of parliament. In 1993 she presented a bill in parliament proposing changes in the law on polygamy in the Muslim family code, as discussed in chapter 2.

7. Of course, it is not only Islamists who are concerned about Bangladesh's dependence on foreign aid. Prominent Bangladeshi economists expressed concerns about the potential for such dependence very early in Bangladesh's history. See, for example, Community Development Library n.d.; Faaland 1981; and R. Sobhan 1982.

8. Interview, Chittagong, March 13, 1996.

9. As we saw in chapter 3, to the extent that the mohrana requirement is enforced, it is only when the man initiates the divorce and in that case is seen as compensation. When a woman initiates a divorce, she is effectively renouncing all claims to the mohrana. Yet the mohrana is supposed to be a condition of marriage, not in any way connected to divorce.

10. Interview, Chittagong, March 16, 1996.

11. Interview, Chittagong, March 13, 1996.

12. A notable example of an NGO that has focused on political and social mobilization rather than income generation is Nijera Kori (We Do It Ourselves).

13. Microcredit in particular is guilty of hindering class solidarity and meaningful collective action. I discuss microcredit in greater detail later in this chapter.

14. Personal communications from civil servants, Dhaka, March 1995.

15. The World Economic Forum's 2007 Gender Gap report, released in November 2007, placed Bangladesh at 100 out of a longer list of 128 countries. Perhaps not surprisingly, this news received no attention in the Bangladeshi media. The 2007 report is available at www.weforum.org/en/initiatives/gcp/Gender%20Gap/index.htm. Accessed November 25, 2007.

16. While I do not explicitly engage with that literature here, I must acknowledge my indebtedness to the extensive work by Amartya Sen on continually expanding the very notion of development. See, for example, Sen 1999.

17. An earlier version of this discussion appeared in Shehabuddin 2004.

18. The corresponding figures for male literacy in that same period are 32.9 percent and 45 percent.

19. Bangladesh Television, *Sobinoye Jante Chay* (If you don't mind, we'd like to know), June 4, 1996.

20. For example, the Muslim Family Code requirement that a man must have the permission of his first wife if he wishes to have a second wife; for many, this stipulation is in violation of Islamic law as they understand it.

21. *Bhorer Kagoj*, April 15 and 17, 1994.

22. See, for instance, *Daily Star*, December 7, 1995; Shehabuddin 1999a: 162–163.

23. Under this program, a qualified Grameen Bank borrower can lease a mobile phone from the bank and earn an income by charging fellow villagers who wish to make or receive calls. For more information on the scheme, see www.grameen-info.org/grameen/gtelecom/index.html.

24. Interview, Dhaka, May 8, 1996.

25. During his waazes, Saidi often sets aside a half-day session exclusively for women, when they can pose questions to him about the movement or more generally about Islam.

26. "Maulana Delawar Hussain Saidi's Public Meeting with Women, Parade Grounds, Chittagong, 1997," audiocassette recording (Dhaka: Spondon Audio-Visual Centre, n.d.).

27. Interview, Chittagong, February 24, 1996.

28. To remedy this situation, NGOs have begun to develop special programs targeting the very poorest such as BRAC's Targeted Ultra Poor Programme (Hossain and Matin 2007).

29. Interview, Chittagong, February 19, 1996.

30. Ibid.

31. Ibid. See also Goetz and Sen Gupta 1996 for instances of NGO workers, under pressure to disburse loans, actively persuading men to urge their wives to join NGOs and accept loans that they can then appropriate.

32. The hajj is the pilgrimage to Mecca prescribed as a religious duty for all Muslims who can afford to undertake it.

5. DEMOCRACY ON THE GROUND

1. The situation in South Asia stands in sharp contrast to the political rights of Muslim women in some countries in the so-called heartland of the Islamic world. Kuwaiti women received the right to vote as recently as May 2005. Badran 1998 identifies pressure from Saudi Arabia, a large neighbor and source of support in the Gulf War, as an important factor in the Kuwaiti state's past resis-

tance to women's enfranchisement. In Saudi Arabia, women still do not have any voting rights while men's are severely restricted.

2. Personal communication, Princeton, New Jersey, February 6, 1997.

3. "Women and Politics," moderated by Farah Kabir, Bangladesh Television (BTV), May 1996.

4. I borrow this apt term from the title of Siddiqi 1996a.

5. See, for example, the U.S. Department of State's "Bangladesh Country Report on Human Rights Practices for 1996," available at www.usemb.se/human/human96/banglade.html. Accessed August 2005.

6. Interview, Chittagong, February 25, 1996.

7. Some seats were reserved for women in the 1937 elections to the provincial legislatures in British India, marking what Gail Pearson describes as "an important shift in gendered notions of citizenship . . . [that] ensured that women were elected, encouraged the election of women to seats not specifically reserved and set a pattern of strong 'women' legislators and government ministers" (2004: 196).

8. In the U.S. context, for example, Elizabeth Dole cited her inability to compete against the funds raised by her male rivals George W. Bush and John McCain when she abandoned her bid for the White House in October 1999. See Karam 2006 and Shvedova 2006 for a comparative analysis of obstacles faced by women seeking elected office.

9. A union is the lowest elected administrative unit of local government. Each union parishad (council) comprises ten to fifteen villages and a population of fifteen to twenty thousand. There are 4,451 unions in the country. Each union is divided into nine wards, each represented by a union parishad member; however, each of the three seats reserved for a woman encompasses three wards and thus a larger constituency.

10. For a discussion of similar problems faced by women elected to city corporations as ward commissioners, see Mehtab 2004.

11. While a significantly larger female presence in parliament certainly might alter the terms of discussion, it would be imprudent to assume that very dramatic changes would follow. It is essential to keep in mind that all women do not necessarily represent or support women's interests and ultimately it is more important that male and female legislators alike recognize the centrality of women's rights and issues to general human development and reorganize their priorities accordingly.

12. See Akhter 2002 for a detailed look at the social backgrounds, experiences, and performance of selected women UP members.

13. Interview, Chittagong, March 16, 1996. Maududi's sexual division on labor evokes, of course, the cult of domesticity that prevailed in antebellum America and again in the 1950s. Historian Nancy Cott (1997) credits Barbara Welter (1966) with coining the term "cult of true womanhood" and Aileen S. Kraditor

(1968) with "cult of domesticity." See *Journal of Women's History* 14 (Spring 2002) for a retrospective analysis of Welter's original article.

14. For a discussion of the importance attached to mothers in the Quran and hadith, see Schleifer 1986. See Linda Kerber's early essay on Republican Motherhood in the U.S. context (1976); work on similar notions in the French context (such as Landes 1988 and Hunt 1992) has recently been subject to some rethinking (e.g., Desan 2004).

15. I am grateful to Vickie Langohr for drawing my attention to this article at a critical moment in my writing.

16. For the purposes of comparison, the World Values Survey found that 71 percent of citizens in Bangladesh believe that "politicians who do not believe in God are unfit for public office." Responses in other countries ranged from 88 percent in Egypt to 71 percent in the Philippines and about 40 percent in the United States (Inglehart and Norris 2003: 66–67).

17. There is a story that Ershad, on having learnt from CNN weather broadcasts that a long dry spell was about to be broken, called for a mass prayer and led the gathering in begging God for rain. When rain it did, he naturally announced that it was because God had heard his prayer.

18. Interview, Dhaka, May 19, 1996. See Brenner 1996 for an insightful discussion of the foreignness of the new Islamic dress in the Javanese context.

19. Interview, Dhaka, May 12, 1996.

20. Interview, Satkania, Chittagong, January 16, 1997.

21. Ibid. Shortly after this interview, Sheikh Hasina had dispensed with the black scarf completely, though she still drew the *anchol* over her head.

22. Interview (by telephone from Princeton, N.J.), Washington, D.C., February 5, 1997.

23. "Historic Women's Meeting with Hazrat Maulana Delawar Hussain Saidi, 1996," audiocassette recording (Dhaka: Spondon Audio-Visual Centre, n.d.).

24. He is referring to Quran 66:10.

25. Interestingly, in a similar move before the January 2005 elections in Iraq, Grand Ayatollah Ali al-Sistani issued a fatwa ordering women to vote independently of their husbands. See Nordland 2005.

26. Interview, Satkkhira, June 14, 1996.

27. Another source of the centrist parties' positions on women's issues is a survey of five hundred electoral candidates undertaken by Gonotantrik Uddyog (Democratic Initiative) just before the parliamentary elections in 1991. This survey found interesting differences across the three parties in their support for change in the personal laws. Among the AL candidates, 72 percent were in favor of reform, while 22 percent felt they should remain unchanged. The corresponding figures among BNP candidates were 45 and 30 percent, and among the JP candidates, 50 and 45 percent. Very few of the candidates interviewed, however,

supported a drastic move such as the establishment of the Uniform Family Code (Gonotantrik Uddyog 1991). Moreover, the election manifestos of the parties did not explicitly include any proposals for legal reform.

28. According to the Bangladesh election commission, the Jamaat received just 3 percent of the popular vote in 1996. Our sample was deliberately not representative because we made a special effort to seek out Jamaat supporters.

29. Interview, Jessore, June 12, 1996 (Election Day).

30. Interview, Baruthan, Chittagong, March 22, 1996.

31. Group discussion at Gender Issues Workshop, Banchte Shekha office, Jessore, June 15, 1996.

32. "Historic Women's Meeting with Hazrat Maulana Delawar Hussain Saidi, 1996."

33. Interview, Jessore, June 12, 1996.

34. Interview, Satkania, Chittagong, January 16, 1997.

35. Interview, Baruthan, Chittagong, February 20, 1996.

36. Interview, Baruthan, Chittagong, February 25, 1996.

37. Interview, Baruthan, Chittagong, February 25, 1996. Dung sticks are a traditional, resource-efficient, and environment-friendly source of fuel in South Asia. Similarly, old cotton saris are recycled for use in quilts.

38. Interview, Dhaka, January 29, 1997.

39. Interviews, Baruthan, Chittagong, February 25, 1996.

40. Interview, Chittagong, March 2, 1996.

41. See Keefer and Khemani 2004 for a thought-provoking discussion of the relationship between the credibility of campaign promises and electoral outcomes. I am grateful to Sabeel Rahman for drawing my attention to this article.

42. Interview, Jessore, June 12, 1996 (Election Day).

43. BTV program on women's voting behavior, May 13, 1996.

44. Bangladesh Election Commission website, www.bd-ec.org/election.php3?stat = 1.

6. BEYOND MUSLIM MOTHERHOOD

1. The Freedom House Survey of 2001, for example, identified eleven Muslim countries as electoral democracies: Albania, Bangladesh, Djibouti, the Gambia, Indonesia, Mali, Niger, Nigeria, Senegal, Sierra Leone, and Turkey. "Of the 31 non-Arab countries, 11 are electoral democracies, while none of the 16 majority-Arab countries has a democratically elected government" (Karatnycky 2002: 104).

2. The ratio of women to men is a common measure of women's status in society and particularly useful for cross-country comparisons. While males generally outnumber females at birth, in the population at large, women tend to outlive

and outnumber men. In the industrialized world, in the United States and Japan, for instance, the ratio is 105 or 106 women to 100 men. The ratio is very different, however, in certain other areas. In China, West Asia, and South Asia, the ratio is 0.94 or even lower. According to economist and Nobel laureate Amartya Sen, this is the result of neglect of the nutritional and health-care needs of females, sex-selective abortions, and limited opportunities. He calculates the number of women who might have been around had the ratio been 1.05 and concludes that "a great many more than 100 million women are 'missing.' These numbers tell us, quietly, a terrible story of inequality and neglect leading to the excess mortality of women" (1990).

3. Interview, Baruthan, Chittagong, March 22, 1996.

4. Interview, Chittagong, March 13, 1996.

5. Interview, Dhaka, June 22, 1996.

6. Interview, Chittagong, March 13, 1996.

7. Interviews, Satkania, Chittagong, January 16, 1997.

8. Interview, Dhaka, May 12, 1996.

9. While it would be interesting to trace the genealogy of these methods—for example, did the Islamists take the idea from the NGOs they constantly criticize?—it is important to note that rote learning is common in both religious and secular educational contexts in Bangladesh. Young children routinely memorize not simply multiplication tables and the different surahs required for the daily prayers but also entire essays that, in many schools, they are then expected to reproduce verbatim during exams.

10. In her study of educated Islamist activists in Egypt, Carrie Wickham also highlights the importance of this sense of a religious obligation to propagate the Islamist message to the success of Islamist recruitment in particular Cairo neighborhoods (2002).

11. An optional prayer that is said in the middle of the night.

12. Interview, Chittagong, August 3, 2001.

13. I have deliberately omitted details about her husband's position and the couple's location in order to preserve her anonymity.

14. Interview, Chittagong, August 3, 2001.

15. See F. Ahmed 2003 for a discussion of NGOs' need to incorporate male relatives in gender empowerment programs.

16. "Allama Delawar Hussain Saidi: Views on the Elections," audiocassette recording (Dhaka: Spondon Audio-Visual Centre, n.d.). He repeated many of these charges at a massive gathering in his home constituency of Pirojpur during the 2001 election campaign that was attended by research associates Raqibul Hassan Rana and Jessmin Nahar.

17. See, for example, Mookherjee 2003 and www.gendercide.org/case_bangladesh.html; www.drishtipat.org/1971/index.htm; www.adhunika.org/issues/wpawc71.html. Accessed June 2005.

18. See Shehabuddin 1999b for an account of how village women used burkas and local plant extracts (that could remove the polling stations' supposedly indelible ink) to cast multiple votes for a major party in exchange for money.

19. Pirojpur meeting, September 2001. Information about the 2001 campaign in Pirojpur is from the notes of research assistants Rokibul Hasan Rana and Jessmin Nahar taken during the 2001 study coordinated by Zakir Hossain and myself.

20. Unless indicated otherwise, information about the 2001 campaign in Satkkhira is from the notes of Sharif Mohammad Bari, a research assistant, taken during the 2001 study coordinated by Zakir Hossain and myself.

21. Sharif noted that the Jamaat candidate had not used his last name—Mandol—on any of the campaign posters, though it did appear on the official ballots.

22. The burka is a very common sight in this area so the Jamaat women's burkas are worthy of comment only to the extent that they covered more of the female form than those traditionally worn locally.

23. interview, August 3, 2001, Chittagong, Bangladesh.

24. Interview, Chittagong, August 3, 2001.

25. "*Shibir*" is shorthand for ICS, the male student wing of the Jamaat. Very active on college and university campuses throughout the country, the shibir have gained notoriety for violent acts and terror tactics against their political and ideological opponents (Hashmi 1994; Hossain and Siddiquee 2004).

26. Interview, Chittagong, August 3, 2001.

27. Kerber suggests that the deferential citizen is an intermediary stage in the process of political socialization discussed in Almond and Verba 1963 in which citizens "end by thinking of themselves as *actors*, who force governments to respond to them" (1976: 203 n. 36; emphasis in original).

28. For a discussion of the "path to moderation" of Islamism in the less open national political context of Egypt, see Wickham 2004.

CODA

1. Interview, Chittagong, February 25, 1996.

WORKS CITED

Abu-Lughod, Lila. 2002. "Do Muslim Women Really Need Saving? Anthropological Reflections on Cultural Relativism and Its Others." *American Anthropologist* 104 (3): 783–790.

——. 2005. *Dramas of Nationhood: The Politics of Television in Egypt*. Chicago: University of Chicago Press.

——, ed. 1998. *Remaking Women: Feminism and Modernity in the Middle East*. Princeton: Princeton University Press.

Ackerly, Brooke. 1995. "Testing the Tools of Development: Credit Programmes, Loan Involvement, and Women's Empowerment." *Institute of Development Studies Bulletin* 26 (3): 56–68.

——. 2001. "Women's Human Rights Activists as Cross-Cultural Theorists." *International Feminist Journal of Politics* 3 (3): 311–346.

ADAB (Association of Development Agencies in Bangladesh). 1994. "Fact Sheet on NGO Activities" (Bengali). Dhaka: ADAB.

Adamson, Clarissa. 2007. "Gendered Anxieties: Islam, Women's Rights, and Moral Hierarchy in Java." *Anthropological Quarterly* 80 (1): 3–37.

Adelkhah, Fariba. 2000. *Being Modern in Iran*. New York: Columbia University Press.

Adnan, Shapan. 1993. "Birds in a Cage: Institutional Change and Women's Position in Bangladesh." In Nora Federici, Karen O. Mason, and Solvi Sogner, eds. *Women's Position and Demographic Change*. New York: Oxford University Press.

Afroze, Sultana. n.d.a. *Awareness-raising Adult Education Text, Part 1* (Bengali). Dhaka: Saptagram Nari Swanirvar Parishad.

——. n.d.b. *A Guide to Enhanced Awareness: Adult Education Lessons*. Part 1, *A Teacher's Guide* (English). Trans. Shafiqur Rahman. Dhaka: Saptagram Nari Swanirvar Parishad.

Afshar, Haleh. 1998. *Islam and Feminisms: An Iranian Case-Study*. New York: St. Martin's.

Aftab, Tahera. 2005. "Negotiating with Patriarchy: South Asian Muslim Women and the Appeal to Sir Syed Ahmed Khan." *Women's History Review* 14 (1): 75–97.

Ahmad, Mokbul Morshed. n.d. "Roots of Funding, Roots of Trust: The Struggle for Survival and Credibility Among the Religious NGOs (Non-Governmental Organisations) in Bangladesh." Unpublished paper, available at www.jhu.edu/~istr/conferences/toronto/workingpapers/ahmad.mokbul.morshed.pdf. Accessed May 2005.

——. 2001. "The State, Laws and Non-Governmental Organizations (NGOs) in Bangladesh." *International Journal of Not-for-Profit Law* 3 (3). Available at www.icnl.org/journal/vol3iss3/ar_ahmad.htm. Accessed May 2005.

——. 2003. "Distant Voices: The Views of the Field Workers of NGOs in Bangladesh on Microcredit." *Geographical Journal* 169 (1): 65–74.

——. 2005. "New Threat to Development? The NGO (Non-Governmental Organisations)-Fundamentalist Conflict in Bangladesh." *Journal of Rural Development* (India) 24 (1): 71–88.

Ahmad, Tahmina and Md. Maimul Ahsan Khan, eds. 1998. *Gender in Law*. Dhaka: Adtam.

Ahmed, Fauzia Erfan. 2003. "Low-income Progressive Men: Microcredit, Gender Empowerment, and the Redefinition of Manhood in Rural Bangladesh." Ph.D. diss., Brandeis University.

Ahmed, Inam. 1995. "A Quiet Revolution: Changing Social Structures in Rural Bangladesh." *Daily Star*, December 30.

Ahmed, Leila. 1992. *Women and Gender in Islam: Historical Roots of a Modern Debate*. New Haven: Yale University Press.

Ahmed, Nizam. 2003. "From Monopoly to Competition: Party Politics in the Bangladesh Parliament (1973–2001)." *Pacific Affairs* 76 (1): 55–77.

Ahmed, Rafiuddin. 1981. *The Bengal Muslims, 1871–1906: A Quest for Identity*. Delhi: Oxford University Press.

——. 1994. "Redefining Muslim Identity in South Asia: The Transformation of the Jamaat-i-Islami." In Martin E. Marty and R. Scott Appleby, eds., *Accounting for Fundamentalisms: The Dynamic Character of Movements*. Chicago: University of Chicago.

——, ed. 2001a. *Understanding the Bengal Muslims: Interpretative Essays*. New Delhi: Oxford University Press.

——, ed. 2001b. *Religion, Identity and Politics: Essays on Bangladesh*. Colorado Springs: International Academic Publishers.

Ahmed, Rahnuma. 1985. "Women's Movement in Bangladesh and the Left's Understanding of the Woman Question." *Journal of Social Studies* 30: 41–56.

——. 1987. "Changing Marriage Transactions and the Rise of Demand System in Bangladesh." *Economic and Political Weekly* (April): WS22–WS26.

Ahmed, Rahnuma and Milu Shamsun Naher, eds. 1987. *Brides and the Demand System in Bangladesh*. Dhaka: Center for Social Studies, Dhaka University.

Ahmed, Sania Sultan and Sally Bould. 2004. "'One Able Daughter Is Worth 10 Illiterate Sons': Reframing the Patriarchal Family." *Journal of Marriage and Family* 66: 1332–1341.

Akhter, Farida. 1992. *Depopulating Bangladesh: Essays on the Politics of Fertility*. Dhaka: Narigrantha Prabartana.

Akhter, Salma. 2002. "Status of Women's Leadership in Bangladesh: Problems and Prospects." *Pakistan Journal of Women's Studies: Alam-e-Niswan* 9 (2): 1–29.

Alam, S. M. Nurul. 1995. "NGOs Under Attack: A Study of Socio-cultural and Political Dynamics of NGO Operations in Bangladesh." Unpublished paper. Sponsor: PRIP-PACT.

——. 1996. "Understanding NGO Operations in Bangladesh: Views from the Field." Unpublished paper.

Alam, Shamsul. 1985. *Islam and Family Planning*. Dhaka: Islamic Foundation.

Albelda, Randy. 2005. *The Dilemmas of Lone Motherhood: Essays from Feminist Economics*. New York: Routledge.

Ali, Azra Asghar. 2000. *The Emergence of Feminism Among Indian Muslim Women, 1920–1947*. Karachi: Oxford University Press.

Ali, Shaheen Sardar. 2000. "Law, Islam and the Women's Movement in Pakistan." In Shirin M. Rai, ed., *International Perspectives on Gender and Democratization*. New York: Palgrave.

Ali, Tariq. 1983. *Can Pakistan Survive?—The Death of a State*. New York: Penguin.

Almeder, Robert. 1994. "Liberal Feminism and Academic Feminism." *Public Affairs Quarterly* 8: 299–315.

Almond, Gabriel and Sidney Verba. 1963. *The Civic Culture: Political Attitudes and Democracy in Five Nations*. Princeton: Princeton University Press.

Alvarez, Sonia E. 1992. *Engendering Democracy in Brazil: Women's Movements in Transition Politics*. Princeton: Princeton University Press.

Amin, Aasha Mehreen. 1996. "Why So Marginalized?" *Daily Star Magazine*, May 31, 4–9.

Amin, M. Ruhul. 1994 [1991]. *Islamer Dristithey Nari Netrityo* (Female leadership in the sight of Islam). Dhaka: Bangladesh Islamic Centre.

Amin, Sajeda and Sara Hossain. 1995. "Women's Reproductive Rights and the Politics of Fundamentalism: A View from Bangladesh." *American University Law Review* 44 (4): 1319–1343.

Amin, Sonia Nishat. 1996. *The World of Muslim Women in Colonial Bengal, 1876–1939*. Leiden: E. J. Brill.

——. 2001. "The Changing World of Bengali Muslim Women: The 'Dreams' and Efforts of Rokeya Sakhawat Hossein." In Rafiuddin Ahmed, ed., *Understanding the Bengal Muslims: Interpretative Essays*. New Delhi: Oxford University Press.

Aminuzzaman, Salahuddin, Harald Baldersheim, and Ishtiaq Jamil. 2003. "Talking Back! Empowerment and Mobile Phones in Rural Bangladesh: A Study of the Village Phone Scheme of Grameen Bank." *Contemporary South Asia* 12 (3): 327–348.

Anderson, Norman. 1976. *Law Reform in the Muslim World*. London: Athlone.

Ansar, Begum Rokeya. 1991. *Islami Andoloner Mohila Kormir Daityo o Kortobyo* (A woman worker's responsibilities and duties in the islamic movement). Dhaka: Raihan Prokashoni.

Anwary, Afroza. 2003. "Acid Violence and Medical Care in Bangladesh: Women's Activism as Carework." *Gender and Society* 17 (2): 305–313.

ASK (Ain o Salish Kendra [Law and Mediation Centre]). 1994a. *Eclipse* (documentary, Bengali and English). Dhaka: ASK.

——. 1994b. "Polygamy and the Law." Special issue, *Sanglap* 1 (January).

——. 1996. "Oppression Against Women in Bangladesh Through Fatwas and Shalishes, 1993–95 (Compiled by ASK on the Basis of Newspaper Reports)" (Bengali). Dhaka: ASK.

——. 1997. "Oppression Against Women 1995–1996: Incidences of Fatwa and Shalish in Bangladesh (ASK Informative Report from the National Dailies)." Dhaka: ASK.

Azim, Firdous. 2001. "Formulating an Agenda for the Women's Movement: A Review of Naripokkho." *Inter-Asia Cultural Studies* 2 (3): 389–394.

——. 2005. "Feminist Struggles in Bangladesh." *Feminist Review* 80: 194–197.

Aziz, Khursheed K. 1976. *Party Politics in Pakistan, 1947–58*. Islamabad: National Commission on Historical and Cultural Research.

Badran, Margot. 1998. "Gender, Islam, and the State: Kuwaiti Women in Struggle, Pre-Invasion to Postliberation." In Yvonne Yazbeck Haddad and John L. Esposito, eds., *Islam, Gender, and Social Change*. New York: Oxford University Press.

Balchin, Cassandra. 2003. "With Her Feet on the Ground: Women, Religion and Development in Muslim Communities." *development* 46 (4): 39–49.

Baldwin, Ruth. 2002. "The 'Talibanization' of Bangladesh." *The Nation*, May 18. www.thenation.com/doc/20020527/baldwin20020517. Accessed November 2004.

Banu, Nilufar, Rowshan Qadir, Khadija Khatun, and Najma Siddiqi. 1997. *Voting Behaviour of Women in Dhaka City and Some Selected Districts in Bangladesh*. Dhaka: Women for Women.

Banu, U. A. B. Razia Akter. 1992. *Islam in Bangladesh*. Leiden: E. J. Brill.

Basu, Amrita. 1992. *Two Faces of Protest: Contrasting Modes of Women's Activism in India*. Berkeley: University of California Press

——. 1995. Introduction to Amrita Basu, ed., *The Challenge of Local Feminisms: Women's Movements in Global Perspective*. Boulder, Colo.: Westview.

——. 2000. "Globalization of the Local/Localization of the Global: Mapping Transnational Women's Movements." *meridians* 1 (1): 68–84.

Basu, Aparna and Bharati Ray. 1990. *Women's Struggle: A History of the All India Women's Conference, 1927–1990*. Delhi: Manohar.

Bates, Lisa M., Sidney Ruth Schuler, Farzana Islam, and Md. Khairul Islam. 2004. "Socioeconomic Factors and Processes Associated with Domestic Violence in Rural Bangladesh." *International Family Planning Perspectives* 30 (4): 190–199.

Baxi, Upendra. 1992. "'The State's Emissary': The Place of Law in Subaltern Studies." In Partha Chatterjee and Gyanendra Pandey, eds., *Subaltern Studies VII: Writings on South Asian History and Society*. Delhi: Oxford University Press.

Bebbington, Anthony, David Lewis, Simon Batterbury, Elizabeth Olson, and M. Sharmeen Siddiqi. 2007. "Of Texts and Practices: Empowerment and Organisational Cultures in World Bank-Funded Rural Development Programmes." *Journal of Development Studies* 43 (4): 597–621.

Begum, Maleka. 1993. "By Her Death, Nurjahan Proved that the Rule of Law Is Yet to Be Established" (Bengali). *Bhorer Kagoj*, January 23.

Begum, Suraiya. 1994. "Fundamentalism and Women in Bangladesh: A Discussion" (Bengali). *Samaj Nirikkhon* 54: 1–19.

Benford, Robert and David Snow. 2000. "Framing Processes and Social Movements: An Overview and Assessment." *Annual Review of Sociology* 26: 611–639.

Berger, Julia. 2003. "Religious Nongovernmental Organizations: An Exploratory Analysis." *Voluntas: International Journal of Voluntary and Nonprofit Organizations* 14 (1): 15–39.

Bergeron, Suzanne. 2004. *Fragments of Development: Nation, Gender, and the Space of Modernity*. Ann Arbor: University of Michigan Press.

Bernasek, Alexandra. 2003. "Banking on Social Change: Grameen Bank Lending to Women." *International Journal of Politics, Culture and Society* 16 (3): 369–385.

Bose, Sugata and Ayesha Jalal. 1998. *Modern South Asia: History, Culture, Political Economy*. London: Routledge.

Boserup, Ester. 1970. *Women's Role in Economic Development*. New York: St. Martin's.

Bowen, John R. 1993. *Muslims Through Discourse: Religion and Ritual in Gayo Society*. Princeton: Princeton University Press.

BRAC. 2004. *BRAC: Annual Report 2003*. Available at www.brac.net/aboutb. htm. Accessed May 2005.

Brenner, Suzanne. 1996. "Reconstructing Self and Society: Javanese Muslim Women and 'The Veil.'" *American Ethnologist* 23 (4): 673–697.

Bruck, Connie. 2006. "Millions for Millions." *New Yorker*, October 23. www. newyorker.com/fact/content/articles/061030fa_fact1. Accessed March 2007.

Burton, Antoinette. 1994. *Burdens of History: British Feminists, Indian Women, and Imperial Culture, 1865–1915*. Chapel Hill: University of North Carolina Press.

Calman, Leslie. 1985. *Protest in Democratic India: Authority's Response to Challenge*. Boulder, Colo.: Westview.

Caton, Annie R. 1930a. Introduction to Annie R. Caton, ed., *The Key of Progress: A Survey of the Status and Conditions of Women in India*. Oxford: Oxford University Press.

——. 1930b. "Women in Public Life (Including Civil and Political Status)." In Annie R. Caton, ed., *The Key of Progress: A Survey of the Status and Conditions of Women in India*. Oxford: Oxford University Press.

CEDAW. 2003. "Fifth Periodic Report of State Parties: Bangladesh." Available at www.un.org/womenwatch/daw/cedaw/31sess.htm. Accessed June 2005.

Chant, Sylvia. 2003. "Female Household Headship and the Feminisation of Poverty: Facts, Fictions and Forward Strategies." London School of Economics, Gender Institute, New Working Paper Series. Available at www.lse.ac.uk/collections/genderInstitute/pdf/femaleHouseholdHeadship.pdf. Accessed May 2006.

Chatterjee, Partha. 1989. "The Nationalist Resolution of the Women's Question." In Kumkum Sangari and Sudesh Vaid, eds., *Recasting Women: Essays in Colonial History*. New Delhi: Kali for Women.

Chatterjee, Piya. 2001. *A Time for Tea: Women, Labor, and Post/Colonial Politics on an Indian Plantation*. Durham, N.C.: Duke University Press.

Chaudhuri, Nupur and Margaret Strobel, eds. 1992. *Western Women and Imperialism: Complicity and Resistance*. Bloomington: Indiana University Press.

Chen, Martha. 1983. *A Quiet Revolution: Women in Transition in Rural Bangladesh*. Cambridge, Mass.: Schenkman.

Choudhury, Dilara. 1995. "Women's Participation in the Formal Structure and Decision-Making Bodies in Bangladesh." In Roushan Jahan, Sayeda Rowshan Qadir, Hamida A. Begum, and Jahanara Huq, eds., *Empowerment of Women: Nairobi to Beijing (1985–1995)*. Dhaka: Women for Women.

——. 1999. "Women, Society, and Politics in Bangladesh." *Daily Star*, November 22.

——. 2000. "Women and Democracy: A Bangladesh Perspective." *Round Table* 357: 563–576.

Chowdhury, A. Mushtaque R., Samir R. Nath, and Rasheda K. Choudhury. 2002. "Enrolment at Primary Level: Gender Difference Disappears in Bangladesh." *International Journal of Educational Development* 22: 191–203.

Chowdhury, Elora H. 2005. "Feminist Negotiations: Contesting Narratives of the Campaign Against Acid Violence in Bangladesh." *meridians* 6 (1): 163–192.

Chowdhury, Farah D. 1999a. "Voting Behaviour of Women in the Seventh Parliamentary Election in Bangladesh: A Case Study of Rajshahi City." *Empowerment: A Journal of Women for Women* 6: 29–40.

——. 1999b. "Women and Election: Issues in Bangladesh." *Pakistan Journal of History and Culture* 20 (1): 93–107.

Chowdhury, Mahfuzul H. 1993. "Popular Attitudes, Legal Institutions and Dispute Resolution in Contemporary Bangladesh." *Legal Studies Forum* 17 (3): 291–300.

Chowdhury, Najma. 1994. "Bangladesh: Gender Issues and Politics in a Patriarchy." In Barbara J. Nelson and Najma Chowdhury, eds., *Women and Politics Worldwide*. New Haven: Yale University Press.

———. 2001. "The Politics of Implementing Women's Rights in Bangladesh." In Janet H. Bayes and Nayereh Tohidi, eds., *Globalization, Gender, and Religion: The Politics of Women's Rights in Catholic and Muslim Contexts*. New York: Palgrave.

———. 2002. "The Implementation of Quotas: Bangladesh Experience—Dependence and Marginality in Politics." Paper presented at workshop hosted by International Institute for Democracy and Electoral Assistance, Jakarta, Indonesia, September 25.

Chowdhury, Nina. 1995. "What's the Flavour of the Month?" *Daily Star*, April 17.

CIA. 2007. *The World Factbook*. Available at www.cia.gov/library/publications/the-world-factbook/. Accessed May 2007.

Clark, Janine A. 2004. "Islamist Women in Yemen: Informal Nodes of Activism." In Quintan Wiktorowicz, ed., *Islamic Activism: A Social Movement Theory Approach*. Bloomington: Indiana University Press.

Clark, Janine A. and Jillian Schwedler. 2003. "Who Opened the Window? Women's Activism in Islamist Parties." *Comparative Politics* 35 (3): 293–312.

Clarke, Gerard. 1998. *The Politics of NGOs in South-East Asia: Participation and Protest in the Philippines*. New York: Routledge.

Cochrane, Susan H. 1979. *Fertility and Education: What Do We Really Know?* World Bank Staff Occasional Papers, No. 26. Baltimore: Johns Hopkins University Press.

Community Development Library. n.d. *Food Aid to Bangladesh: Whose Benefit?* Dhaka: The Library.

Cott, Nancy F. 1997. *The Bonds of Womanhood: "Woman's Sphere" in New England, 1780–1835*. Reprint with new preface. New Haven: Yale University Press. (Orig. pub. 1977.)

Counts, Alex. 1996. *Give Us Credit*. New York: Times Books.

Crook, Clive. 1989. "Poor Man's Burden: Missing Entrepreneurs." *The Economist*, September 23, 44–46.

Custers, Peter. 1987. *Women in the Tebhaga Uprising: Rural Poor Women and Revolutionary Leadership, 1946–47*. Calcutta, India: Naya Prokash.

Deeb, Lara. 2006. *An Enchanted Modern: Gender and Piety in Shia Lebanon*. Princeton: Princeton University Press.

Desan, Suzanne. 2004. *The Family on Trial in Revolutionary France*. Berkeley: University of California Press.

Develtere, Patrick and An Huybrechts. 2005. "The Impact of Microcredit on the Poor in Bangladesh." *Alternatives* 30: 165–189.

Devji, Faisal F. 1994. "Gender and the Politics of Space: The Movement for

Women's Reform, 1857–1900." In Zoya Hasan, ed., *Forging Identities: Gender, Communities and the State in India*. Boulder, Colo.: Westview.

Diamond, Larry. 1992. "Economic Development and Democracy Reconsidered." In Larry Diamond and Gary Marks, eds., *Reexamining Democracy: Essays in Honor of Seymour Martin Lipset*. Newbury Park, Calif.: Sage.

van Doorn-Harder, Pieternella. 2006. *Women Shaping Islam: Indonesian Women Reading the Qur'an*. Urbana: University of Illinois Press.

Economist. 2000. "Sins of the Secular Missionaries." *Economist*, January 29, 25–27.

——. 2003. "Being Well-Meaning Is No Protection: When Humanitarianism Gets Caught Up with Politics." *Economist*, March 15, 39.

Edwards, Michael and David Hulme. 1996. *Beyond the Magic Bullet: NGO Performance and Accountability in the Post-Cold War World*. West Hartford, Conn.: Kumarian.

Eickelman, Dale F. and James Piscatori. 1996. *Muslim Politics*. Princeton: Princeton University Press.

El Guindi, Fadwa. 1999. *Veil: Modesty, Privacy and Resistance*. New York: Berg.

Elson, Diane. 1991. "Male Bias in the Development Process: An Overview." In Diane Elson, ed., *Male Bias in the Development Process*. Manchester: Manchester University Press.

Esposito, John L. 1982. *Women in Muslim Family Law*. Syracuse: Syracuse University Press.

——. 1998a. "Introduction: Women in Islam and Muslim Societies." In Yvonne Yazbeck Haddad and John L. Esposito, eds., *Islam, Gender, and Social Change*. New York: Oxford University Press.

——. 1998b. *Islam and Politics*. Syracuse: Syracuse University Press.

Faaland, Just, ed. 1981. *Aid and Influence: The Case of Bangladesh*. London: Macmillan.

Fair, F. Christine. 2007. "On the Issues: Bangladesh." USIP (U.S. Institute of Peace) interviews with USIP experts, April 27, 2007, available at www.usip. org/on_the_issues/bangladesh.html. Accessed May 2007.

Farooq, Mohammad Omar. 2002. "In Search of the Bottom: Focus on the Top." *Daily Star*, August 25.

Feldman, Shelley. 1998. "(Re)presenting Islam: Manipulating Gender, Shifting State Practices, and Class Frustrations in Bangladesh." In Patricia Jeffery and Amrita Basu, eds., *Appropriating Gender: Women's Activism and Politicized Religion in South Asia*. London: Routledge.

——. 2001a. "Exploring Theories of Patriarchy: A Perspective from Contemporary Bangladesh." *Signs* 26 (4): 1097–1127.

——. 2001b. "Gender and Islam in Bangladesh: Metaphor and Myth." In Rafiuddin Ahmed, ed., *Understanding the Bengal Muslims: Interpretative Essays*. New Delhi: Oxford University Press.

——. 2001c. "NGOs and Civil Society: (Un)stated Contradictions." In Rounaq Jahan, ed., *Bangladesh: Promise and Performance*. Dhaka: University Press Limited.

———. 2003. "Paradoxes of Institutionalisation: The Depoliticisation of Bangladeshi NGOs." *Development in Practice* 13 (1): 5–26.

Ferguson, James. 1994. *The Anti-Politics Machine: "Development," Depoliticization, and Bureaucratic Power in Lesotho*. Minneapolis: University of Minnesota Press.

Fish, M. Steven. 2002. "Islam and Authoritarianism." *World Politics* 55: 4–37.

Foley, Rebecca. 2004. "Muslim Women's Challenges to Islamic Law: The Case of Malaysia." *International Feminist Journal of Politics* 6 (1): 53–84.

Forbes, Geraldine. 1996. *Women in Modern India*. Cambridge: Cambridge University Press.

Fraser, Arvonne S. and Irene Tinker, eds. 2004. *Developing Power: How Women Transformed International Development*. New York: Feminist Press at the City University of New York.

Freitag, Sandria. 1985. "Collective Crime and Authority in North India." In Anand A. Yang, ed., *Crime and Criminality in British India*. Tucson: University of Arizona Press.

Fruttero, Anna and Varun Gauri. 2005. "The Strategic Choices of NGOs: Location Decisions in Rural Bangladesh." *Journal of Development Studies* 41 (5): 759–787.

Gardner, Katy. 1998. "Women and Islamic Revivalism in a Bangladeshi Community." In Patricia Jeffery and Amrita Basu, eds., *Appropriating Gender: Women's Activism and Politicized Religion in South Asia*. London: Routledge.

Ghuznavi, Farah. 1995. "Education Is Power!" *Daily Star*, November 23.

Gilani, Syed Asad. 1978 [1962]. *Maududi: Thought and Movement*. Lahore: Farooq Hasan Gilani.

Gluck, Sherna B. and Daphne Patai, eds. 1990. *Women's Words: The Feminist Practice of Oral History*. New York: Routledge.

Goetz, Anne Marie. 1998. "Mainstreaming Gender Equity to National Development Planning." In Carol Miller and Shahra Razavi, eds., *Missionaries and Mandarins: Feminist Engagements with Development Institutions*. London: Intermediate Technology Publications and United Nations Research Institute for Social Development.

Goetz, Anne Marie and Rina Sen Gupta. 1996. "Who Takes the Credit? Gender, Power and Control Over Loan Use in Rural Credit Programs in Bangladesh." *World Development* 24 (1): 45–64.

Göle, Nilüfer. 1996. *The Forbidden Modern: Civilization and Veiling*. Ann Arbor: University of Michigan Press.

Golub, Stephen. 2007. "The Rule of Law and the UN Peacebuilding Commission: A Social Development Approach." *Cambridge Review of International Affairs* 20 (1): 47–67.

Gonotantrik Uddyog (Democratic Initiative). 1991. *Election 1991* (Bangla). Dhaka: MECB.

Government of Bangladesh (GoB). 1973. *First Five-Year Plan*. Dhaka: Ministry of Planning.

———. 1994. *The Constitution of the People's Republic of Bangladesh*. Dhaka: Bangladesh Forms and Publishing Office.

——. 1995a. *Country Paper—Bangladesh*. Prepared for World Summit for Social Development, Copenhagen, Denmark, March 1995. Dhaka: GoB.

——. 1995b. "Women in Bangladesh: Equality, Development and Peace—National Report to the Fourth World Conference on Women, Beijing 1995." Dhaka: Ministry of Women and Children's Affairs.

Government of India. 1983. *The Constitution of India*. New Delhi: Government of India, Ministry of Law, Justice and Company Affairs.

Grameen Bank. 2004. *Grameen Bank: Annual Report 2003*. Dhaka: Grameen Bank. Available at www.grameen-info.org/annualreport/2003/index.html. Accessed May 2005.

Gray, H. 1968. "The Progress of Women." In L.S.S. O'Malley, ed., *Modern India and the West*. London: Oxford University Press.

Griswold, Eliza. 2005. "The Next Islamist Revolution?" *New York Times Magazine*, January 23.

Guha, Ranajit and Gayatri Spivak, eds. 1988. *Selected Subaltern Studies*. New York: Oxford University Press.

Guhathakurta, Meghna. 1985. "Gender Violence in Bangladesh: The Role of the State." *Journal of Social Studies* 30:57–76.

——. 1994. "The Women's Agenda and the Role of Political Parties." In Najma Chowdhury, Hamida Akhtar Begum, Mahmuda Islam, and Nazmunnessa Mahtab, eds., *Women and Politics*. Dhaka: Women for Women.

——. 1997. *Contemporary Feminist Perspectives*. Dhaka: University Press Limited.

——. 2004. "Women Negotiating Change: The Structure and Transformation of Gendered Violence in Bangladesh." *Cultural Dynamics* 16 (2/3): 193–211.

Haeri, Shahla. 2002. *No Shame for the Sun: Lives of Professional Pakistani Women*. Syracuse: Syracuse University Press.

Hagerty, Devin T. 2007. "Bangladesh in 2006: Living in 'Interesting Times.'" *Asian Survey* 47 (1): 105–112.

Hale, Sondra. 1998. *Gender Politics in Sudan: Islamism, Socialism, and the State*. Boulder, Colo.: Westview.

Halliday, Fred. 1997. Review of *The Clash of Civilizations and the Remaking of World Order*. *New Statesman*, April 4, 42.

Haque, M. Shamsul. 2002. "The Changing Balance of Power Between the Government and NGOs in Bangladesh." *International Political Science Review* 23 (4): 411–435.

Hardon, Anita P. 1992. "The Needs of Women Versus the Interests of Family Planning Personnel, Policy-Makers and Researchers: Conflicting Views on the Safety and Acceptability of Contraceptives." *Social Science and Medicine* 35 (6): 753–766.

Hartmann, Betsy. 1995 [1987]. *Reproductive Rights and Wrongs: The Global Politics of Population Control and Contraceptive Choice*. New York: Harper and Row.

Hartmann, Betsy and James K. Boyce. 1983. *A Quiet Violence: View from a Bangladesh Village*. London: Zed.

———. 1990 [1979]. *Needless Hunger: Voices from a Bangladesh Village*. San Francisco: Institute for Food and Development Policy.

Hartmann, Betsy and Hilary Standing. 1985. *Food, Saris and Sterilisation: Population Control in Bangladesh*. London: Bangladesh International Action Group.

Hashemi, Syed M. 1991. "Conscientisation in Bangladesh: The NGO Way." In Clinton B. Seely, ed., *Calcutta, Bangladesh, and Bengal Studies: 1990 Bengal Studies Conference Proceedings*. East Lansing: Asian Studies Center, Michigan State University.

———. 1996. "NGO Accountability in Bangladesh: Beneficiaries, Donors, and the State." In Michael Edwards and David Hulme, eds., *Beyond the Magic Bullet: NGO Performance and Accountability in the Post-Cold War World*. West Hartford, Conn.: Kumarian.

Hashemi, Syed and Sidney Schuler. 1992. *State and NGO Support Networks in Rural Bangladesh: Concepts and Coalitions for Control*. Copenhagen: Centre for Development Research.

Hashmi, Taj I. 1994. "Islam in Bangladesh Politics." In Hussin Mutalib and Taj I. Hashmi, eds., *Islam, Muslims and the Modern State*. London: Macmillan.

———. 2000. *Women and Islam in Bangladesh: Beyond Subjection and Tyranny*. New York: St. Martin's.

Hefner, Robert W. 2000. *Civil Islam: Muslims and Democratization in Indonesia*. Princeton: Princeton University Press.

———. 2001. "Public Islam and the Problem of Democratization." *Sociology of Religion* 62 (4): 491–514.

Hilsdon, Anne-Marie and Santi Rozario. 2006. "Introduction: Special Issue on Islam, Gender, and Human Rights." *Women's Studies International Forum* 29: 331–338.

Hirschkind, Charles. 2006. *The Ethical Soundscape: Cassette Sermons and Islamic Counterpublics*. New York: Columbia University Press.

Hirschkind, Charles and Saba Mahmood. 2002. "Feminism, the Taliban, and Politics of Counter-Insurgency." *Anthropological Quarterly* 75 (2): 339–354.

Holcombe, Susan H. 1995. Managing to Empower: The Grameen Bank's Experience of Poverty Alleviation. Atlantic Highlands, N.J.: Zed.

Holloway, Richard. 1998. *Supporting Citizens' Initiatives: Bangladesh's NGOs and Society*. London: Intermediate Technology Publications.

Horvatich, Patricia. 1994. "Ways of Knowing Islam." *American Ethnologist* 21 (4): 811–826.

Hossain, Hameeda. 1994. "More Crumbs for Women." *Daily Star*, August 12.

———. 1998. "Women Enter the Union Councils." *Grameen Poverty Research* 4 (1): 6–7.

———, ed. 2002. *Human Rights in Bangladesh 2001*. Dhaka: ASK.

Hossain, Ishtiaq and Norre Alam Siddiquee. 2004. "Islam in Bangladesh Politics: The Role of Ghulam Azam of Jamaat-i-Islami." *Inter-Asia Cultural Studies* 5 (3): 384–399.

Hossain, Mahabub. 1984. *Credit for the Rural Poor: The Experience of Grameen Bank in Bangladesh*. Dhaka: Bangladesh Institute of Development Studies.

Hossain, Naomi. 1999. "How Do Bangladeshi Elites Understand Poverty?" Institute of Development Studies Working Paper 83. Brighton: IDS Publications Office, University of Sussex

Hossain, Naomi and Imran Matin. 2007. "Engaging Elite Support for the Poorest? BRAC's Targeted Ultra Poor Programme for Rural Women in Bangladesh." *Development in Practice* 17 (3): 380–392.

Hossain, Naomi, Ramya Subrahmanian, and Naila Kabeer. 2002. "The Politics of Educational Expansion in Bangladesh." Institute of Development Studies Working Paper 167. Brighton: IDS Publications Office, University of Sussex.

Hossain, Sara. 2001 [2002]. "High Court Nails Fatwa." *Holiday*, January 5. Reprinted in *interventions* 4 (2): 220–223.

Hossain, Shawkat Ara and Najma Siddiqui. 2001. "Women's Political Rights: Bangladesh Perspective." In Khaleda Salahuddin, Roushan Jahan, and Latifa Akanda, eds., *State of Human Rights in Bangladesh: Women's Perspective*. Dhaka: Women for Women.

Houghton, Ross. 1877. *Women of the Orient: An Account of the Religious, Intellectual, and Social Condition of Women in Japan, China, India, Egypt, Syria and Turkey*. Cincinnati: Hitchcock and Walden.

Hours, Bernard. 1993. *Islam et Développement au Bangladesh* (Islam and development in Bangladesh). Paris: L'Harmattan.

Hoveyda, Fereydoun. 2004. "Summary of the Roundtable on Democratic Reform and the Role of Women in the Muslim World (Held on March 29, 2004)." *American Foreign Policy Interests* 26: 279–296.

Huda, Shahnaz. 2001. "Protection of Women's Human Rights in Bangladesh: Legal Framework." In Khaleda Salahuddin, Roushan Jahan, and Latifa Akanda, eds., *State of Human Rights in Bangladesh: Women's Perspective*. Dhaka: Women for Women.

Hulme, David. 2004. "Thinking 'Small' and the Understanding of Poverty: Maymana and Mofizul's Story." *Journal of Human Development* 5 (2): 161–176.

Hunt, Lynn. 1992. *The Family Romance of the French Revolution*. Berkeley: University of California Press.

Hunt, Juliet and Nalini Kasynathan. 2001. "Pathways to Empowerment? Reflections on Microfinance and Transformation in Gender Relations in South Asia." *Gender and Development* 9 (1): 42–52.

Huntington, Samuel P. 1968. *Political Order in Changing Societies*. New Haven: Yale University Press.

——. 1991. *The Third Wave: Democratization in the Late Twentieth Century*. Norman: University of Oklahoma Press.

——. 1993a "The Clash of Civilizations?" *Foreign Affairs* 72 (3): 22–49.

——. 1993b. "If Not Civilizations, What? Paradigms of the Post-Cold War World." *Foreign Affairs* 72 (5): 186–194.

——. 1996. *The Clash of Civilizations and the Remaking of World Order.* New York: Simon and Schuster.

Huq, Maimuna. 2005. "Pursuing Peace in Both Worlds: The Formation and Contestation of a Female Islamist Subjectivity in Bangladesh." Paper presented at Workshop on Islamic Reform Movements in South Asia, School of Oriental and African Studies, University of London, May.

Husain, Syed Anwar. 2001. "Islamic Fundamentalism in Bangladesh: Internal Variables and External Inputs." In Rafiuddin Ahmed, ed., *Religion, Identity and Politics: Essays on Bangladesh.* Colorado Springs: International Academic Publishers.

Hussain-Patel, Rashida Mohammad. 2003. *Women Versus Man: Socio-Legal Gender Inequality in Pakistan.* Karachi: Oxford University Press.

Inglehart, Ronald and Pippa Norris. 2003. "The True Clash of Civilizations." *Foreign Policy* (March/April): 63–70.

International IDEA (Institute for Democracy and Electoral Assistance). 2006. *Women in Parliament: Beyond Numbers.* Stockholm: International IDEA.

International Monetary Fund (IMF). 2005. "Bangladesh: Poverty Reduction Strategy Paper." IMF Country Report No. 05/410. Washington, D.C.: IMF.

Islam, Tabibul. 2000a. "Bangladesh Women Not Capable Enough for Public Life?" *Dawn,* July 12.

——. 2000b. "NGOs Face New Opposition from Gov't." IPS-Inter Press Service/Global Information Network, July 31.

——. 2003. "Women Suffer Under Mullah Power, Activists Say." IPS-Inter Press Service/Global Information Network, January 3.

Jacobsohn, Gary J. 2005. *The Wheel of Law: India's Secularism in Comparative Constitutional Context.* Princeton: Princeton University Press.

Jaggar, Alison M. and Paula R. Struhl. 1978. *Feminist Frameworks: Alternative Theoretical Accounts of the Relations Between Women and Men.* New York: McGraw-Hill.

Jahan, Rounaq. 1987 [1980]. *Bangladesh Politics: Problems and Issues.* Dhaka: University Press Limited.

——. 1994 [1972]. *Pakistan: Failure in National Integration.* Dhaka: University Press Limited.

——. 1995. *The Elusive Agenda: Mainstreaming Women in Development.* Dhaka: University Press Limited.

——, ed. 2000. *Bangladesh: Promise and Performance.* Dhaka: University Press Limited.

Jahan, Roushan. 1988. "Rokeya: An Introduction to Her Life." In Rokeya Hossain, *Sultana's Dream.* New York: Feminist Press, CUNY.

——. 1995. "Men in Seclusion, Women in Public: Rokeya's Dream and Women's Struggles in Bangladesh." In Amrita Basu, ed., *The Challenge of Local Feminisms: Women's Movements in Global Perspective.* Boulder, Colo.: Westview.

——. 2001. "Right to Education and Bangladeshi Women: Concerns and Challenges." In Khaleda Salahuddin, Roushan Jahan, and Latifa Akanda, eds.,

State of Human Rights in Bangladesh: Women's Perspective. Dhaka: Women for Women.

Jahangir, Asma. 1998. "The Origins of the MFLO: Reflections for Activism." In Farida Shaheed, Sohail A. Warraich, Cassandra Balchin, and Aisha Gazdar, eds., *Shaping Women's Lives: Laws, Practices, and Strategies in Pakistan.* Lahore: Shirkat Gah.

Jalal, Ayesha. 1991. "The Convenience of Subservience: Women and the State of Pakistan." In Deniz Kandiyoti, ed., *Women, Islam and the State.* London: Macmillan.

——. 1995. *Democracy and Authoritarianism in South Asia: A Comparative and Historical Perspective.* Cambridge: Cambridge University Press.

Jamaat-i-Islami Bangladesh. 1996. *Manifesto.* Dhaka: Al-Falah.

Jayawardena, Kumari. 1986. *Feminism and Nationalism in the Third World.* London: Zed.

——. 1995. *The White Woman's Other Burden: Western Women and South Asia During British Colonial Rule.* New York: Routledge.

Jeffery, Patricia. 1998. "Women's Agency, Resistance and Activism." In Patricia Jeffery and Amrita Basu, eds., *Appropriating Gender: Women's Activism and Politicized Religion in South Asia.* London: Routledge.

Jeffery, Patricia and Amrita Basu, eds. 1998. *Appropriating Gender: Women's Activism and Politicized Religion in South Asia.* London: Routledge.

Jeffery, Patricia and Roger Jeffery. 1998. "Silver Bullet or Passing Fancy?—Girls' Schooling and Population Policy." In Cecile Jackson and Ruth Pearson, eds., *Feminist Visions of Development: Gender Analysis and Policy.* New York: Routledge.

Jeffery, Patricia, Roger Jeffery, and Andrew Lyon. 1989. *Labour Pains and Labour Power: Women and Childbearing in India.* London: Zed.

John, Mary. 1999. "Gender, Development and the Women's Movement: Problems for a History of the Present." In Rajeswaru S. Rajan, ed., *Signposts: Gender Issues in Post-Independence India.* New Brunswick, N.J.: Rutgers University Press.

Joseph, Betty. 2004. *Reading the East India Company, 1720–1840: Colonial Currencies of Gender.* Chicago: University of Chicago Press,

Kabeer, Naila. 1988. "Subordination and Struggle: Women in Bangladesh." *New Left Review* 168: 95–121.

——. 1991. "The Quest for National Identity: Women, Islam and the State of Bangladesh." In Deniz Kandiyoti, ed., *Women, Islam and the State.* London: Macmillan.

——. 1994a. *Reversed Realities: Gender Hierarchies in Development Thought.* New York: Verso.

——. 1994b. "Women's Labour in the Bangladesh Garment Industry: Choice and Constraints." In Camillia el-Solh and Judy Mabro, eds., *Muslim Women's Choice: Religious Belief and Social Reality.* Oxford: Berg.

——. 2000. *The Power to Choose: Bangladeshi Women and Labor Market Decisions in London and Dhaka.* London: Verso.

——. 2001. "Conflicts Over Credit: Re-Evaluating the Empowerment Potential of Loans to Women in Rural Bangladesh." *World Development* 29 (1): 63–84.

——. 2004. "Globalization, Labor Standards, and Women's Rights: Dilemmas of Collective (In)action in an Interdependent World." *Feminist Economics* 10 (1): 3–35.

Kabeer, Rokeya R. n.d. Foreword to Sultana Afroze, *A Guide to Enhanced Awareness: Adult Education Lessons Part 1. A Teacher's Guide* (English), trans. Shafiqur Rahman. Dhaka: Saptagram Nari Swanirvar Parishad.

Kabir, B. M. Manoar. 2001. "The Politics of Religion: The Jamaat-i-Islami in Bangladesh." In Rafiuddin Ahmed, ed., *Religion, Identity and Politics: Essays on Bangladesh*. Colorado Springs: International Academic Publishers.

Kabir, B. M. Manoar and Anwara Begum. 2005. "The Jamaat-e-Islami Bangladesh's Electoral Setback in 1996 and the Aftermath." *Journal of South Asian and Middle Eastern Studies* 29 (1): 1–35.

Kabir, Nurul. 1998. "Upazila Parishad Bill: Constitutional Provisions Ignored." *Daily Star*, October 31.

Kabir, Shahriar. 1995. "Resurgence of Fundamentalism in Bangladesh." In Shahriar Kabir, ed., *Resist Fundamentalism: Focus on Bangladesh*. Dhaka: Nirmul Committee.

Kadioglu, Ayse. 1994. "Women's Subordination in Turkey: Is Islam Really the Villain?" *Middle East Journal* 48 (4): 645–660

Kahf, Mohja. 1997. *Western Representations of the Muslim Woman: From Termagant to Odalisque*. Austin: University of Texas Press.

Kaiser, Shahidullah. 1993. *Shagshaptak* (Bengali). Dhaka: Pallab.

Kalimullah, Nazmul A. and Caroline B. Fraser. 1990. "Islamic Non-Government Organisations in Bangladesh with Reference to Three Case Studies." *Islamic Quarterly* 34 (2): 71–92.

Kamal, Sultana. 1995a. *Fearless Mind* (Bengali). Dhaka: ASK.

——. 1995b. "Law as an Instrument of Women's Empowerment." In Roushan Jahan, Sayeda Rowshan Qadir, Hamida A. Begum, and Jahanara Huq, eds., *Empowerment of Women: Nairobi to Beijing (1985–1995)*. Dhaka: Women for Women.

Karam, Azza. 2006. "Conclusions." In International IDEA, *Women in Parliament: Beyond Numbers*. Stockholm: International IDEA.

Karatnycky, Adrian. 2002. "Muslim Countries and the Democracy Gap." *Journal of Democracy* 13 (1): 99–112.

Karim, Lamia. 2001. "Development and Its Discontents: NGOs, Women and the Politics of Social Mobilization in Bangladesh." Ph.D. diss., Rice University.

——. 2004. "Democratizing Bangladesh: State, NGOs, and Militant Islam." *Cultural Dynamics* 16 (2/3): 291–318.

Kasper, Wolfgang. 2005. "Can Islam Meet the Challenges of Modernity?" *Quadrant* 49 (5): 8–19.

Keefer, Philip and Stuti Khemani. 2004. "Why Do the Poor Receive Poor Services?" *Economic and Political Weekly*, February 28.

Kerber, Linda. 1976. "The Republican Mother: Women and the Enlighten-ment—An American Perspective." *American Quarterly* 28 (2): 187–205.

Khan, Farida C. 2005. "Gender Violence and Development Discourse in Bangla-desh." *ISSJ* 184: 219–230.

Khan, Mazhar ul Haq. 1972. *Purdah and Polygamy: A Study in the Social Pathol-ogy of the Muslim Society.* Peshawar, Pakistan: Nashiran-e-Ilm-Taraqiyet.

Khan, Mizanur Rahman. 1996. *Fatwabaz* (Bangla). Dhaka: Anupan Prokashoni.

Khan, Mohammad Mohabbat. 2003. "State of Governance in Bangladesh." *Round Table* 370: 391–405.

Khan, Muhammad Musa. 1993. "We Are Mortified, We Are Concerned" (Ban-gla). *Banglabazaar Patrika,* January 18.

Khan, Salma. 2001. "The Central Issue of Women's Equality and the Role of the Convention on the Elimination of All Forms of Discrimination Against Women." In Khaleda Salahuddin, Roushan Jahan, and Latifa Akanda, eds., *State of Human Rights in Bangladesh: Women's Perspective.* Dhaka: Women for Women.

Khan, Shahnaz. 2004. "Locating the Feminist Voice: The Debate on the Zina Ordinance." *Feminist Studies* 30 (3): 660–685,

Khan, Syed Ahmed. 2000 [1873]. *The Causes of the Indian Revolt.* Karachi: Ox-ford University Press.

Khan, Zillur Rahman. 1985. "Islam and Bengali Nationalism." *Asian Survey* 25 (8): 834–851.

Kibria, Nazli. 1995. "Culture, Social Class, and Income Control in the Lives of Women Garment Workers in Bangladesh." *Gender and Society* 9 (3): 289–309.

Kilby, Patrick. 2006. "Accountability for Empowerment: Dilemmas Facing Non-Governmental Organizations." *World Development* 34 (6): 951–963.

Klein, Joe. 1995. "Mothers vs. Mullahs: A Program Favored by Hillary Clinton Meets Islamic Resistance." *Newsweek,* April 17, 56.

Kohli, Atul. 1984. *The State and Poverty in India: The Politics of Reform.* Cam-bridge: Cambridge University Press.

Kotalova, Jitka. 1996. *Belonging to Others: Cultural Construction of Womanhood in a Village in Bangladesh.* Dhaka: University Press Limited.

Kraditor, Aileen S. 1968. *Up from the Pedestal: Selected Writings in the History of American Feminism.* Chicago: Quadrangle.

Lakoff, Sanford. 2004. "The Reality of Muslim Exceptionalism." *Journal of De-mocracy* 15 (4): 133–139.

Lambert-Hurley, Siobhan. 2007. *Muslim Women, Reform and Princely Patronage: Nawab Sultan Jahan Begam of Bhopal.* London: Routledge.

Landes, Joan B. 1988. *Women and the Public Sphere in the Age of the French Revolu-tion.* Ithaca: Cornell University Press.

Langohr, Vickie. 2001. "Of Islamists and Ballot Boxes: Rethinking the Relation-ship Between Islamisms and Electoral Politics." *International Journal of Mid-dle East Studies* 33: 591–610.

Lateef, Shahida. 1990. *Muslim Women in India: Political and Private Realities, 1890s-1980s*. Atlantic Highlands, N.J.: Zed.

———. 1994. "Defining Women Through Legislation." In Zoya Hasan, ed., *Forging Identities: Gender, Communities and the State in India*. Boulder, Colo.: Westview.

Lazreg, Marnia. 1990. "Gender and Politics in Algeria: Unraveling the Religious Paradigm." *Signs* 15 (4): 755–780.

———. 1994. *The Eloquence of Silence: Algerian Women in Question*. New York: Routledge.

Leve, Lauren. 2007. "'Failed Development' and Rural Revolution in Nepal: Rethinking Subaltern Consciousness and Women's Empowerment." *Anthropological Quarterly* 80 (10): 127–172.

Levine, Daniel, ed. 1986. *Religion and Political Conflict in Latin America*. Chapel Hill: University of North Carolina Press.

Lewis, Bernard. 1990. "The Roots of Muslim Rage: Why So Many Muslims Deeply Resent the West and Why Their Bitterness Will Not Be Easily Mollified." *Atlantic Monthly* 266 (September).

Lewis David, and Babar Sobhan. 1999. "Routes of Funding, Roots of Trust? Northern NGOs, Southern NGOs, Donors, and the Rise of Direct Funding." *Development in Practice* 9 (1/2): 117–129.

Lifschultz, Lawrence. 1979. *Bangladesh: The Unfinished Revolution*. London: Zed.

Lucas, Marie-Aimee Helie and Harsh Kapoor. 1996. *Fatwas Against Women in Bangladesh*. Grabel, France: Women Living Under Muslim Laws.

Lutzker, Edythe. 1973. *Edith Pechey-Phipson, M. D.: The Story of England's Foremost Pioneering Woman Doctor*. New York: Exposition.

McCarthy, Florence. 1993. "Development From Within: Forms of Resistance to Development Processes Among Rural Bangladeshi Women." In Alice W. Clark, ed., *Gender and Political Economy: Explorations of South Asian Systems*. Delhi: Oxford University Press.

Macaulay, Thomas Babington. 1970. *Macaulay: Prose and Poetry*. Ed. C. M. Young. Cambridge: Harvard University Press.

MacLeod, Arlene. 1992. *Accommodating Protest: Working Women, the New Veiling, and Change in Cairo*. New York: Columbia University Press.

Mahmood, Saba. 2005. *Politics of Piety: The Islamic Revival and the Feminist Subject*. Princeton: Princeton University Press.

———. 2006. "Secularism, Hermeneutics, and Empire: The Politics of Islamic Reformation." *Public Culture* 18 (2): 323–347.

Mahmud, Simeen. 2003. "Actually How Empowering Is Microcredit?" *Development and Change* 34 (4): 577–605.

Majumdar, Badiul Alam. 2004. "Increasing Women's Representation in Parliament: What Is the Best Alternative?" *Daily Star*, March 14.

Mallick, Ross. 2002. "Implementing and Evaluating Microcredit in Bangladesh." *Development in Practice* 12 (2): 153–163.

Mani, Lata. 1989. "Contentious Traditions: The Debate on *Sati* in Colonial India." In Kumkum Sangari and Sudesh Vaid, eds., *Recasting Women: Essays in Colonial History*. New Delhi: Kali for Women.

Maniruzzaman, Talukder. 1988. *The Bangladesh Revolution and Its Aftermath*. Dhaka: University Press Limited.

——. 1994. *Politics and Security of Bangladesh*. Dhaka: University Press Limited.

——. 2001. "Bangladesh Politics: Secular and Islamic Trends." In Rafiuddin Ahmed, ed., *Religion, Identity and Politics: Essays on Bangladesh*. Colorado Springs: International Academic Publishers.

Manji, Irshad. 2004. *The Trouble with Islam: A Muslim's Call for Reform in Her Faith*. New York: St. Martin's.

Mannan, M. A. 2000. "Female-headed Households in Rural Bangladesh: Strategies for Well-Being and Survival." Paper 10, Center for Policy Dialogue–United Nations Population Fund Programme on Population and Sustainable Development. Dhaka: Center for Policy Dialogue.

——. 2002. *Widowhood and Poverty: Well-Being and Survival in Rural Bangladesh*. Dhaka: Grameen Trust.

Martelli, E. 1930. "Section on Purdah." In Annie R. Caton, ed., *The Key of Progress: A Survey of the Status and Conditions of Women in India*. Oxford: Oxford University Press.

Mason, Karen O. 1985. *The Status of Women. A Review of Its Relationships to Fertility and Mortality*. New York: Rockefeller Foundation.

Matin, Neela. 2002. "Women's Rights: Freedom of Participation and Freedom from Violence." In Hameeda Hossain, ed., *Human Rights in Bangladesh, 2001*. Dhaka: ASK.

Maududi, S. Abul A'la. 1960. *The Islamic Law and Constitution*. Trans. and ed. Khurshid Ahmad. Lahore: Islamic Publications.

——. 1972 [1997]. *Al-Hijab: Purdah and the Status of Women in Islam*. Trans. Al-Ash'ari. Reprint. Lahore: Islamic Publications.

——. 1981–1982. *Selected Speeches and Writings of Maulana Maududi*. 2 vols. Trans. S. Zakir Aijaz. Karachi: International Islamic Publishers.

Mayuzumi, Kimine. 2004. "Rethinking Literacy and Women's Health: A Bangladesh Case Study." *Health Care for Women International* 25: 504–526.

Mehtab, Nazmunessa. 2004. "In Letter, Not in Spirit: Tokenism Marks Women's Political Participation in Bangladesh." *Manushi* 142 (May 1): 26–29.

Metcalf, Barbara. 1994. "Reading and Writing About Muslim Women in British India." In Zoya Hasan, ed., *Forging Identities: Gender, Communities and the State in India*. Boulder, Colo.: Westview.

Mia, Ahmadullah. 2005. "Complementary Provision: State and Society in Bangladesh." In Nitya Rao and Ines Smyth, eds., *Partnerships for Girls' Education*. Oxford: Oxfam.

Migdal, Joel, Atul Kohli, and Vivienne Shue, eds. 1994. *State Power and Social Forces: Domination and Transformation in the Third World*. Cambridge: Cambridge University Press.

Minault, Gail. 1983. "Shaikh Abdullah, Begum Abdullah, and Sharif Education for Girls at Aligarh." In Imtiaz Ahmed, ed., *Modernization and Social Change Among Muslims in India*. New Delhi: Manohar.

——. 1990. "Sayyid Mumtaz Ali and *'Huquq un-Niswan'*: An Advocate of Women's Rights in Islam in the Late Nineteenth Century." *Modern Asian Studies* 24 (1): 147–172

——. 1999. *Secluded Scholars: Women's Education and Muslim Social Reform in Colonial India*. New Delhi: Oxford University Press.

Mir-Hosseini, Ziba. 1994. "Strategies of Selection: Differing Notions of Marriage in Iran and Morocco." In Camillia Fawzi el-Solh and Judy Mabro, eds., *Muslim Women's Choices: Religious Belief and Social Reality*. Oxford: Berg.

Mitchell, Timothy. 1991. "The Limits of the State: Beyond Statist Approaches and Their Critics." *American Political Science Review* 85 (1): 77–96.

Mitra, Sharmila. 2006. "The Movement for Women's Emancipation Within the Bengali Muslim Community in India." *Women's History Review* 15 (3): 413–422.

Moghadam, Valentine M. 2005. "Is Gender Inequality in Muslim Societies a Barrier to Modernization and Democratization?" In Shireen T. Hunter and Huma Malik, eds., *Modernization, Democracy, and Islam*. Westport, Conn.: Praeger.

Moghissi, Haideh. 2000. *Feminism and Islamic Fundamentalism: The Limits of Postmodern Analysis*. London: Zed.

Mohanty, Chandra T. 1991. "Under Western Eyes: Feminist Scholarship and Colonial Discourses." In Chandra T. Mohanty, Ann Russo, and Lourdes Torres, eds., *Third World Women and the Politics of Feminism*. Bloomington: Indiana University Press.

Monsoor, Taslima. 1999. *From Patriarchy to Gender Equity: Family Law and Its Impact on Women in Bangladesh*. Dhaka: University Press Limited.

Mookherjee, Nayanika. 2003. "Gendered Embodiments: Mapping the Body-Politic of the Raped Woman and the Nation in Bangladesh." In Nirmal Puwar and Parvati Raghuram, eds., *South Asian Women in the Diaspora*. New York: Berg.

Moore, Erin B. 1998. *Gender, Law, and Resistance in India*. Tucson: University of Arizona Press.

Mukhopadhyay, Carol C. and Susan Seymour, eds. 1994. *Women, Education and Family Structure in India*. Boulder, Colo.: Westview.

Mumtaz, Khawar and Farida Shaheed. 1987. *Women of Pakistan: Two Steps Forward, One Step Back?* Lahore: Vanguard.

Munir, Muhammad. 1981. *From Jinnah to Zia*. Delhi: Akbar.

Murshid, Ghulam. 1983. *Reluctant Debutante: Response of Bengali Women to Modernization, 1849–1905*. Rajshahi: Sahitya Samsad, Rajshahi University.

Murshid, Tazeen. n.d. "Women, Islam and the State: Subordination and Resistance." Available at www.lib.uchicago.edu/e/su/southasia/Tazeen.html. Accessed April 2007.

——. 1996. *The Sacred and the Secular: Bengal Muslim Discourses, 1871–1977.* Dhaka: University Press Limited.

Nagata, Judith. 1994. "How to Be Islamic Without Being an Islamic State: Contested Models of Development in Malaysia." In Akbar S. Ahmed and Hastings Donnan, eds., *Islam, Globalization and Postmodernity.* London: Routledge.

Naher, Ainoon. 1996. "Gender, Religion and Rural Development in Bangladesh." M.A. thesis, University of Sussex.

Nair, Janaki. 1991. "Reconstructing and Reinterpreting the History of Women in India." *Journal of Women's History* 3 (1): 131–136.

——. 1996. *Women and Law in Colonial India—A Social History.* New Delhi: Kali for Women.

Nasr, Seyyed Vali Reza. 1994. *The Vanguard of the Islamic Revolution: The Jamaat-i Islami of Pakistan.* Berkeley: University of California Press.

——. 1996. *Mawdudi and the Making of Islamic Revivalism.* New York: Oxford University Press.

——. 2005. "The Rise of 'Muslim Democracy.'" *Journal of Democracy* 16 (2): 13–27.

Nasrin, Taslima. 2000. "They Wanted to Kill Me." *Middle East Quarterly* 7 (3): 67–74.

Nations, Richard. 1971. "The Economic Structure of Pakistan: Class and Colony." *New Left Review* 68 (July–August): 3–26.

NGO Affairs Bureau. 1998. *Flow of Foreign Grant Fund Through NGO Affairs Bureau at a Glance.* Dhaka: NGO Affairs Bureau, Prime Minister's Office.

Noman, Omar. 1990. *Pakistan: Political and Economic History Since 1947.* New York: Kegan Paul International.

Nordland, Rod. 2005. "The Cities Were Not Bathed in Blood." MSNBC, February 9. Available at www.msnbc.msn.com/id/6887461/site/newsweek/. Accessed April 2005.

Nuthall, Keith. 2002. "Bank Loan Allows Girls to Choose Schooling Over Marriage." *Times Educational Supplement,* March 29, 16.

Odeh, Loma Abu. 1993. "Post-Colonial Feminism and the Veil: Thinking the Difference," *Feminist Review* 43: 26–37.

O'Hanlon, Rosalind. 1992. "Issues of Widowhood: Gender and Resistance in Colonial Western India." In Douglas Haynes and Gyan Prakash, eds., *Contesting Power: Resistance and Everyday Social Relations in South Asia.* Berkeley: University of California Press.

Oldenburg, Veena T. 2002. *Dowry Murder: The Imperial Origins of a Cultural Crime.* New York: Oxford University Press.

Oxford Policy Management. 2004. "DFID Rural and Urban Development Case Study—Bangladesh." Available at passlivelihoods.org.uk/. Accessed June 2005.

Papachristou, Alexander. 1984. "The Colonial Experience of Law: Islamic Law in British India." LL.M. thesis, Harvard Law School.

Papanek, Hanna. 1971. "Purdah in Pakistan: Seclusion and Modern Occupations for Women." *Journal of Marriage and the Family* 33 (3): 517–530.

——. 1973. "Purdah: Separate Worlds and Symbolic Shelter." *Comparative Studies in Society and History* 15 (3): 289–325.

Pearson, Gail. 2004. "Tradition, Law and the Female Suffrage Movement in India." In Louise Edwards and Mina Roces, eds., *Women's Suffrage in Asia: Gender, Nationalism, and Democracy*. London: RoutledgeCurzon.

Pearson, Ruth and Cecile Jackson. 1998. "Introduction: Interrogating Development—Feminism, Gender and Policy." In Cecile Jackson and Ruth Pearson, eds., *Feminist Visions of Development: Gender Analysis and Policy*. New York: Routledge.

Peletz, Michael G. 1996. *Reason and Passion: Representations of Gender in a Malay Society*. Berkeley: University of California Press.

——. 2002. *Islamic Modern: Religious Courts and Cultural Politics in Malaysia*. Princeton: Princeton University Press.

Pereira, Faustina. 2000. "Fatwa in Bangladesh—Patriarchy's Latest Sport." In Kelly D. Askin and Dorean M. Koenig, eds., *Women and International Human Rights Law*. Ardsley, N.Y.: Transnational.

——. 2002a. "Dossier on Fatwa in Bangladesh." *interventions* 4 (2): 212–214.

——. 2002b. *The Fractured Scales: The Search for a Uniform Personal Code*. Dhaka: University Press Limited.

Pitt, Mark M., Shahidur R. Khandker, and Jennifer Cartwright. 2003. "Does Micro-Credit Empower Women? Evidence from Bangladesh." World Bank Policy Research Working Paper 2998. Washington, D.C.: World Bank. Also available at econ.worldbank.org.

Putnam, Robert D. 1993. *Making Democracy Work: Civic Traditions in Modern Italy*. Princeton: Princeton University Press.

Pye, Lucien. 1990. "Presidential Address to APSA, 1989." *American Political Science Review* (March): 3–21

Qadir, Sayeda R. 1994. "Participation of Women in Local Level Politics: Problems and Prospects." In Najma Chowdhury, Hamida A. Begum, Mahmuda Islam, and Nazmunnessa Mahtab, eds., *Women and Politics*. Dhaka: Women for Women.

Qadir, Sayeda R. and Mahmuda Islam. 1987. *Women Representatives at the Union Level as Change Agent of Development*. Dhaka: Women for Women.

Rafi, Mohammad and A. M. R. Chowdhury. 2000. "Human Rights and Religious Backlash: The Experience of a Bangladeshi NGO." *Development in Practice* 10 (1): 19–30.

Raheja, Gloria G. and Ann Gold. 1994) *Listen to the Heron's Words: Reimagining Gender and Kinship in North India*. Berkeley: University of California Press.

Rahim, Enayetur. 2001. "Bengali Muslims and Islamic Fundamentalism: The Jama'at-i-Islami in Bangladesh." In Rafiuddin Ahmed, ed., *Understanding the Bengal Muslims: Interpretative Essays*. New Delhi: Oxford University Press.

Rahman, Aminur. 1999a. "Micro-credit Initiatives for Equitable and Sustainable Development: Who Pays?" *World Development* 27 (1): 67–82.

——. 1999b. *Women and Microcredit in Rural Bangladesh: Anthropological Study of the Rhetoric and Realities of Grameen Bank Lending.* Boulder, Colo.: Westview.

Rahman, Atiur and Shoumi Mustafa. 1995. "Governance and Participation: The NGO Experience in Bangladesh." *Morning Sun,* March 15.

Rahman, Sabeel. 2006. "Development, Democracy and the NGO Sector: Theory and Evidence from Bangladesh." *Journal of Developing Societies* 22 (4): 451–473.

Ramusack, Barbara N. 1992. "Cultural Missionaries, Maternal Imperialists, Feminist Allies—British Women Activists in India, 1865–1945." In Nupur Chaudhuri and Margaret Strobel, eds., *Western Women and Imperialism—Complicity and Resistance.* Bloomington: Indiana University Press.

Rashiduzzaman, M. 1994. "The Liberals and the Religious Right in Bangladesh." *Asian Survey* 34 (11): 974–990.

——. 1997. "The Dichotomy of Islam and Development: NGOs, Women's Development and Fatawa in Bangladesh." *Contemporary South Asia* 6 (3): 239–246.

Riaz, Ali. 2004. *God Willing: The Politics of Islamism in Bangladesh.* Lanham, Md.: Rowman and Littlefield.

Richter, Linda K. 1990. "Exploring Theories of Female Leadership in South and Southeast Asia." *Pacific Affairs* 63 (4): 524–540.

Robinson, Francis. 2000. Introduction to Syed Ahmed Khan, *The Causes of the Indian Revolt.* Karachi: Oxford University Press.

Robinson, Glenn E. 1997. "Can Islamists Be Democrats? The Case of Jordan." *Middle East Journal* 51 (3): 373–387.

Rothschild, Emma. 1976. "Food Politics." *Foreign Affairs* 54 (2): 285–307.

Rowlands, Jo. 1998. "A Word of the Times, but What Does It Mean? Empowerment in the Discourse and Practice of Development." In Haleh Afshar, ed., *Women and Empowerment: Illustrations from the Third World.* New York: St. Martin's.

Roy, Olivier. 2004. *Globalized Islam: The Search for a New Ummah.* New York: Columbia University Press.

Roy, Sandip. 2001. "In Bangladesh Fears of Talibanization." *Pacific News Service,* November 20, available at www.alternet.org/story/11940.

Rozario, Santi. 1992. *Purity and Communal Boundaries: Women and Social Change in a Bangladeshi Village.* London: Zed.

——. 1998. "Disjunctions and Continuities: Dowry and the Position of Single Women in Bangladesh." In Carla Risseeuw and Kamala Ganesh, eds., *Negotiation and Social Space: A Gendered Analysis of Changing Kin and Security Networks in South Asia and Sub-Saharan Africa.* Walnut Creek, Calif.: AltaMira.

——. 2004. *Building Solidarity Against Patriarchy.* Dhaka: Rural Livelihoods Program, CARE Bangladesh.

Rudolph, Lloyd I. and Susanne H. Rudolph. 1967. *The Modernity of Tradition: Political Development in India*. Chicago: University of Chicago Press.

Saidi, Allama Delawar Hossain. 2003. *Mohila Shomabeshey Proshner Jobabe* (In response to questions posed at the women's gatherings). 2 vols. Dhaka: Global Publishing Network.

Saikia, Yasmin. 2004. "Beyond the Archive of Silence: Narratives of Violence of the 1971 Liberation War of Bangladesh." *History Workshop Journal* 58: 275–287.

Saktanber, Ayse. 2002. *Living Islam: Women, Religion and the Politicization of Culture in Turkey*. London: I. B. Tauris.

Salahuddin, Khaleda, Roushan Jahan, and Latifa Akanda, eds. 2001. *State of Human Rights in Bangladesh: Women's Perspective*. Dhaka: Women for Women.

Salahuddin, Khaleda, Roushan Jahan, and Mahmuda Islam, eds. 1997. *Women and Poverty*. Dhaka: Women for Women.

Salim, M. Abdus. 1995. "NGOs in Bangladesh and Some Pertinent Matters." *Dainik Shangram*, August 8.

Salway, Sarah, Sonia Jesmin, and Shahana Rahman. 2005. "Women's Employment in Urban Bangladesh: A Challenge to Gender Identity?" *Development and Change* 36 (2): 317–349.

Samad, Ataus. 1995. "Cold War Between Government and NGOs." *Holiday*, March 31.

Sangari, Kumkum and Sudesh Vaid, eds. 1989. *Recasting Women: Essays in Colonial History*. New Delhi: Kali for Women.

Sarat, Austin and Thomas R. Kearns, eds. 1993. *Law in Everyday Life*. Ann Arbor: University of Michigan Press.

Schaffer, Howard B. 2002. "Back and Forth in Bangladesh." *Journal of Democracy* 13 (1): 76–83.

Schleifer, Aliah. 1986. *Motherhood in Islam*. Cambridge: Islamic Academy.

Scott, James C. 1976. *The Moral Economy of the Peasant*. New Haven: Yale University Press.

——. 1985. *Weapons of the Weak: Everyday Forms of Resistance*. New Haven: Yale University Press.

——. 1999. *Seeing Like a State: How Certain Schemes to Improve the Human Condition Have Failed*. New Haven: Yale University Press.

Selimuddin. 1996. "Prohibited by Law, yet Child Marriages Persist." *Sangbad*, January 31.

Sen, Amartya K. 1981. *Poverty and Famines: An Essay on Entitlement and Deprivation*. Oxford: Clarendon.

——. 1990. "More Than 100 Million Women Are Missing." *New York Review of Books*, December 20. Available at www.nybooks.com/articles/3408. Accessed March 2007.

——. 1999. *Development as Freedom*. New York: Anchor.

Shaarawi, Huda. 1987. *Harem Years: The Memoirs of an Egyptian Feminist*. Trans. and ed. Margot Badran. New York: Feminist Press, CUNY.

Shaheed, Farida. 1998. "The Other Side of the Discourse: Women's Experiences of Identity, Religion, and Activism in Pakistan." In Patricia Jeffery and Amrita Basu, eds., *Appropriating Gender: Women's Activism and Politicized Religion in South Asia*. London: Routledge.

Shehabuddin, Elora (as Rahnuma Shehabuddin). 1992. *Empowering Rural Women: The Impact of Grameen Bank in Bangladesh*. Dhaka: Grameen Bank.

——. 1997. "Women's Participation in Community Dispute Resolution." Unpublished research study prepared for ASK and Asia Foundation.

——. 1999a. "Beware the Bed of Fire: Gender, Democracy, and the Jamaat-i Islami in Bangladesh." *Journal of Women's History* 10 (4): 148–171.

——. 1999b. "Contesting the Illicit: The Politics of Fatwas in Bangladesh." *Signs* 24 (4): 1011–1044.

——. 2004 [2007]. "'Development' Revisited: A Critical Analysis of the Status of Women in Bangladesh." *Journal of Bangladesh Studies* 6 (1–2): 1–19. Reprinted in M. Faizul Islam and Syed Saad Andaleeb, eds. *Development Issues in Bangladesh-III: Human Development and Quality of Life*. Dhaka: University Press Limited.

Shehadeh, Lamia Rustum. 2003. *The Idea of Women Under Fundamentalist Islam*. Gainesville: University Press of Florida.

Shvedova, Nadezhda. 2006. "Obstacles to Women's Participation in Parliament." In International IDEA, *Women in Parliament: Beyond Numbers*. Stockholm: International IDEA.

Siddiqi, Dina M. 1991. "Discipline and Protect: Seclusion and Subversion Among Women Garment Workers in Bangladesh." *Grassroots, An Alternative Development Quarterly* 1 (2): 42–49.

——. 1996a. "The Festival of Democracy: Media and Elections in Bangladesh." *Asian Journal of Communication* 6 (2): 30–42.

——. 1996b. "Women in Question: Gender and Labor in Bangladeshi Factories." Ph.D. diss., University of Michigan.

——. 2003a. *Paving the Way to Justice: The Experience of Nagorik Uddyog*. London: One World Action.

——. 2003b. "Religion, Rights and the Politics of Transnational Feminism in Bangladesh." Center for Northeast India, South and Southeast Asia Studies (CENISEAS) Papers 2. Guwahati, India: CENISEAS.

——. 2003c. "The Sexual Harassment of Industrial Workers: Strategies for Intervention in the Workplace and Beyond." Center for Policy Dialogue–United Nations Population Fund Paper 26. Dhaka: Center for Policy Dialogue.

——. 2006a. *Ain O Salish Kendra: Twenty Years on the Frontline*. Dhaka: ASK.

——. 2006b. "In the Name of Islam? Gender, Politics and Women's Rights in Bangladesh." *Harvard Asia Quarterly* 10 (1), available at www.asiaquarterly. com/content/view/165/40/. Accessed March 2007.

Singerman, Diane. 1995. *Avenues of Participation: Family, Politics, and Networks in Urban Quarters of Cairo*. Princeton: Princeton University Press.

Singh, Priyam B. 1993. "Colonial State, Women Victims and Criminals: The

North-western Provinces and Oudh, (India), 1870–1910." Ph.D. diss., Temple University.

———. 1996. "Women, Law, and Criminal Justice in North India: A Historical View." *Bulletin of Concerned Asian Scholars* 28 (1): 27–38.

Sinha, Mrinalini. 1994. "Reading *Mother India*: Empire, Nation, and the Female Voice." *Journal of Women's History* 6 (2): 6–44.

———. 1995. *Colonial Masculinity: The "Manly Englishman" and the "Effeminate Bengali" in the Late Nineteenth Century*. New York: Manchester University Press.

———. 2006. *Specters of Mother India: The Global Restructuring of an Empire*. Durham, N.C.: Duke University Press.

Smillie, Ian. 1997. *Words and Deeds: BRAC at 25*. Dhaka: BRAC Centre.

Smith-Hefner, Nancy. 2007. "Javanese Women and the Veil in Post-Soeharto Indonesia." *Journal of Asian Studies* 66 (2): 389–420.

Sobhan, Rehman. 1979. "The Politics of Food and Famine in Bangladesh." *Economic and Political Weekly* 14 (December): 1973–1980.

———. 1982. *The Crisis of External Dependence: The Political Economy of Foreign Aid to Bangladesh*. London: Zed.

———. 1993. *Bangladesh: Problems of Governance*. Dhaka: University Press Limited.

Sobhan, Salma. 1978. *Legal Status of Women in Bangladesh*. Dhaka: Bangladesh Institute of Law and International Affairs.

Sonbol, Amira el-Azhary. 1996. *Women, the Family, and Divorce Laws in Islamic History*. Syracuse: Syracuse University Press.

Spivak, Gayatri C. 1988. "Can the Subaltern Speak?" In Cary Nelson and Lawrence Grossberg, eds., *Marxism and the Interpretation of Culture*. Urbana: University of Illinois Press.

———. 1996. "'Woman' as Theatre: United Nations Conference on Women, Beijing 1995." *Radical Philosophy* 75 (January/February): 2–4.

———. 2004. "Righting Wrongs" *South Atlantic Quarterly* 103 (2/3): 523–581.

Stansell, Christine. 1986. *City of Women: Sex and Class in New York, 1789–1860*. New York: Knopf.

Stark, Jan. 2005. "Beyond 'Terrorism' and 'State Hegemony': Assessing the Islamist Mainstream in Egypt and Malaysia." *Third World Quarterly* 26 (2): 307–327.

Stepan, Alfred. 2003. "An 'Arab' More Than 'Muslim' Electoral Gap." With Graeme B. Robertson. *Journal of Democracy* 14 (3): 30–44.

Stepan, Alfred and Graeme B. Robertson. 2004. "Arab, Not Muslim Exceptionalism." *Journal of Democracy* 15 (4): 140–146.

Stiles, Kendall W. 2002a. *Civil Society by Design: Donors, NGOs, and the Intermestic Development Circle in Bangladesh*. Westport, Conn.: Praeger.

———. 2002b. "International Support for NGOs in Bangladesh: Some Unintended Consequences." *World Development* 30 (5): 835–846.

Sullivan, Denis J. 1994. *Private Voluntary Organizations in Egypt: Islamic*

Development, Private Initiative, and State Control. Gainesville: University Press of Florida.

Summers, Lawrence H. 1993. Foreword to Elizabeth M. King and M. Anne Hill, eds., *Women's Education in Developing Countries: Barriers, Benefits and Policies.* Baltimore: John Hopkins University Press.

Suran, Luciana, Sajeda Amin, Lopita Huq, and Kobita Chowdury. 2004. "Does Dowry Improve Life for Brides? A Test of the Bequest Theory of Dowry in Rural Bangladesh." Policy Research Division Working Paper 195. New York: Population Council.

Al-Suwaidi, Jamal. 1995. "Arab and Western Conceptions of Democracy." In David Garnham and Mark Tessler, eds., *Democracy, War, and Peace in the Middle East.* Bloomington: Indiana University Press.

Swarup, Hem Lata, Niroj Sinha, Chitra Ghosh, and Pam Rajput. 1994. "Women's Political Engagement in India: Some Critical Issues." In Barbara J. Nelson and Najma Chowdhury, eds., *Women and Politics Worldwide.* New Haven: Yale University Press.

Tahmina, Qurratul Ain. 2005. "Bangladesh: Women's Policy Sneakily Changed by Gov't." PeaceWomen–Women's International League for Peace and Freedom Website, www.peacewomen.org/news/International/July05/Bangladesh.html. Accessed May 2007.

Taraki, Lisa. 1995. "Islam Is the Solution: Jordanian Islamists and the Dilemma of the 'Modern Woman.'" *British Journal of Sociology* 46 (4): 643–661.

——. 1996. "Jordanian Islamists and the Agenda for Women: Between Discourse and Practice." *Middle Eastern Studies* 32 (1): 140–158.

Taylor, Verta and Leila Rupp. 1991. "Researching the Women's Movement: We Make Our Own History, but Not Just As We Please." In Mary Margaret Fonow and Judith A. Cook, eds., *Beyond Methodology: Feminist Scholarship as Lived Research.* Bloomington: Indiana University Press.

Teays, Wanda. 1991. "The Burning Bride: The Dowry Problem in India." *Journal of Feminist Studies in Religion* 7 (2): 29–52.

Townsend, J.G. and A.R. Townsend. 2004. "Accountability, Motivation and Practice: NGOS North and South." *Social and Cultural Geography* 5 (2): 271–284.

Tucker, Judith E. 1998. *In the House of the Law: Gender and Islamic Law in Ottoman Syria and Palestine.* Berkeley: University of California Press.

Umar, Badruddin. 1996. "On the Subject of NGOs" (Bengali). *Ajker Kagoj,* April 26.

UNDP. 2002. "Human Development Balance Sheet." *Human Development Report 2002.* hdr.undp.org/reports/global/2002/en/pdf/HDR PR_balance.pdf. Accessed April 2005.

——. 2003. *Human Development Report 2003.* hdr.undp.org/reports/global/2003/pdf/presskit/HDR03_PKE_HDI.pdf. Accessed November 2004.

——. 2004. *Human Development Report 2004.* hdr.undp.org/statistics/data/cty/cty_f_BGD.html. Accessed November 2005.

USAID. 1991. *Democracy and Governance*. Washington: USAID, Directorate for Policy.

———. 1994. *Strategies for Sustainable Development*. Washington: USAID, Directorate for Policy.

Vlassoff, Carol. 1996. "Against the Odds: The Changing Impact of Education on Female Autonomy and Fertility in an Indian Village." In Roger Jeffery and Alaka Basu, eds., *Girls' Schooling, Women's Autonomy and Fertility Change in South Asia*. Newbury Park, Calif.: Sage.

Voll, John O. 2005. "Islam and Democracy: Is Modernization a Barrier?" In Shireen T. Hunter and Huma Malik, eds., *Modernization, Democracy, and Islam*. Westport, Conn.: Praeger.

Waines, David. 1982. "Through a Veil Darkly: The Study of Women in Muslim Societies." *Comparative Studies in Society and History* 24 (4): 642–659.

Weiner, Myron. 1986. "Institution Building in South Asia." In R. A. Scalapino, Seizaburo Sato, and Jusuf Wanandi, eds., *Asian Political Institutionalization*. Berkeley: Institute of East Asian Studies, University of California.

Weiss, Anita. 1998. "The Slow Yet Steady Path to Women's Empowerment in Pakistan." In Yvonne Yazbeck Haddad and John L. Esposito, eds., *Islam, Gender, and Social Change*. New York: Oxford University Press.

Welter, Barbara. 1966. "The Cult of True Womanhood: 1820–1860." *American Quarterly* 18 (2-1): 151–174.

Westergaard, Kirsten. 1996. "People's Empowerment in Bangladesh: NGO Strategies." *Journal of Social Studies* 72 (April): 27–57.

———. 2000. "Decentralization in Bangladesh: Local Government and NGOs." Paper presented at the Colloquium on Decentralization and Development at the Department of Political Science, Yale University, April 7.

White, Jenny B. 2002. *Islamist Mobilization in Turkey: A Study in Vernacular Politics*. Seattle: University of Washington Press.

White, Sarah. 1992. *Arguing with the Crocodile: Gender and Class in Bangladesh*. London: Zed.

———. 1999. "NGOs, Civil Society, and the State in Bangladesh: The Politics of Representing the Poor." *Development and Change* 30:307–326.

Wickham, Carrie Rosefsky. 2002. *Mobilizing Islam: Religion, Activism, and Political Change in Egypt*. New York: Columbia University Press.

———. 2004. "The Path to Moderation." *Comparative Politics* 36 (2): 205–228.

Wiktorowicz, Quintan. 2001. *The Management of Islamic Activism: Salafis, the Muslim Brotherhood, and State Power in Jordan*. Albany: SUNY Press.

———, ed. 2004. *Islamic Activism: A Social Movement Theory Approach*. Bloomington: Indiana University Press.

Winter, Bronwyn. 2001. "Fundamental Misunderstandings: Issues in Feminist Approaches to Islamism." *Journal of Women's History* 13 (1): 9–41.

Women for Women. 1995. *Women and Politics: Orientation of Four Political Parties on Women's Empowerment Issues*. Dhaka: Women for Women.

World Bank. 1994a. *Governance: The World Bank's Experience*. Washington, D.C.: World Bank.

——. 1994b. "The World Bank and Participation: Report on the Learning Group on Participatory Development." Washington, D.C.: Operations Policy Department, World Bank.

——. 1999. "South Asia Brief: Pioneering Support for Girls Secondary Education: The Bangladesh Female Secondary School Assistance Program." Available at wbln0018.worldbank.org/lo%20web%20sites/bangladesh%20web. nsf/0704a4348e105b2e462566720023975f/a693f20497df2449462567l8002b f583?OpenDocument. Accessed December 2007.

World Economic Forum. 2005. Press Release. weforum.org/gendergap. Accessed May 2005.

Yang, Yongzheng and Montfort Mlachila. 2007. "The End of Textile Quotas: A Case Study of the Impact on Bangladesh." *Journal of Developing Studies* 43 (4): 675–699.

Yunus, Muhammad and Alan Jolis. 2001. *Banker to the Poor: The Autobiography of Muhammad Yunus, Founder of the Grameen Bank*. New York: Oxford University Press.

Zahidi, Saadia and Augusto Lopez-Claros. 2005. *Women's Empowerment: Measuring the Global Gender Gap*. Geneva: World Economic Forum. Available at www.weforum.org/gendergap. Accessed May 2005.

Zaman, Muhammad Qasim. 2002. *The Ulama in Contemporary Islam: Custodians of Change*. Princeton: Princeton University Press.

Zaman, Mustafa. 2006. "Women Against the Odds." *Star Weekend Magazine*, February 3. Available at www.thedailystar.net/magazine/2006/02/01/index. htm. Accessed May 2006.

Page numbers in italics refer to illustrations.